ENJOY!!

D1523291

The Joy of Trash

NATHAN RABIN'S HAPPY PLACE'S
DEFINITIVE GUIDE
TO THE VERY WORST OF
EVERYTHING

BY NATHAN RABIN
ILLUSTRATIONS BY FELIPE SOBREIRO

ENJOY!!!

CONTENTS

INTRODUCTION

Life is about stealing joy from a world that can be stingy in doling out happiness and obscenely generous when it comes to disseminating pain.

As a pop culture writer and trash culture obsessive, I have found that joy in eviscerating entertainment that is terrible on a historic level: the literature of disgraced figures like Doug Hutchison, Lou Pearlman, Joan Crawford, Steven Seagal, Milo Yiannopoulos, and Rachel Dolezal and the films of *Loqueesha* writer-director-star Jeremy Saville.

The entertainment I like writing about most offends me on a moral as well as an aesthetic level. There's something deeply cathartic about working through my rage at an insult like *Loqueesha,* a natural high that comes from knowing that I'm doing what I was put on earth to do.

In *The Joy of Trash* I explore the endlessly fascinating transgressions of a rogue's gallery of scoundrels and hustlers, criminals and con artists, phonies and degenerates. It's a kooky compendium of creative crimes that overlap and reflect each other at odd angles.

It's empowering as well as cathartic to derive something of worth out of the ostensibly worthless. In the essays that follow I alchemize pain into pleasure, trash into treasure, the unforgivable into the unforgettable.

Welcome to my nightmare.

Welcome to my paradise.

Welcome to *The Joy of Trash.*

THE WORST OF
LITERATURE

JOAN CRAWFORD'S
MY WAY OF LIFE
(1971)

Reading disgraced boy band Svengali Lou Pearlman's *Bands, Brands & Billions: My Top 10 Rules for Making Any Business Go Platinum,* I was struck by the chutzpah of a man whose career was built upon a lie giving readers an inside look into his money-making psyche.

Pearlman knew that the "secret" of his success involved running one of the world's largest Ponzi schemes. Yet, he nevertheless felt the need to take quill to paper for the sake of spinning a fictional, feel-good story of his life to inspire other dreamers.

On a similar note, it seems counterintuitive for a woman whose name and cult classic biopic (*Mommy Dearest*) have become synonymous with monstrous, abusive show-business mothers to pen a guide to entertaining, marriage, beauty, and all-around fabulousness.

Yet, Joan Crawford wrote a lifestyle guide in 1971 entitled *My Way of Life,* a manic manifesto that feels like the product of someone who ate a bowl of speed for breakfast and then sat down with a tape recorder to chronicle for posterity, in a motormouthed, free-associative blur, everything in their fascinatingly scrambled mind that felt important, which was everything.

In *My Way of Life,* Crawford is Alfred Molina in *Boogie Nights* discoursing on "Jesse's Girl" in a coked-up frenzy. She's Patrick Bateman monologuing about Huey Lewis and the News. Every line begs to be not just read aloud but *performed* by drag queens.

Here, for example, is Crawford providing a superhero or supervillain origin story for her famous love of domestic work when she writes, "In the second school I was the only helper in a fourteen room house accommodating thirty students and, in true Dickensian fashion, I was thrown down the stairs and beaten with a broom handle. This should have turned me off housework forever, but the funny thing is that I still love scrubbing and ironing and especially cooking, and I could no sooner leave a bed unmade than I could fly to the moon."

Crawford casually references being the subject of barbaric cruelty, but only to provide context for her love of cleaning. For the author, the important part isn't that she was thrown down the stairs and beaten with a broom handle. That's just life. That's just being a woman. What matters is the super-cleaning superpowers she derived from that abuse.

Crawford has a Little Edie–like flair for accidental poetry, like when she begins a chapter by musing theatrically, "Everybody has strong ideas about marriage. And why not? It's the most intriguing situation a woman has in life."

Crawford has strong ideas about this most intriguing of situations. Judging by her book, she also prides herself on being busier than the president with her acting career, running her household and toiling endlessly as an executive and goodwill ambassador for Pepsi.

Jesus didn't take his role as savior of humanity as seriously as Crawford does a job that requires her to travel the world spreading the gospel of Pepsi, smiling and signing autographs and selling herself along with soda pop. That endless pitch includes her fizzy, dizzy, moderately psychotic lifestyle manual, which might as well be called *Pepsi Presents the Joan Crawford Pepsi Way of Life, Brought to You by Pepsi*.

My Way of Life is a cross between a campaign speech from someone who does not know what office they're running for and a literary nervous breakdown. But it's also a business/lifestyle guide from someone uniquely qualified and unqualified to tell other people how to live.

Crawford's life is at once a Hollywood Cinderella success story and a harrowing cautionary tale. We've envied, pitied, and misunderstood Crawford. We've vilified the Oscar winner and laughed at her, in her lifetime but also afterward when portrayed by Faye Dunaway and Jessica Lange in *Mommy Dearest* and *Feud,* respectively.

In *My Way of Life,* the fairer sex must be superwomen to prove themselves as partners. After all, your hubby gave you a last name, put a rock on your finger, puts on a suit, and goes to work in an office. You would literally be criminally insane to even think about wanting more than that.

Crawford writes scoldingly of the worrisome case of a mother and wife who "realized, while her babies were still toddlers, that she was totally engrossed in them, and that her husband was being made to take a back seat. And that he might not feel like occupying it alone for very long. He was getting ahead rapidly as an electrical engineer and he loved talking about it; if he couldn't talk to her, she realized, he just might find someone else."

Crawford seems brainwashed enough by her own rhetoric that she genuinely believes that by not boning up on electrical engineering this wife is not only risking her marriage but also costing herself an opportunity to have a man explain the world to her. Today this phenomenon is known as "mansplaining" and Crawford thinks it's just wonderful, an opportunity for women to learn something important *and* feed their husband's sense that he is the center of the universe at the same time.

It's essential that a wife find her husband's agonizingly dull life mesmerizing. It doesn't work the other way around. Crawford writes of her final late husband, "When we were alone, if he wanted to talk business, so did I. I was interested, and he knew it. I never regaled him with an account of what the children had done, the lateness of deliveries because of traffic, or the neighborhood gossip (unless it was a particularly juicy bit!). There's nothing less stimulating for a man than the day-to-day business of raising four children.

That's women's work. If she's lucky she revels in it. If not, she gets it done in the time allotted for it."

Elsewhere, Crawford writes worriedly, "I've heard of men who were permanently stymied in their careers because their wives flatly refused to leave their hometowns. That's not right. A man's job has to come first and women have to draw on their natural adaptability."

After behaving for seventy pages or so as if every woman is the housewife of a businessman, Crawford grudgingly acknowledges that it's 1971, so pretty much all the women she knows work. And she knows some *pretty* famous people. Noel Coward. Cole Porter. Cary Grant. F. Scott Fitzgerald. She could go on. And she does!

Crawford is predictably sympathetic to men who have a problem with their wives working. Crawford writes, in a strange attempt at humor, "Men put up all sorts of objections, all of which cover up their real, subconscious fear that 'she'll come home tired and won't want to go to bed with me.' They wonder what's going to happen to them sexually. But the fact is that when a woman feels she's done a good job and accomplished something, she's charged. She's ready for sex. Maybe *he'll* be too tired that night. And maybe he'll get raped!"

Crawford observes witheringly of women who have attained professional success at the cost of their femininity, "Men who are prejudiced against women in executive positions have usually had a bad experience with one who swaggered in with a chip on her manly shoulder believing that she had to fight her way up, and fight men to do it. A gal like that can make it tough for the rest of us. Many in the woman's liberation movement have done that— but few of them are executives and few are very good to look at. They have nothing to lose but their uncombed hair."

It's not working outside the home that's the real sin for Crawford: it's being unladylike. Crawford has no problem with a woman running a Fortune 500 company as long as she's as elegant as Grace Kelly. It's okay in Crawford's book (literally) for a woman to hold a job, so long as it doesn't interfere with her being a sex goddess, hostess, and the image of glamorous femininity with a body devoid of cellulite, imperfections, and those love handles *nobody* loves.

Crawford encourages women to have a "friend" photograph them from the most unflattering possible angles possible and then have the images blown up into an 8 by 10, so that they can obsess about every imperfection. Do you have stubby knees or bony ankles, but don't know it? Then you're a liar, a monster, and a fraud and you should be ashamed of yourself.

Thankfully, once you know about these shamefully stubby knees, you can pursue exercise or cosmetic surgery to fix yourself. As Crawford writes sensitively, "The shock of taking a photographic inventory may send the average woman to bed for a week. But it could be the best thing that ever happened to her."

Crawford isn't entirely unsympathetic to the plight of people who do not conform to society's impossible standards of beauty. Of readers looking to lose weight she writes, "Regular exercise, all alone, can be boring. If you just can't schedule it for yourself, organize a little neighborhood club. Get all the pleasingly plump girls together *regularly* at a certain hour on certain days of the week—and compete. Competition is often just the stimulus you need.

"At the first session, weigh in, take all the crucial measurements, and put them on charts. Do the weighing in and measuring every week on the same day. A woman will give up anything—from a hot fudge sundae to a dry martini or a grilled cheese sandwich—to beat her fellow club members to a slim finish. She may lose a friend or two, but she'll gain loveliness, and her husband's pride and admiration. *That*'s worth a couple of fat friends!"

Deep into *My Way of Life*, I had a realization. Crawford did not write her strange and ultimately achingly sad book for her readers' sake. It is not a book of advice for people who might learn from Crawford's elegantly unhinged example.

No, *My Way of Life* is Crawford giving herself a brutal bible to live by. But it's deeper than that. Advice can be gentle, kind, a matter of subtle suggestion. That is not the tone here. It's more a matter of Crawford angrily ordering herself around, being cruel and uncompromising to someone she knew could withstand abuse, internal and external, and come out smiling because smiling was not only a huge part of her job as an actress and public figure; it was also her mask to conceal almost inconceivable pain.

Crawford is sternly telling herself more than her readers that you must be perfect to be worthy of love. The camp icon so thoroughly internalized the misogyny of the country that elevated her to a god and destroyed her psychologically that she adopted society's hatred of women as her own personal philosophy.

My Way of Life was intended as lifestyle porn/self-help. Instead, it's a riveting, darkly funny, and utterly revealing book-length exercise in self-loathing.

MARABEL MORGAN'S
THE TOTAL WOMAN
(1973)

Marabel Morgan's *The Total Woman*, the best-selling nonfiction book of 1974, with sales of over ten million copies, inhabits a stodgy alternate reality where feminism didn't happen, nor did the counterculture, black power, or gay rights movement.

The rest of the world might have been experimenting with sensory derangement and alternate forms of spirituality when *The Total Woman* was released in 1973, but within the book's pages, the world was still a smutty *Playboy* cartoon wherein wives in bathrobes nagged their husbands while men gleaned their truest satisfaction from smoking cigars on the golf course with their buddies, and secretaries were busty sexpots being chased around desks by horny businessmen.

Morgan told a nation simultaneously confused, titillated, and threatened by massive cultural changes that it didn't need to bother with self-examination or spiritual seeking because there was already a book with all the answers. It was called the Christian Bible and, according to Morgan, it preached that in order to experience true happiness, women must worship, love, and obey their husbands and also God, if not necessarily in that order.

She advised women to remake themselves in the image of whatever their husbands desire most. Hubby loves hockey? Learn to skate, study up on hockey history, and read the sports pages regularly. And be sincere in your newfound love of hockey because if you're insincere when you ask him about a new trade he'll know instantly and will rightfully punish you any way he sees fit.

What if you don't like hockey? Jesus, this isn't about you, you inflexible bitch! What are you interested in, knitting and talking about feelings? Why would any man be interested in that? Those are lady things and consequently are garbage, so never waste your husband's valuable time when you could be bringing him a beer and complimenting him on how regal he looks in his beat-up recliner of a throne.

Part of *The Total Woman*'s notoriety comes from the surprisingly central role sex plays in an otherwise deeply

Christian book written in a tone that screams, "I'm just a dumb girl, but these are the silly thoughts rattling around in the goofy wad of cotton candy I call a brain!"

It's difficult, if not impossible, to parody a book with passages like the following:

"That great source book, the Bible, states, 'Marriage is honorable in all, and the bed undefiled' . . . In other words, sex is for the marriage relationship only, but within those bounds, anything goes. Sex is as clean and pure as eating cottage cheese."

That's good news for married men, and less welcome news for married women, because according to the Marabel Morgan method you really should have sex with your husband any time he wants, however he wants, and be sincere about it!

The empowering message of *The Total Woman* is that if you're a woman in an unhappy marriage, everything is your fault. If he's a loser, it's because *you* made him one. It's up to you to make him a winner.

Thankfully, since housewives are to blame for all the problems in their marriages, there's a surefire, can't-miss, quick-fix solution: become everything you imagine your husband wants in a wife, partner, lover, and sex slave. Transform yourself into a perpetually ready sex-bomb, and your husband will have no choice but to love and respect you.

As an evangelical Christian, Morgan would never condone adultery, but if a housewife were to gain five pounds, can she really blame her poor husband for sleeping with his secretary?

In developing The Total Woman program, Morgan transformed the pathological self-negation of what appears to be a deeply troubled marriage between an almost impressively dull lawyer and a sad, lonely woman into an all-encompassing strategy to save any troubled marriage that fits within its narrow confines.

Basically, if you're not a middle-class or upper-middle-class Christian housewife eager to learn how to be servile to your husband, you do not exist in Morgan's world. Then again, even if you *do* fit within the runaway best-seller's parameters, it still can't do anything for you. I suspect that of the 10 million copies of *The Total Woman* that were sold, 9.9 million of them were bought by men eager to have a woman tell their wives that happiness lies in finding freedom in slavery and empowerment in servility.

Make yourself a slave to your husband's every whim and the world will open up to you. Because who, ultimately, is treated better than a slave?

It'd be nice to think that Marabel Morgan's way of thinking is a relic of the past. That Donald Trump, a probable sex criminal, did better with white female voters than Hillary Clinton, the living embodiment of everything Morgan abhorred, in the 2016 presidential election suggests, however, that while Morgan and her book may be mostly forgotten, her ideas remain disturbingly in vogue.

LOU PEARLMAN'S
BANDS, BRANDS & BILLIONS: MY TOP 10 RULES FOR MAKING ANY BUSINESS GO PLATINUM
(2003)

When he published the memoir/business manual *Bands, Brands & Billions: My Top 10 Rules for Making Any Business Go Platinum* in 2003, disgraced boy band Svengali Louis J. Pearlman was decades into running one of the largest Ponzi schemes in American history.

He was only three years away from getting arrested in Indonesia after going on the lam as A. Incognito Johnson and only thirteen years away from dying in prison as one of the most reviled figures in the history of American popular music, a field not lacking in scoundrels.

If anyone's life should not have been an open book, it was Pearlman's. Before reading Pearlman's loving tribute to his own greatness, I wondered what could have moved a man with everything to lose, and everything to hide, to write a book about his life, but more specifically about his businesses, many of which were crooked or nonexistent.

Why would you release a book promising to give aspiring moguls the secret to your success when your "success" is predicated on robbing investors out of hundreds of millions of dollars utilizing an endless series of fraudulent schemes, many blimp-related?

The answer is rooted in Pearlman's narcissism. Pearlman couldn't resist an opportunity to spend an entire book bragging about his success and generosity.

Besides, despite the author's claims, by 2003 Pearlman had undeniably peaked as a musical force. He was deep into a steep professional slide that would end with his arrest, imprisonment, and death. Pearlman's two cash cows—Backstreet Boys and *NSYNC—sued to get out of their contracts. Diddy had taken over *Making the Band* after a first season where Lou Pearlman discovered O-Town. Pearlman's twenty-million-dollar teen movie/vanity project *Longshot* went direct-to-video.

Bands, Brands & Billions afforded Pearlman an opportunity to try to change the narrative of his life as an unlikely music mogul.

He could portray himself not as he was—a career criminal desperately trying to re-create his earlier musical success and stay one step ahead of Johnny Law—but as he wanted to be seen, as a big shot, a macher, a Jewish Berry Gordy Jr., beloved by his employees, investors, and artists for his Midas touch and Santa Claus–like generosity. In *Bands, Brands & Billions*, Pearlman isn't just a great businessman. He's also a great guy! Maybe the best!

Pearlman's literary valentine to himself opens on a note of supreme triumph, or rather a note of faux triumph. He's at the 2001 Super Bowl and everywhere he looks he's reminded of his incredible successes. As he writes at the beginning of this epic exercise in bibliographic autoeroticism: "The Bud blimp is now operated by another company, but that didn't stop the boys from Budweiser at the Super Bowl from saying, 'Look up! It's Lou's blimps! Look down! It's Lou's bands! He's everywhere! He's everywhere!'"

Ah, but it wasn't just the blimps floating above the stadium that now belonged to someone else. That was equally true of "Lou's" acts performing at the big game. The lawyers for Backstreet Boys and *NSYNC made sure of that. The biggest-selling album of 2000 was *NSYNC's *No Strings Attached,* a giant fuck-you to Lou Pearlman. In case Lou didn't get the hint, the big single was pointedly titled "Bye, Bye, Bye." Yet, despite these professional travails, Pearlman had the audacity to watch the bands with a paternal sense of ownership.

Pearlman returns repeatedly to the Super Bowl as a moment of ultimate victory, but the truth is that Lou wasn't anywhere. Those blimps floating above the stadium didn't belong to Lou. Neither did the acts singing the National Anthem (Backstreet Boys) or performing the halftime show (*NSYNC and Britney Spears, who was briefly part of a Pearlman-managed girl group named Innosense).

Pearlman was never one to let facts get in the way of a good story. If you're going to lie, you might as well lie big, and *Bands, Brands & Billions* is full of doozies. A man who never actually owned many blimps brags about having "the world's largest blimp business."

Pearlman depicts himself as a born "helium head" (blimp aficionado) and lovable, endlessly enthusiastic dreamer with an innate genius for business who conquered the world of blimps and charter airlines before a group Pearlman had never heard of called New Kids on the Block rented one of his planes for 250,000 dollars in cash.

Pearlman was blown away that the teeny bopper idols could afford something so expensive. Sensing a hole in the market, Pearlman set about creating a new, improved New Kids on the Block, first with Backstreet Boys, then with *NSYNC, and, finally, with an endless series of lesser copycats, including Natural, an act Pearlman pimps relentlessly because they were one of the only groups that had not split acrimoniously from the notorious embezzler by that point.

Pearlman, with the assistance of ghostwriter Wes Smith, makes *Bands, Brands & Billions* a deeply unearned book-length victory lap/literary infomercial for Pearlman's various businesses. It's written in an indefatigably peppy, upbeat manner festooned with terrible dad jokes, groaning pop culture references, and exclamation points designed to really drive home just how excited Pearlman is to be a fabulously successful, deeply moral dream-maker and mogul.

It's also full of observations about the music biz that would only make sense to people who know nothing about pop culture. One of the book's most fascinatingly insane passages involves Pearlman delineating the characteristics of the four primary groups of teen consumers.

Pearlman writes, "After studying the teen consumer market—including reports from the US Census, the Gallup Poll, and newspaper accounts of research done on my target audience—I figured this market was one I could bank on. Our primary audience was teenaged girls between the ages of 12 and 19. Specifically, our strategic bull's eye was those teen girls from a group I call the 'Mainstreamers.' Researchers characterize these teens as mainstream kids who make up 49 percent of the teen market. They are profiled as 'normal,' sociable teens who have a large group of friends, love to shop at malls; participate in school activities; follow fashion trends; and wear Nike, Tommy Hilfiger, Old Navy, Lee, Fila, Guess, American Eagle, I.E.I, and Gap clothing and Claire Accessories."

This is in sharp contrast to a group Pearlman dubs "Individualists." Here's how Pearlman describes their salient characteristics: "This group, which is said to represent about 21 percent of teens, is a predominantly male group that includes brainier kids, the class clowns, artistic kids and others who are not as focused on socializing or following trends of any kind."

What do these brainiacs, geeks, and rebels wear and listen to? How do they express their rugged individuality and belief in personal expression? Poppa Lou's got the scoop and is willing to share it: "They tend to wear fashions by Levi, Lee, Wrangler, Arizona, Nike, and Adidas. Their musical tastes run to Janet Jackson, LeAnn Rimes, Matchbox Twenty, Third Eye Blind and Barenaked Ladies. Some are also sports fans, but not so much participants."

Of course, a Pearlman group should never be edgy enough to appeal to the kind of radical individualists who listen to Matchbox Twenty and LeAnn Rimes, but he could nevertheless tap into this market with a "more introspective" boy band member for the Individualists.

Late in the book we're treated to another fascinatingly random combination of names when Pearlman dreams out loud about Church Street Station, a giant entertainment Mecca in Orlando he's setting up as the headquarters of his business Trans Continental (how perfect that "Con" is in the company's name) as well as a tourist attraction.

Pearlman writes, "My dream is to have my friends in the entertainment business serve as guest lecturers so that our visitors could get 'real life' tips from people like Howie D and Justin Timberlake from *NSYNC, Nick Carter of Backstreet Boys, Mandy Moore, Kenny Rogers, Ringo Starr, Davy Jones, Carrot Top, Gilbert Gottfried, Jose Feliciano, the members of Natural, my 'cuz' Art Garfunkel and others we work with."

Sadly, Pearlman's dream of a pop utopia where "Professors" like Top, Gottfried, and Starr would share their wisdom with excited tourists never came to fruition, nor did most of the big plans he shamelessly promotes here.

Speaking of Timberlake, who later accused Pearlman of "financial rape," Pearlman doesn't address his falling out with Backstreet Boys and *NSYNC until the end of the book. By that point, presumably, he imagines that readers will be so wowed by his uncanny business genius and purity of spirit that they'll believe any old line of hokum.

In this chapter, Poppa Lou's mask of guileless, childlike enthusiasm slips, and he grows uncharacteristically defensive and angry. Not at the members of *NSYNC or Backstreet Boys, of course. In Pearlman's telling, they're all deeply appreciative of everything he's done to make them stars; rather, it's the evil, parasitic, and worst of all, *greedy* (the only thing Saint Pearlman hates more than greed is dishonesty) lawyers and relatives out to break up Poppa Lou's happy family by tricking Pearlman's "boys" into thinking they've been treated unfairly.

Here's Pearlman on his professional "guilt": "Yes I'm guilty of making a profit after taking a huge risk. And I'm guilty of making multimillionaires out of a bunch of young singers too! I don't think that makes me a bad person, but it has made me the target of money-hungry people and their lawyers."

Bands, Brands & Billions is full of advice that Pearlman himself should have taken to heart, like when he advises readers, "If you want to avoid public scrutiny and frequent lawsuits, stay out of the music business."

Here's another gem that could have kept Pearlman out of trouble: "My best advice to you is to know the law, stay within it, and treat people fairly."

The surreally unselfconscious Pearlman peppers his rapturous ode to self with whoppers like, "I value my reputation as a good and fair businessman," and, "My associates often give me a hard time for being 'too nice' in negotiations and deal-making because of my emphasis on relationships." On the book's final page comes this surreal mischaracterization of his life's work: "When you help people as a way of life, they tend to pass it on. That is the greatest thing about what I do."

sex tape with porn star James Deen that, unsurprisingly, became public in a way that netted its star a small fortune and launched a career in pornography.

In 2012, as part of her pre-pornography promotional blitz, Abraham took time out of her busy schedule of doing whatever it is that people like her do to release a memoir accompanied by her debut album, both entitled *My Teenage Dream Ended.*

The dream of the title is her poignantly deluded belief that, had the Grim Reaper not intervened, she was destined for a happy ending for her fairy-tale teen romance with Derek, the handsome, cocky, insanely endowed man-child of her dreams.

Farrah Abraham and Derek are like Romeo and Juliet if Romeo was a cross between Beavis, Butthead, Ronnie from the *Jersey Shore,* and a sentient bottle of Axe body spray; and Juliet was a cold, manipulative mean girl who comes off as the villain even when telling her own story.

Nobody admits they were popular in high school. Instead, everyone pretends that they were an outcast even if they were famous, a star football player, or the Homecoming Queen.

That's true of everyone *except* for Abraham. She will have you know that as a pretty, athletic cheerleader, she was *very* popular, and when she started dating Derek, they amplified each other's popularity in a way that made lesser girls seethe with jealousy.

Derek was her Prince until their seemingly charmed relationship ran into an endless series of obstacles. When he wasn't making Farrah happy with his enormous penis, Derek was breaking Farrah's heart by lying, chasing women, getting into fights, and generally behaving like human garbage.

Reading *My Teenage Dream Ended*, I kept thinking about Abraham's daughter eventually reading the book to find out what kind of a man her father was and being confronted with the following passage, about Derek's response to learning that his ex-girlfriend had slept with an African American basketball player after they'd broken up:

"Derek started yelling, 'I loved you and you went and had sex with a n*****. I fucking hate black people.'

I let him vent and get all of his anger out. He was devastated and crying. Derek wasn't a racist. He had black friends and I had never heard him say anything racist before. I think he was just so angry at the thought that I had slept with another guy that he was lashing out and trying to say the most awful, hurtful thing he could think of. This sounds crazy, but it showed me how much he really cared about me."

I was legitimately gobsmacked by this paragraph.

In case you're keeping score, **these are things Abraham holds against her daughter's dead father:**

* Working at Burger King
* Having unflattering blonde tips
* Flirting with ugly girls
* Flirting with pretty girls
* Sleeping with pretty girls
* Cheating on her on her birthday
* Giving her a ring in an unsatisfactorily romantic fashion that made her feel like she had to reject it
* Getting arrested for unsuccessfully trying to pull a Gas-and-Go
* Lying about the severity of the Gas-and-Go incident
* Selling weed

* Smoking weed
* Doing pills that he gets from weird girls at college parties
* Having loser stoner friends
* Getting killed in an irresponsible and careless manner that was almost assuredly his fault (in Abraham's mind, at least)
* Lying about his beloved uncle being dead
* Lying about pretty much everything

These are ways Derek expressed his love for Abraham, in her mind at least:

* Dropping an N bomb
* Saying "I fucking hate black people" in a fit of rage
* Wearing one of Farrah's shirts the last time she saw him, even if he was, unsurprisingly, in the company of a girl who Abraham feels duty bound to inform us, both "got around" and "smoked weed"
* Signing a letter "Cheese Nuts," Abraham's pet name for him

If I were Abraham's editor or ghostwriter, I would never let that paragraph make it into the book. I would warn her that it reflects terribly not only on the dead father of her daughter but also on her. In another context, this might qualify as candor. Instead, it makes Abraham seem perversely shallow, but also fine with racism and racial slurs as long as they feed her ego.

My Teenage Dream Ended is an endless catalog of Derek's shortcomings as a boyfriend and human being. Here's a typical paragraph where a mortified Abraham gazes sadly at her soulmate's grim personal downward spiral from a place of unearned superiority:

"I went home and that night I thought about whether or not I should talk to Derek and give him another chance. I knew I should never take a guy back who smoked, did drugs and worked at Burger King, especially after he tried to make me jealous with some other girl. That all screamed, 'Loser!' to me. But I still loved him and I couldn't help wanting things to work out between us."

Abraham never stops loving Derek or wanting things to work out between them, but when she gets pregnant and MTV cameras start following her around school, she actively lies to Derek about both her pregnancy and his paternity.

With exquisitely myopic teenage logic, Abraham reckons that she won't tell Derek that he's going to be a father until he illustrates that he's ready for the responsibilities ahead.

The author doesn't understand that some readers may view continuously lying to the father of your unborn child about your pregnancy and his role in it as wrong. In Farrah's delusional world, it makes perfect sense.

Abraham's romantic life is unmistakably a tragedy, but it's also unintentionally a very dark comedy about a pair of teenaged nightmares who could not have been more wrong or more right for each other. On that level, and that level alone, it's a voyeuristic guilty pleasure, heavy on the guilt.

MILO YIANNOPOULOS'S
DANGEROUS
(2017)

Cheeky Alt-Right provocateur Milo Yiannopoulos's doomed manifesto *Dangerous* was self-published on July 4, 2017, after Threshold Editions, Simon & Schuster's Conservative imprint, joined the rest of the world in getting out of the Milo Yiannopoulos business once audio was released of him seemingly endorsing pedophilia as a healthy rite of passage.

Milo's career-killing words on the subject are, "In the homosexual world, particularly, some of those relationships between younger boys and older men are coming of age relationships in which those older men have helped those young boys to discover who they are and give them security and safety and provide them with love and a reliable—and sort of a rock where they can't speak to their parents."

Milo learned the hard way that you can say incendiary things and be elevated to superstardom for your outrageousness. But when you start asking what's so unhealthy about adults and thirteen-year-olds having intimate relationships, allies and institutions are going to abandon you in droves.

On Facebook, Milo claimed, "My usual blend of British sarcasm, provocation and gallows humor might have come across as flippancy, a lack of care for other victims or, worse, 'advocacy.' I deeply regret that," but what stands out about that quote after reading *Dangerous* is how uncharacteristically earnest the words that killed Milo's career are. *Dangerous* is sarcastic, provocative, full of gallows humor, and flippant about everything. It reads nothing like the words that sent the Milo movement hurtling into a brick wall.

Dangerous was published well into Donald Trump's presidency. Yet it feels like ancient history. For starters, the book is an endless victory lap from a dude whose winning streak was about to snap dramatically, with the whole world watching and cheering along.

In *Dangerous'* epilogue, Milo boasts, "I dare to be dangerous every day, and, well, I can't *stop* winning." Milo is like Donald Trump in that his idea of winning looks like an endless series of defeats from the outside.

Those defeats include Simon & Schuster parting ways with Milo after his comments about pedophilia came out. An indignant Milo sued Simon & Schuster. Then, in an unexpected gift from the universe, the complete text of Yiannopoulos's *Dangerous,* along with his editor's extensive notes, was made public due to legal wrangling.

A schadenfreude-happy public delighting in Yiannopoulos's downfall were able to experience Milo's manifesto as it was meant to be read: through the disapproving lens of an editor cursed with having to transform the troll's racism, sexism, Islamophobia, fat jokes, lesbian jokes, Kardashian jokes, Ben Shapiro jokes, and self-loathing into a book he and his employers wouldn't be ashamed to be associated with.

The conflict between Milo and his editor is not political. The editor is a Republican who works on conservative books for a right-wing imprint. The difference, instead, is generational and attitudinal, between an online culture of shock and provocation, where it's enough to make an impact and bait the right people, and a literary culture where arguments must be supported with facts and logic and not jokes about feminists being crazy cat ladies.

When Milo references Leslie Jones or the female *Ghostbusters* reboot, it's with the arrogance of someone who knows he just needs to drop the right buzzwords to get his audience to lose their shit. Milo thinks that he doesn't need to explain how his harassment of Jones got him kicked off Twitter, or the basics of GamerGate to readers because they are both such historic triumphs that poets write rapturous odes to the epic victory that ensued when the Great Milo slew the silly movie about the women busting ghosts, saving humanity in the process.

The editor continually tries to tame his wayward author by arguing that sexist, racist, homophobic, uniformly unfunny jokes, and personal insults detract from his argument and his authority.

But the truth is that as an author, Milo has no authority and the sexist, racist, homophobic, uniformly unfunny jokes *are* his argument. Oh, sure, Milo lays out plenty of conservative talking points about the evil posed by what he refers to as Muslim "rape-fugees" and radical feminists in academia and video games, but really he's just agitating for a return to an era where you could joke about Democratic women all being man-hating lesbians and cab drivers smelling like curry without facing consequences. He's in it for the LOLs and the hate. Mostly the hate.

A good example of what his poor editor was up against can be found in an early digression where Milo confidently asserts, "Speaking of witchcraft, the Clintons have turned into such villains that the demons summoned through their 'spirit cooking' sessions take notes on *them*. It's like a masterclass in demonic behavior. The demons wonder how she has done it all in one human lifetime. If you want a great example of media bias, imagine if the Trump campaign had been participating in satanic trials involving blood and semen. The closest thing Donald Trump has to occult ritual is his infamous habit of eating KFC with a knife and fork. But even that I think is one of Daddy's elaborate trolls.

You have to feel for poor Bill. Every time he hears 'gender' and 'gap' in the same sentence he gets hard, then he sees Hillary's crossed eyes and evil smile and he's booking another flight on the Lolita Express."

How do you respond to nonsense of that magnitude? If you're the editor, you break out the ALL CAPS for emphasis and insist, "This entire paragraph is just repeating fake news. There was NO blood, NO semen and there was NO Satanism. Delete."

A passage reading, "Still, I suppose the lesbians need somewhere to go. Look at any gender studies faculty in America and you're likely to find a list that goes something like, dyke, dyke, dyke, divorcée, dyke, 'genderqueer,' dyke, dyke. Lesbians should be thrown out of academia altogether and put back where they belong—porn! God hates fags, but he hates feminists more," meanwhile, merits a rightfully aghast "DELETE UGH."

DELETE UGH applies to the whole book, but the editor had to pick his battles.

Milo fills *Dangerous* with charming sentiments like, "I am a gay anomaly—like a lesbian without a violent girlfriend," that cause the editor to complain, "Leave the lesbians out of it!"

When the editor pleads, "This is not the time or place for a black dick joke," he could literally be referring to over a dozen passages.

Dangerous makes transgression toothless, provocation lame, trolling tame. You know how you can tell that Milo isn't hip? Because he spends the book bragging about how hip he is. Nobody who is genuinely hip needs to broadcast their hipness.

Milo also spends much of the book joking about how unbelievably sexy he is, much to his editor's irritation. Given the level of humor on display here, his endless comments about his good looks end up feeling less like the campy theatricality of a queer diva thrusting their sexuality onto the public and more like a corny uncle joking about how hot his new mustache makes him look.

The same is true of Milo's endless comments about his predilection for having sex with black men, something he seems to think makes it impossible for him to be racist. He similarly can't imagine how people might think he's a self-loathing homosexual even though he literally devotes a chapter of his book to arguing that homosexuals should go back into the closet and procreate with women.

The editor says of this particularly problematic section, "This chapter is in the worst shape of any chapter in the book—and it will be one of the most scrutinized. You can't just toss off poorly thought out theories about going back in the closet, as you might in a college lecture. People will come to this chapter with legitimate questions about how a gay man goes against the gay/liberal grain. You have to meet their curiosity with an appropriate level of intellectual rigor."

The chapter on why gays need to go back into the closet has fierce competition for "roughest shape" with a chapter attacking the fat acceptance movement so dire the editor deems it irredeemable, arguing gravely, "The whole chapter is a problem in tone. Your usual style NEGATES any value your information might have. The presence of the chapter in the book destroys the rest of the book."

Milo makes so many errors that no one editor can catch them all. Milo prides himself on being pop culture literate, in sharp contrast to dreary establishment Republicans. Yet, he nevertheless asserts of the sinister trend of evil black people trying to make white people feel bad about slavery by occasionally making fact-based films about American history, "There's a huge trend in movies that seek to channel white guilt over slavery, with movies like *Django Unchained*, *10 Years a Slave* [*sic*] and *MLK* [*sic*]. The villains in these movies, always white males, get progressively more sadistic and irredeemable."

The assertion that the bad guys in those three films are all white should come as a surprise to anybody who remembers Samuel L. Jackson's revered performance in *Django Unchained* as a house slave who is just about the evilest motherfucker alive. Oh, and there is no movie called *MLK*, you dunce. It's *Selma*.

A more eagle-eyed editor would have caught that the film Milo was so apoplectic about is titled *12 Years a Slave* although it's understandable how a film that ancient (four years old) and obscure (it only won Oscars for Best Picture, Adapted Screenplay, and Supporting Actress) could be misremembered by someone who spends much of the book scolding the media for getting facts wrong.

Dangerous is less a manifesto than the transcription of an endless open-mic stand-up comedy routine. Only instead of playing to his core audience of cultists and fanboys, Milo is performing for an audience of one—his editor—who does Milo and the world an incredible service in constantly stopping Milo's set to inform him that the joke that he just told was not funny.

To keep himself sane, the editor finds different ways to tell Milo that his sense of humor sucks, his jokes are terrible, and that he should be ashamed of himself. After Milo quips of Mark Zuckerberg, "He's basically like a Jewish girl who moves in bed, it shouldn't be a big deal but is considering the competition," the editor grouses, "Gets in the way of the point you're making and is not even funny."

The editor's response to Milo's assertion that "women have been nothing more than two faced backstabbing bitches except Mother Theresa . . . and even she's suspect" is funnier in and of itself than Milo's book is in its entirety. With wry understatement, the editor deadpans, "The use of a phrase like 'two faced backstabbing bitches' diminishes your overall point."

The editor puts his foot down more than once in the name of human decency. When Milo insists, "It turns out that the Hollywood Left is even more racist than the high-level Nazis," the editor nixes Nazi analogies. When Milo refers to trans people as "mentally ill," the editor fires back, "I will not accept a manuscript that labels an entire class of people 'mentally ill.'" But when Milo insists that Progressives are only interested in protecting, "tr—nies, Muslims and lonely hambeasts in their thirties," our editor pal is left to inquire what a "hambeast" is.

Milo predictably thinks that a chapter on what he depicts as the culture-destroying lie of Rape Culture is the perfect place for rape jokes.

Milo can't even make a statement like, "Rape is terrible," without immediately undercutting it with a paragraph quipping, "Well, I assume it's terrible for most people. Personally, I've never gotten off faster than when I've had a gun to my temple. My boyfriend will tell you I can't even get hard these days without a knife to my throat."

The editor is like the world's most useful heckler, a heckler who can keep the rest of the world from being subjected to abysmal jokes.

At times the editor seems rightfully astonished at Milo's ignorance, like when he corrects his assertion that "when America landed on the moon, the Cold War essentially ended" by reminding the hate-filled polemicist: "Moon landing was 1969. Berlin Wall didn't fall until 1990."

Throughout the book, the editor takes Milo to task for embodying everything he rails against, from shameless self-promotion to online harassment. The editor taps into the ridiculous, pearl-clutching hypocrisy at the book's core when he answers Milo's indignant assertion, "No one should ever be investigated for hate speech, as Mustafa was, but it's clear from the example of (feminist writer Jessica) Valenti, who once wrote the headline 'Feminists Don't Hate

Men, But It Wouldn't Matter if We Did,' that hate speech is permissible if it's done under a byline"—with an indignant, "If that headline is hate speech, THIS WHOLE BOOK is hate speech."

That's an accurate description for a toxic tome with passages like the following:

* "San Francisco has an online map of human fecal waste. If you bring enough Muslims over, you'll need a poop map and a rape zone map. Remind me again why that's a good idea?"

* "When it comes to Islamic immigration, assimilation doesn't seem to be an option. At least not yet. It's 'When in Rome, rape and kill everyone and then claim welfare.'"

* "The next time a leftist asks you what you're doing to fight rape culture, or intolerance, or homophobia, take out a Quran and burn it in front of his face."

Reading *Dangerous* would be a much different experience without the editor's notes. They transform an odious monologue into a hilarious two hander whose plentiful laughs are rooted in the culture clash between Milo and his editor.

Milo never stops trying to be funny. He never succeeds. His editor never tries to be funny and is hilarious from the first page to the last. And he didn't have to rely on cruel humor or racism or a potty mouth to make people laugh, albeit unintentionally. Milo could learn from a guy like him, in more ways than one.

I somehow expected more from *Dangerous*. I assumed that because Milo had catapulted to fame and infamy there must be something to his cult, some spark of wit or insight.

Milo may present himself as a cross between Ayn Rand, John Belushi in *Animal House*, and a human Spuds Mackenzie out to liberate our campuses. But there's nothing liberating or fun about *Dangerous*. It tries to make Islamophobia, homophobia, and racism hip and rebellious, something all the cool kids are doing, the new punk rock. It fails.

In *Dangerous*, Emperor Milo, Trickster God of the Righteous Right-Wing Trolls, was inviting an endlessly fascinated public to check him out in all his outrageous literary finery. Alas, it was evident to everyone that this Emperor had no clothes. But one heroic soul cursed with having to transform Milo into an actual author made that realization before anyone else and, through a crazy series of twists, was able to share his book-length revulsion with a morbidly fascinated public more interested in laughing at Milo than in laughing with him.

Dangerous isn't a book so much as it is a book-length self-own.

STEVEN SEAGAL AND TOM MORRISSEY'S THE WAY OF THE SHADOW WOLVES: THE DEEP STATE AND THE HIJACKING OF AMERICA (2017)

The Way of the Shadow Wolves: The Deep State and the Hijacking of America, Steven Seagal's 2017 debut novel, is a gift to the camp gods about a Mexican cartel-Jihadist-Obama conspiracy to bring down the Great Satan with a series of devastating terrorist attacks at the Grand Canyon and Camp Snoopy, and a pack of preternaturally gifted Native Americans known as "Shadow Wolves."

In Seagal's feverish Alt-Right fantasy, Shadow Wolves are law enforcement agents with the powers of Luke Skywalker and the political opinions of your racist aunt who won't stop sending you anti-Obama memes even though he's not in office anymore.

In a spectacularly clumsy opening gambit, the novel opens with our protagonist watching the end of a documentary about Native Americans with clumsily expository narration that, in angry defiance of everything we know about documentaries, continues after the film ends and well into the end credits, specifically:

"Native Americans have an innate and powerful spiritual connection with the earth and its creatures. An understanding of the 'true nature' of all that is on this planet and how it works in the perfect balance of cause and effect. An elite group within the Native American communities, known as Shadow Wolves, are part of this perfect balance and are the 'best of the best,' with the ability to see what can't be seen with the eyes. They know without having to be taught. They blend easily with the night. True right and wrong is ingrained in their souls, which makes them able to stand against evil no matter the cost. To see footprints on rock."

The authors could have just opened *The Way of the Shadow Wolves* with a few paragraphs conveying the same information as the fictional film's "narration." Yet, Seagal apparently felt it was more "cinematic" to open the film with the protagonist sitting in a darkened theater and watching a documentary that could never exist, let alone be theatrically shown.

In the space of just a few pages, Seagal and his coauthor usher us into a world that makes no sense, and dehumanize Native Americans by depicting them not as human beings, but rather as superhuman entities with a special spiritual connection to the Earth.

Our hero, John Nan Tan Gode, is one of these preternaturally wise Native Americans who commune with the Great Spirit. This powerful connection to the land has led him to know the true nature of Crooked Hillary, O'Bummer, and the Demoncrats, as we learn in the following paragraph:

"His spirit was totally connected to this land. He knew that when he walked this desert, he was stepping where many brave, bold and sometimes naive men who preceded him once walked. He could feel their energy and sense their spirit with the way things were playing out in the culture. How they had been led down a path of total dependency by an elite group of politicians who were concerned only with absolute power, nothing less, nothing more."

Yes, the true tragedy of Native Americans lies in too many governmental handouts, not in our country being built on the genocide of indigenous people.

John shares the fervently held beliefs of an InfoWars addict, as evidenced by passages like the following:

"The Deep State within the mainstream media kept the eyes of the country on the flood of illegals that were coming across the border. They painted them as simple people in need of a better life. It was a cunning distraction to take the eyes off the drugs that billionaire drug lords were pumping into the US."

Shadow Wolves proposes that a bought-and-paid-for media is working in collusion with Mexican Drug Lords and the Obama administration to flood our country with illegals and hard drugs. But the authors have more on his mind than just that. He's concerned about the Obama-*New York Times*-Mexican Drug Lord alliance, but he's even more concerned about what the novel dubs OTM (other than Mexicans) similarly flooding into the country to establish a "jihadi caliphate."

John has learned much about the "Old Ways" from a spiritual teacher who is such a ridiculous caricature of a wise Native American shaman that his name might as well be Chief MuchGood SpiritualWisdom. We learn, for example, that John has the "spirit of the snake in his bloodline," which consequently "gave him power over some people and many snakes."

At one point evil federal agents are discussing how they'll sneak Jihadi-minded terrorists over the border by positing them as "crisis actors," those fabled figures of far right-wing conspiracies who fake tragedies like the Sandy Hook shooting as part of a plan to steal everyone's guns and make Obama King for Life. *Shadow Wolves* is like a Russian nesting doll of insane conspiracy theories.

In chapter four, ominously titled "Inside the Federal Building,"we learn the exact nature of the sinister conspiracy: the president of the United States is colluding with Mexican cartels and Muslim terrorists to allow hundreds of Jihadists over an open border so they can do crimes.

As a Mexican law enforcement officer eloquently states, "It is crystal clear to all of us that the USG (United States government) is completely penetrated, and this trafficking of human jihadists is approved by the president himself and being protected by rogue elements of the CIA FBI and DEA—the same rogue elements that have been smuggling drugs, guns, gold, cash, and small children for the American elite ever since Allen Dulles and J. Edgar Hoover first created a secret state within a state."

The gorgeous thing about a passage like that is that it conveys information, but it also soars as dialogue. Seagal and Morrissey have an unerring ear for the way people talk.

The novel's protagonist is named John, but one of his most trusted associates (and fellow Shadow Wolf) is also named John. They even have distractingly similar last names (Gode and Noche) and nearly identical personalities.

The Shadow Wolves are perfect spiritual beings living in harmony with nature, but weirdly enough, they all talk and act like the profane, rasping action hero Steven Seagal plays in all his movies.

Giving lead characters nearly identical names, personalities, and backgrounds proves incredibly confusing, but if you were to dream up an original name like "John" for a character, you'd want to use it as often as possible, regardless of the confusion it creates.

The bad guys don't just plan on unleashing a hell storm upon the Great Satan that will make 9/11 seem like a pleasant afternoon in the park: they also stage murder drug orgies that combine the beheading of infidels, opium, and the finest women of ill repute filthy Muslim oil money can buy.

What kind of parties? Here's a description from late in the book:

"The tents were up and the activities were beginning as a group of women arrived and began moving about the encampment, kissing any man who came into their path. Middle Eastern music was blaring through the speakers, placed throughout the encampment, and the smell of hashish filled the air."

Whoa, there are women at these hashish-fueled murder orgies who will kiss *any* man who comes into their path?

We're also treated to the authors' thoughts on the counterculture. In a wonderfully/horrifyingly representative passage, the authors write, "(Nefarious Deep State villain Wilson) walked him towards a group who was toasting the night, some waving their arms like hippies at a rock concert.

"As he approached them, Wilson thought, 'I wonder when they're going to pull out their cigarette lighters and hold them over their heads as they begin to dig the scene.' He chuckled to himself because what he was watching [*sic*] firmed his conviction that the hippie culture was the easiest led. And usually led by charismatic fools. He wondered if some of these people were just looking to party anytime, anywhere, like Deadheads."

In *Shadow Wolves*, everyone talks like a cranky sixty-something white Republican. Think Native Americans might have issues with the Washington Redskins or being called Indians? Stupid butthurt snowflake!!! Why don't you crawl into your safe space with your participation trophies? These are real Americans, so they dismiss those concerns as the kind of political correctness that allows murderous illegals to flood into our country en masse to rape our white women, steal our jobs, rape our jobs, and then steal our white women.

Like the authors, the insane, decadent Jihadists believe strongly that all our problems are caused by political correctness, like when one of any number of hateful, bigoted stereotypes of Jihadists taunts, "I'll handle (one of the Johns) and his band of disappearing monkeys, or, as the weak-minded insist that they be called, 'Native Americans,' so they don't get there [*sic*] feelings hurt by calling them Indians. What do they call that nonsense, 'political correctness'!"

Seagal and his cowriter have terrorists think things like, "What fools these Americans are. They brought upon themselves their own destruction by their naive concept of justice and fairness."

Shadow Wolves is strongly against justice and fairness and in favor of law and order. It's against wishy-washy girly-men politicians and in favor of angry strongmen like Comrade Putin and Glorious Commandant Trump.

Shadow Wolves is flooded with loving homages to *Billy Jack*—including the timeless dialogue, "Billy Jack was a fictional character who kicked dumb shits, uh, like you, in the nuts. He did that in a lot of his movies"—yet boasts an even more juvenile conception of Native American mystical perfection than Tom Laughlin's vehicles, where, it should be noted, he did not spend too much time kicking people in the nuts. There's not a lot of honor in kicking dudes in the testicles, and Billy Jack was all about honor.

It's possible that Seagal is confusing Billy Jack for Cock Puncher, a character he played in *The Onion Movie*. Cock Puncher was, in fact, a fictional character who punched a lot of dumb shits in the cock.

What of the writing? These are real passages from the book:

> "When he parked at the casino a half hour later, Jimmy had no idea that he was being watched by a shadowy man with a heart as empty as a cave."

"General Clap did not understand the way of the ancient warrior. However, the Shadow Wolves did."

"This great, half-white father who lives in DC has released people from Gitmo who went right back into the battlefield killing my brothers in arms."

"The task force commander was pulling his leadership persona out of his back pocket."

"If all we had to depend on to do it was the US government, then we'd all be toast, and you'd wind up wearing a head scarf, if you still had a head, and all the men would be on prayer rugs five times a day."

"He produced a crucifix from under his shirt. (Muslims) treat these things like Vampires treat them."

"What he had going for him was that being Native American, they could not violate their political correctness position."

"It all comes down to money. The jihadists have plenty of it, and the Catholics who are working with them want plenty of it."

Wolves asks what it imagines is a timely and important question: What if everyone who illegally crosses the United States' borders is actually Osama Bin Laden, even the babies and women? It doesn't realize that that might be the single stupidest question ever asked about the War on Terror and immigration.

Shadow Wolves closes with the titular superheroes stopping Obama's planned Muslimgeddon and a final chapter promising a new hope in the form of a certain orange gentlemen revered by racist morons everywhere: "Finally, there was a feeling of tremendous change that began sweeping across the land as a new president was sworn into office and was immediately beset upon by the Deep State and those left behind from the previous administration. But he was stronger and smarter and far more adept than any of them had ever imagined."

Stronger, smarter, and more adept than anyone could ever imagine—those are three things that could never honestly be said of Donald Trump. But Seagal and company have sucked down the Alt-Right Kool Aid and begged for more, leading to one of the central camp artifacts of the Trump era and the poisonously xenophobic mindset behind it.

RACHEL DOLEZAL'S
IN FULL COLOR: FINDING MY PLACE IN A BLACK AND WHITE WORLD
(2017)

When an obscure president of the Spokane branch of the NAACP named Rachel Dolezal became national news after her estranged biological parents outed her as having been born white rather than the woman of color she was pretending to be, the road to public redemption seemed clear.

The media and public were fascinated and mortified by the surreal and unlikely turn of events. Yet if Dolezal had publicly apologized, explaining that her self-identification as black was an extreme response to trauma, and then set out to live a more authentic existence, the public probably would have forgiven her. She could then leverage her weird fame for strange, exploitive opportunities, including the requisite memoir and reality television show deal.

Instead of backing down, however, Dolezal doubled down. She insisted that she was not a white woman pretending to be black, but rather a Black woman who had the misfortune to be born into a race that was not her own, although she's also big on the idea that race is purely a social construct with no biological elements.

To Dolezal, it didn't matter that her parents were both white, or that she was fair-skinned, freckled, and blonde as a child. Dolezal insisted that she was "transracial" and that people who denied her identity as, in the un-ironic words of her memoir, a "woke" "soul sista" were being bigots who'd end up on the wrong side of history, even if they were black.

The backlash against Dolezal was culture-wide and wildly disproportionate to the level of power she held. Trans activists were offended by Dolezal's attempts to link her struggle to theirs. Conservatives snorted derisively at Dolezal and used her as a tool to attack trans rights, as well as an example of the ultimate "Social Justice Warrior," more obsessed in broadcasting righteousness than pushing for meaningful social change. Progressives were equally mortified. Dolezal wasn't just appropriating a hairstyle or clothes: she was appropriating blackness in its entirety. Despite Dolezal's background as an academic teaching black history, she didn't seem to understand why that was wrong. She still doesn't.

There was so much hostility toward Dolezal that her memoir, *In Full Color: Finding My Place in a Black and White World,* was apparently rejected by dozens of publishing houses before it was published by BenBella Books.

The response to the book was scathing. At Amazon, the book has a dire 2.3-star rating, and in a widely read interview published in *The Stranger,* black writer Ijeoma Oluo depicted Dolezal as not just delusional but also racist.

It's a very popular article, and one I imagine Dolezal despises for reasons that go beyond it starting with "I'm sitting across from Rachel Dolezal and she looks . . . white" and containing sentiments like, "Something else, something even sinister is at work in (Dolezal's) relationship and understanding of blackness."

In her denunciation of Dolezal, Oluo comes to the same conclusion that I did after reading *In Full Color.* Dolezal seems to think that her black identity must be authentic because she's better than people born black at understanding what she sees as the core of blackness.

Dolezal thinks that since she's read all the books, gone to all the protests, joined all the civil rights groups, made all the speeches, and rocked all the natural black hairstyles, then how dare anyone tell her she's not black just because by every standard other than her own, she is not black?

What makes *In Full Color* so heartbreaking is that Dolezal's sense of herself as black comes from a place of deep pain. According to Dolezal, her early life as the daughter of racist, deplorable Jesus Freaks Larry and Ruthanne was a cross between *Little House on the Prairie* and *Carrie*. Dolezal wasn't just white: she was the progeny of the worst, whitest people in existence. Rachel compares her early life to that of a sharecropper forced to toil endlessly in the fields, from morning till night, for food and shelter and nothing more.

It was nothing but elk tongue sandwiches; fiery sermons about the Lord's wrath; and physical, emotional, and sexual abuse for Rachel as a child until she was introduced to another world through images of naked, beautiful Africans in *National Geographic* magazines. The author felt intense feelings of not just fascination but also identification. This was the beginning of a lifelong love affair with black culture that would ultimately lead Dolezal to identify as black.

In Full Color alternately resembles a fairy tale and a superhero origin story. In the fairy-tale version, Dolezal is a beautiful Black princess doomed by a witch's curse to be born with the wrong skin color and live with tiny white oafs who only pretended to be her "real" parents.

In this version, it is not a prince who saves the heroine. Instead, Rachel finds the tools to save not only herself but also the people closest to her—in this case, her son and adopted siblings—and underprivileged black children everywhere by embracing her black identity and working tirelessly not as a white ally but as a proud soul sista.

Though it is certainly not Dolezal's intention to do so, she ends up using the black people she professes to love and honor as props in her hero's journey. They're less people with agency and issues and complications of their own than magical mirrors that reflect Dolezal's black identity back to her in exhilaratingly flattering ways.

In *In Full Color*, Dolezal is forever dealing with gushing compliments from black people about how she could be their sister or how her hair is flawless or how, whatever her biological origins, she's blacker than they'll ever be. In Dolezal's telling at least, a deeply scarred and emotionally traumatized blonde white woman's attempts to pass herself off not just as a black woman but as a black civil rights leader was met by the black community with universal cheers of "you go, girl!"

The only exception to the universal cheers of the black community seems to be the enormous number of black people who were deeply insulted and offended by Dolezal's conception of herself as black. These include her ex-husband/father of her child, a black man Dolezal portrays as a man who hated his own blackness so much that he forced Dolezal to live as a white woman; two of Dolezal's black adopted siblings; and pretty much every black interviewer and talk-show host she encountered while doing press following her outing as a woman born white.

Dolezal pretends that she wants to start a deep, painful, but important conversation about race. She doesn't. She has an opportunity to have that conversation with the black women who interview her during her post-outing press tour, but when she's challenged by these descendants of slaves, she refuses to acknowledge the legitimacy of their arguments because, in her mind, they just don't understand the true nature (and inherent fallacy) of race the way that she does, either because they simply haven't read the same books or because of their internalized racism. Dolezal thinks that she alone understands race and is cursed to share the planet with people who are so unenlightened that they are to be pitied more than hated.

In the superhero origin story version of Dolezal's tale, she was born into humble circumstances yet realized at an early age that she had an identity that set her apart from her family and everyone around her. While the world might look at this little blonde white girl and see a Caucasian moppet, she was secretly a black Superwoman.

In this version, Dolezal set about becoming the guardian and protector of black children everywhere and became so good at what she sees as the essence of blackness—reading about black History, leading marches, doing black hair, protesting, making black art, mentoring black children—that she crossed some invisible line and became black.

Identifying as black didn't constitute part of Dolezal's identity. Dolezal's manufactured blackness instead constitutes her entire identity. Everything she did was rooted not just in an obsession with an idealized and romanticized fantasy conception of blackness but in her own idealized, romanticized blackness.

Dolezal did a lot for the Black communities that she lived in. I know because *In Full Color* is an endless catalog of all the things Dolezal has done for Black communities. If Dolezal won an award, acquired a job skill, held a position, or got a raise, she dutifully records it in the book to the point where her memoir begins to feel like a résumé.

Oluo sees Dolezal as deeply emblematic of white supremacy at its most clueless. It's hard to derive any other conclusion from Dolezal's fierce conviction that she, a woman born white, to racists, should be the voice of black Spokane, and not someone with more legitimate claims to blackness.

Dolezal did not just attend marches and meetings. She sought out media attention and wrote columns about her blackness without ever anticipating that parents she depicts as angry and vindictive might blow her cover.

Dolezal depicts her outing as an attempt on her parents' behalf to discredit her as a witness in her brother's molestation case as well as an attempt by the corrupt police establishment of Spokane to get rid of her. But it seems like Dolezal was always going to be found out. What's surprising is that it took so long.

Late in the book, as terrible argument 379 as to why everyone should just shut up and accept that she's black, Dolezal brags, "When my friend Nikki in college, multiple boyfriends and girlfriends, and a professor at Whitworth all made statements to the effect of, 'Rachel is blacker than most black people'—something that happens to this day—they clearly weren't talking about my complexion or my hair. They were pointing to my commitment to the cause of racial and social justice, my work on behalf of the Black community, and the sense of self it took me multiple decades to fully embrace."

At one point in *In Full Color* Dolezal mentions that because of her childhood, she has no sense of humor. This is tossed off as an aside, just another example of how the author is different from people on both sides of a color line Dolezal wants to erase.

The rest of the book backs up Dolezal's contention that because she grew up in a world without laughter, or humor, she can neither understand what makes something funny or be funny herself. When Dolezal was exposed as someone who grew up white and blonde and freckled in the whitest parts of the white Midwest, yet insisted that she was black, she became an instant punchline to everyone but herself.

Dolezal doesn't understand what made her a figure of fun. She doesn't understand the concept of fun or comedy at all. And that, I think, says something profound about Dolezal and her inability to understand the world, or race, or the way the world sees her. *In Full Color* is fascinating in part because it is a book about a white woman who became the president of an NAACP branch while identifying as black from an author who has no idea why anyone would find her story funny.

We understand the world through religion, through art, through spirituality, philosophy, storytelling, and politics. Just as essentially, we understand the world through humor. This is particularly true when it comes to race. Someone with a sense of humor might interpret a comment like, "Rachel is blacker than most black people," to mean something along the lines of, "Damn, Rachel, you are trying way too damn hard to be black." But Dolezal does not have a sense of humor, nor does she seem capable of understanding nuance, and she's so desperate to have her self-conception as black confirmed by people born black that she's incapable of seeing those comments as anything other than a stirring affirmation that she is a strong black woman.

Because Dolezal cannot understand comedy, or humor, or the roles that either play in how we understand and process life, she fatally misunderstands herself and the world. If she had a sense of humor, Dolezal might have made a joke about the fact that she spends *In Full Color* gushing about the opportunities she's provided for black people, yet when it came time to choose a ghostwriter, she didn't just pick a white guy, but rather a white guy named Storms Reback, whose name sounds like a white supremacist organization.

But Dolezal does not make jokes, nor does she undercut the memoir's relentless self-mythologizing with self-deprecation. Dolezal's humorlessness seems central to her inability to grasp the complexities and ambiguities of the world. The author does not understand why her life is both a dark comedy and a tragedy. Because of Dolezal's fatal lack of self-awareness, a memoir Dolezal intends as a triumph of self-realization reads more like a tragedy of self-delusion.

DOUG HUTCHISON'S
FLUSHING HOLLYWOOD: FAKE NEWS AND FAKE BOOBS: A MEMOIR
(2020)

Doug Hutchison's 2020 memoir, *Flushing Hollywood*, is a book that SHOULD NOT EXIST. *Flushing Hollywood* should not exist, first and foremost, because its author infamously married sixteen-year-old Courtney Stodden (who identifies as nonbinary and uses they/them pronouns) when he was fifty.

Flushing Hollywood is less a memoir than an angry jeremiad against a world that would DARE to judge Doug Hutchison and his marriage to a child despite being ferociously imperfect itself.

Hutchison's accidental but utterly damning confession resembles Dustin Diamond's similarly rancid memoir, *Behind the Bell,* in pointing an accusatory finger in Hollywood's direction and insisting that show business does not have the right to judge ANYONE because it is so infamously a den of sin and iniquity.

In their memoirs, Diamond and Hutchison put HOLLYWOOD on trial, and find it GUILTY! GUILTY of hypocrisy! GUILTY of being phony! GUILTY of greed! GUILTY of flagrantly mistreating good, sensitive people like Dustin Diamond and Doug Hutchison! GUILTY, GUILTY, GUILTY!

Like Diamond, Hutchison makes a special point of insulting the appearances of glamorous Hollywood movie stars on the dubious grounds that pointing out that actors don't look as good without makeup is empowering rather than sexist and gross.

In this passage, Hutchison relays how, actually, his *Batman & Robin* costars Alicia Silverstone and Uma Thurman are total uggos in real life: "On my first day on set I arrived extra early to find myself flipping through the before and after make-up Polaroids of our main stars: Clooney, O'Donnell, Silverstone and Thurman and folks, I know you've probably heard it one thousand times before but I'm here to tell ya the truth: These Hollywood sex symbols look like road kill before the make-up chair. I find Thurman and Silverstone both attractive, but—if you could've seen them in those before pics—you would've barfed up your breakfast."

Behind the Bell and *Flushing Hollywood* posit themselves as shocking, incendiary exposés.

Think everyone in Hollywood is faithful and a paragon of sexual modesty? Think AGAIN, chump! A lot of famous people are screwing around on their wives! Think your favorite stars all refrain from using mood-altering substances because they want to preserve the sacred temples that are their bodies and minds? Hutchison has news for you: they're all cheating on their wives at cocaine parties with Kid Rock and Lars Ulrich where the groupies line up fifty deep!

That's how it is in Holly*weird*, man! It's full of fornicators. And drunks! And the agents: they're SO greedy! And crazy! And not ethical either. Not to mention the Liberals with all their Priuses who think they're so great! What about the paparazzi and the reality shows? Turns out THEY'RE totally gross and sleazy as well! Who knew, other than everyone?

So, what right does a world so awash in sin have to blacklist a dude just for the whole "exploiting a child he thrust into the unforgiving, traumatizing glare of the tabloid spotlight" thing?

Like Diamond, Hutchison doesn't seem to understand that the existence of sin does not absolve him of his own sins. It's not an either/or proposition: Hollywood AND Hutchison are both terrible. Hollywood is sleazy and amoral; Hutchison is rightly notorious for being sleazy and amoral even by Hollywood standards.

The first half of *Flushing Hollywood* is devoted to a series of rambling, misanthropic, sexist, and racist anecdotes about its author's checkered career as a theater, television, and film character actor specializing in playing creepy loners in *The X-Files, Punisher: War Zone,* and *The Green Mile.*

Hutchison knows how deeply it hurts to be judged, yet he nevertheless spends the entire book judging others and letting himself off easy.

Early in his career Hutchison had the honor of brushing up against some of the most respected actors and actresses of his generation. In a development at once surprising and unsurprising, it turns out that they all suck.

Hutchison writes that Lili Taylor, who costarred in the play *Fun* with him when they were both starting out, is a "pretentious, duplicitous ball-busting back stabber."

Even though, by his own account, Hutchison has been deeply wounded by vicious gossip, he nevertheless feels the need to share, "Our paths never cross again but I hear story after story from various sources who work with her that Lili Taylor, queen of the indie world, is nothing but a demanding, self-serving brat who throws tantrums when the slightest tilt of the world is not to her liking."

Hutchison merely insults Taylor's personality. William H. Macy, who would have directed Hutchison in an off-Broadway premiere of *Fun* had the young actor not ditched the production for a big movie payday, gets roasted for his looks, for his personality, AND for being a talentless loser.

The bitterness-poisoned author with the brain full of diseased worms writes of the *Fargo* star, "At first sight— with his howdy doody ears, orangey hair and freckles—Bill Macy resembles something like a troll."

Macy earns Hutchison's undying hatred by asking him not to abandon a play he's directing for a role in the forgotten Andrew McCarthy/Molly Ringwald vehicle *Fresh Horses* mere days before the play is scheduled to open.

That seems reasonable to me, but in Hutchison's eyes, it's proof that Macy is just another phony narcissistic egotistical show-biz shit bag, and a non-talent to boot.

To Hutchison, this monster is as talentless as he is ugly. Hutchison writes of the Oscar nominee, "Macy is one of the worst actors of our generation. His performances, to me, are consistently stilted, over-the-top and transparent— as if he's trying too hard to enunciate every word in that annoying, Mamet-esque staccato style. Simply put: William H. Macy's a fake. He's faking it now when he tries talking me out of my shot at *Fresh Horses,* and he'll continue faking it over the years with his horse-poop acting."

Macy is at least in good company. Here's Hutchison on another beloved yet secretly terrible actor, Samuel L. Jackson: "I can't, for the life of me, figure out why Jackson continues to maintain his A-list movie star status. With rare exceptions (i.e., His stellar performance in 137 and maybe, just maybe, *Pulp Fiction*), Sam Jackson's a one-trick pony. He delivers the same over-arching and unconvincing performances—flaring his nostrils, bugging his eyeballs, and acting 'all angry and shit'—in nearly every single thing he does."

Hutchison has a HUGE problem with black men acting "all angry and shit," onscreen and off.

True, Samuel L. Jackson never appeared in a movie called 137, but that does not undermine Hutchison's assertion that all the best actors are terrible, especially if they're black.

Hutchison writes derisively of Juilliard classmate Andre Braugher's take on Macbeth, "Andre is awful. He over-acts and basically shouts his way throughout the play with a big, bad, bawdy, booming affection of—well, quite frankly, crapola. It's like a bad second-rate attempt at a James Earl Jones impression."

Now, bear in mind, Hutchison is NOT racist. By his own account, he is extremely NON racist, though for the sake of getting into character as a racist for his role in *A Time to Kill* he felt that it was VERY important to use the N word in real life, off the set, and hang out with as many racists as possible. You know, for method acting purposes!

Hutchison is uniquely attuned to the devastating costs of reverse racism when committed by black actors he doesn't like or considers too "arrogant" or "angry" like Samuel L. Jackson, Ving Rhames, Jamie Foxx, Wesley Snipes, and Braugher. Hutchison has nothing but harsh words for black movie stars who think they're so great that they can treat a bona fide white man like Doug Hutchison any old way just because they're rich and famous and successful and powerful.

Hutchison isn't just racist and belligerent, hateful, and overflowing with bitterness and resentment. He is also, unsurprisingly, a creep to women.

Here's Hutchison on his guest appearance on *The X-Files*: "It's August 9th and Gillian's twenty-third birthday when we shoot the scene where (Hutchison's villain character) Tooms squeezes through the heating duct of Scully's apartment, climbs on top of her on the bathroom floor, and is about to extract her liver before Mulder arrives in the nick of time to save the day. On almost every single take, during our struggle, Gillian's blouse insists on popping open and revealing the brassiere beneath. Gillian's a good sport about it. She buttons back up after each take, saying, 'I'm kind of exposing myself here.' I reply teasingly, 'No worries, Gil. I'm certainly enjoying the free show.' Gillian laughs, crimson-faced with embarrassment, but I surmise flattered by the attention, nonetheless.

"At one point, straddling her and holding her wrists down while the director sets up the shot, I decide to flirt with Gillian, whispering, 'You like being restrained. Don't you?' Gillian's eyes become as big as saucers. 'Come on, admit it, Gillian. You're a baaaaad girl, aren't you? You want to be tied up and spanked.'"

Hutchison does not get to tie up and spank his twenty-three-year-old coworker, but he does console himself with the news that the *X-Files* star, like all famous people, devolved into a narcissistic monster once she became successful.

"Rumors abound years from now in *The X Files* circles that Gillian morphs into a self-serving prima-donna after a semblance of success," he insists.

Now bear in mind, Hutchison does not "know" this firsthand. Nonetheless, he feels compelled to share it all the same.

Hutchison's idea of flirting looks an awful lot like sexual harassment, but sexual predators see their actions differently than others do. They don't see their actions as predation, assault, or harassment but rather as flirting, friendship, romance, and sexy fun.

Everyone must find a way to live with themselves and their actions. For Hutchison, that means re-conceiving his parasitic, deeply problematic romantic and sexual relationship with a child as a grand romance destroyed by his ex-wife's evil mother and a world and an industry that would not allow these soulmates to be happy.

In limply defending his marriage to a child, Hutchison trots out all the defenses pedophiles employ. I thought they were WAY older! They're very mature for their age! They're an old soul! We were together in previous lives! Age doesn't matter! Famous people like Charlie Chaplin and

Paul Walker dated or married teenagers and got away with it, mostly! It's legal (with parental consent) so it can't be amoral! The heart wants what it wants!

In a fever of delusion, Hutchison writes, "Courtney's far more mature than a 'typical' sixteen-year-old. They're no pony-tailed high school cheerleader with braces on their teeth and a crush on Justin Bieber. Courtney's well beyond their years and—based on our connection—I'm sensing that they're just as beautiful on the inside as they appear outside. They're an angel. I'm smitten."

Looks don't matter to Hutchison. He writes that he would still consider Stodden the most beautiful person in the world if they were the victim of an acid attack. That's not because he's superficial or cares about looks but because it's important to continually reiterate how smoking hot his child bride was and how everyone wanted to fuck them, something that seems to displease Hutchison and turn him on simultaneously.

Hutchison's relationship with Stodden began online, with the disillusioned thespian and acting coach being blown away by the talent and natural charisma of a beauty he claims to have assumed was in their mid to late twenties.

Depending on the context, Hutchison either doubles down on the "They're SO mature for their age! They're like a forty-year-old in the body of a teenager!" line of defense or implores readers to bear in mind that Stodden was only seventeen—a CHILD—when they were being eviscerated by cast-mates and the public at large during their time on *Couples Therapy*.

Won't someone think about the children! Especially the ones married—HAPPILY!—to creepy fifty-something character actors?

Hutchison insists that Stodden's love for black and white shows like *The Honeymooners*, *I Love Lucy*, and *The Twilight Zone* proved they were mature beyond their years.

Yet those shows are famously beloved by children. I know. I watched them when I was eight; they're pretty much only watched by old people and children, so Doug and Courtney, pretty much.

When Hutchison learned that Stodden was only sixteen years old it did not prove a deal-breaker. Because by that point Hutchison was in love, and, in *Flushing Hollywood* at least, love excuses and justifies all.

Marrying a sixteen-year-old makes Hutchison a pariah in an industry that, to be honest, was never that wild about him to begin with. He becomes unemployable. No reputable production wants to be associated with a notorious cradle robber.

With Hutchison's life savings running out, acting opportunities nonexistent, and Stodden in a furious hurry to launch their career as a singer/actress/model, Hutchison pivots professionally and personally. He stops being a VERY serious actor who takes his art seriously and becomes a shameless tabloid creature desperately chasing down every last dollar and perpetually willing to degrade himself and pimp out his marriage for a payday.

Flushing Hollywood feels pornographic even before Stodden films an ACTUAL pornographic motion picture that is initially rejected by Vivid Video for not being pornographic enough.

Courtney's "momager" Krista, the memoir's primary villain and a figure of Satanic evil, can't help but fall hopelessly in love with her daughter's new husband, at one point asking Hutchison if he'd ever fantasized about having a threesome with his then-wife and his mother-in-law.

Hutchison turns her down because he is, by his own account, a "trustworthy and straight-forward person." While he concedes that he is not perfect—a bold admission given how easy and possible it is to be perfect—he insists, "I am a man of good character. I attribute this to my upbringing.

Like all parents, mine made many, many mistakes but—all in all—I believe they raised me the best they could to be a decent man with honorable values. Proof positive of this is Hollywood. After twenty-five years in this cesspool, I've somehow managed to preserve my character."

Because this man infamous for marrying a child is trustworthy and straightforward, a decent man with honorable values, we can trust him when he tells us that for the better part of the decade pretty much his entire public life with Stodden was a flimsy fiction concocted by desperate opportunists for a paycheck large enough to keep their grubby hustle going.

This includes filming a Las Vegas solo sex video they pretend was taped for Hutchison's erotic benefit alone and then stolen or leaked when it was always intended for the public market. Alas, the pornographers the couple get into bed with professionally don't think it's dirty enough, so an additional scene is filmed involving an ice cream cone being used in an unsavory, unhygienic manner.

The public's interest in this seedy sideshow diminished with time, however. The sad, desperate publicity stunts didn't work, and Hutchison went bankrupt financially as well as morally. These soulmates eventually went their separate ways, with Hutchison retreating back to his home state of Michigan to get his head straight and life right.

The cover of *Flushing Hollywood* is an amateurish photoshop of Doug Hutchison pointing at a toilet indelicately placed on the Hollywood Walk of Fame. The title and cover are only one manifestation of Hutchison's obsession with feces. Hutchison wants us to know that Hollywood acts like its shit doesn't stink when—and this is another explosive revelation—it does!

In what remarkably qualifies as one of the book's less disgusting passages, Hutchison writes about how impressed he was by Tom Hanks' charm and talent on *The Green Mile*, but also how they were in a bathroom together once and the Oscar winner dropped a MONSTER deuce so foul-smelling that it disgusted people three states over.

So even though Hanks is a great guy, his shit not only stinks but is so foul-smelling that decades later Hutchison felt the need to commemorate, for posterity, its grossness.

In that same scatological spirit, *Flushed Hollywood* is complete shit, real horse-poop writing. It was nevertheless EXACTLY what I needed during the early days of the pandemic, because escape is escape even when what you're escaping to is the warped psyche of a grade-A show-business creep.

THE WORST OF
TELEVISION

THE BRADY BUNCH
VARIETY HOUR
(1976-1977)

People know *The Brady Bunch Variety Hour* largely through *The Simpsons*' ingenious parody of it as "The Simpsons Family Smile Time Variety Hour" on the classic episode "The Simpsons Spin-Off Showcase."

It's a parody of spin-offs and tacky variety shows in general, but one variety show in particular: *The Brady Bunch Variety Hour*, the Krofft brothers' notorious attempt to reinvent America's favorite blandly idealized blended family as unlikely vaudevillians.

"The Simpsons Spin-Off Showcase" host Troy McClure pitches the variety show as an opportunity for the Simpsons "to show off the full range of their talents." However, "one family member didn't want that chance," but thanks to some creative casting, you won't even notice her absence.

In "The Simpsons Smile Time Variety Hour" the lone holdout is Lisa Simpson, who understandably would have seen the variety show as beneath her dignity. In *The Brady Bunch Variety Hour* the *Brady Bunch* veteran who is conspicuous in her absence is Eve Plumb, aka the Real Jan.

Plumb may not have been the most popular Brady Kid, but when she opted out of returning, she instantly became not just an important cast member but *the* most important Brady Kid because her absence invalidated an already surreally misconceived project.

Under no circumstances could a variety show vehicle for the Bradys have worked, but replacing Eve Plumb with newcomer Geri Reischl in the role of Jan represents the maraschino cherry placed gingerly atop this three-scoop shit sundae that is *The Brady Bunch Variety Hour.*

The Brady Bunch Variety Hour was so fascinatingly wrong that *The Simpsons'* spoof can't possibly capture all its egregiously bonkers elements.

The set for "The Simpsons Family Smile Time Variety Hour" is tacky and vulgar, but it noticeably lacks the defining feature of *The Brady Bunch Variety Hour's* set: an enormous pool where a dance troupe known as the Krofftettes performed water ballet and soggy slapstick shenanigans. The Kroffts were inspired by their own *Donnie and Marie,* which prominently featured an ice-skating rink because its stars were accomplished skaters.

It's less clear why there's a pool in the *Brady Bunch Variety Hour* set.

The Brady Bunch Variety Hour opens on a note of deliberate, delirious excess, with a frenzy of Busby Berkeley–style choreography and elaborate camerawork showcasing the frenetic exertions of chorus girls all sporting the same plastic amphetamine smiles as they gyrate in unison onstage and in the water.

On a giant screen behind the Bradys we see rapid-fire images of the cast in their *Brady Bunch* days with the notable exception of Reischl, whose presence once again serves to highlight the project's perversely off-brand nature.

The old-school spectacle is designed to distract from the sorry nature of the main attraction. Onstage the Bradys, and Geri Reischl, perform a Branson-style medley that combines the standard "Babyface" with the hot new disco smash "Love to Love You Baby."

An urban legend developed around "Love to Love You Baby" that Donna Summer's cries of sexual ecstasy weren't feigned but rather were the product of genuine masturbation, and that what you're hearing on the disco anthem are real orgasms.

Despite its title, "Love to Love You Baby" is not about love. It's about fucking, about orgasmic delight and female sexual pleasure and pushing the boundaries of explicitness to their breaking point.

It is, in other words, a perverse choice of an opening number for a family group so bland that their name doubles as dismissive shorthand for "white-bread."

Watching the Bradys destroy the Great American Songbook, I came to a realization about "Weird Al" Yankovic's possible motivation for polka medleys. You could not watch television in the 1970s without being inundated by medleys of standards and contemporary hits that weren't just bad—they were crimes against music.

I felt sorry for the songs being performed here. They were good songs, sometimes great. They did nothing to merit being inelegantly shoehorned into the Bradys' muddled post–*Brady Bunch* legacy.

Nothing in any of "Weird Al" Yankovic's many polka medleys has ever been as perverse or comically incongruous as Mike Brady, architect with pipes of rusty aluminum, and now-not-so-little Cindy Brady peppily crooning an infamous explosion of orgasmic ecstasy like "Love to Love You Baby" as a peppy early number on their own ill-fated variety show.

The classically trained Robert Reed, who was nominated for three Emmys for his non-Brady work, famously hated the show and role that made him famous. He rightly considered it pabulum and continually bumped heads with its producers and writers. Reed wanted it to be less terrible. *Gilligan's Island* creator Sherwood Schwartz, however, was comfortable operating at the existing level of shittiness or, possibly, getting even worse.

Yet, Reed apparently enjoyed *The Brady Bunch Variety Hour* despite its mind-boggling awfulness, because it gave him a chance to sing and dance, to express an element of his personality he repressed as a closeted homosexual thespian who took himself very seriously and had the credits (*The Defenders, The Boy in the Plastic Bubble, Roots*) and background (Northwestern, Royal Academy of Dramatic Arts, Actors Studio) to back up his perception of himself as an artist.

Reed thought delivering pat life lessons and canned wisecracks on *The Brady Bunch* was beneath his dignity. Yet, Reed apparently also felt that singing and dancing to "Shake Your Booty" in a sparkly white tuxedo surrounded by his coked-out fake kids in front of a pool was just his speed.

If you want to be generous, you could call *The Brady Bunch Variety Hour* revolutionary in its format in that it was a variety show, but also incorporated elements of sitcom, soap opera, melodrama, sketch, broad physical comedy, puppetry, song, dance, musicals, postmodern motherfuckery, conceptual weirdness, and, of course, underwater ballet.

Though *The Brady Bunch Variety Hour* was a variety show, it maintained a heavy element of narrative storytelling. Within the universe of the show Mike Brady has quit his job as an architect to pursue his musical family's dream of having a national televised showcase for their show-business ambitions.

Reed's inexperience as a singer and dancer was written into the show. *The Brady Bunch Variety Hour* made a running gag of Brady being a show-business novice easily outperformed by his wife and kids. Florence Henderson was a veteran singer while the Brady Kids recorded albums and toured during the show's run.

Reed's inability to sing or dance posed a formidable problem to a show that's mostly singing and dancing, with a healthy side order of baggy pants comical shenanigans. Yet there's something poignant and endearing about Reed's Quixotic efforts to keep up, to will himself into being a competent singer and adequate hoofer.

It makes no sense for Mike Brady, vocally challenged architect, to be at the center of this mostly singing, mostly dancing kitsch extravaganza flaunting his glaring limitations. The clammy, desperate addition of the Bradys' maid, Alice, is even more inexplicable.

After starring in *The Brady Bunch*, Ann B. Davis understandably felt the need to repent. She renounced her sinful show-business ways and retired from the business to serve Christ.

But her resolve crumbled when she was afforded a once-in-a-lifetime opportunity to do the worst work of her career in a project so misconceived that later generations would legitimately wonder how it could have come to pass.

How could Davis resist the opportunity to dress up like a nightmarish hillbilly geriatric Pippi Longstocking and hoof her way through a clattering cover of "Thank God I'm a Country Girl" surrounded by rednecks with grotesque puppet heads?

Watching *The Brady Bunch Variety Hour*, I came to understand why *Saturday Night Live* has been romanticized as revolutionary countercultural comedy when it is so obviously, even transparently, commercial and mainstream, a towering monument to cynical calculation and cowardice.

Compared to the variety shows that flooded the air at the time, including, but not limited to, *Saturday Night Live with Howard Cosell*, *Saturday Night Live* was punk as fuck. It was hailed as subversive largely because Krofft Brothers–produced, Bruce Vilanch–written variety shows set the bar so low for sketch comedy that *Saturday Night Live* couldn't help but soar over it.

The Brady Bunch Variety Hour unsuccessfully tried to resell the Bradys back to the public as an off-brand Partridge Family crossed with Donnie and Marie. By the time the Bradys' new neighbors Lee Majors and Farrah Fawcett, then the hottest TV stars in the world and consequently the Bradys' peers, show up for a spontaneous sleepover because of a termite infestation in their mansion, the mission drift was impossible to ignore.

A show that began as a look at an idealized, blended all-American family had become a glitter-strewn, puppet-infested, inexplicably Esther Williams–inspired variety spectacle about a show-business family that hung out with the biggest celebrities in the world and contended with romantic competition from Charo and Paul Williams.

The core joke of first the influential stage show *The Real Live Brady Bunch*, where future stars like Jane Lynch and Andy Richter performed actual Brady Bunch scripts live for the ironic amusement of Gen Xers in the early 1990s, and then the *Brady Bunch* movies, is that the "normalcy" of the Brady Bunch is, in fact, anything but normal.

What *The Brady Bunch* tried to pass off as sunny Americana was actually utterly bizarre. Plop the Bradys into an approximation of the real world, as *The Brady Bunch Movie* did, and they seem more like space aliens than a typical American family.

Due to music rights clearance issues and a screaming lack of interest, there will probably never be an official release of *The Brady Bunch Variety Hour*. But I have seen it, and can vouch that it exists, improbably, wrongly, but incontrovertibly. Now you can experience it for yourself on YouTube and see firsthand that sometimes the reality is even crazier than the legend.

GET HIGH ON YOURSELF
(1981)

For cultists of Robert Evans, film producer, actor, executive, author, national treasure, and bon vivant, the 1981 special *Get High on Yourself* occupies a small but major place in the great showman's self-mythology.

In the film version of Evans' memoir *The Kid Stays in the Picture*, the author disgraces himself by getting busted for cocaine trafficking. Even worse, Evans does not contact his mentor Sidney Korshak immediately to resolve the situation, irrevocably harming their friendship in the process.

But like a gorgeously tanned Phoenix rising from the ashes, the super-producer transformed a court order to create an anti-drug commercial as part of his punishment into a weeklong celebration of sobriety called *Get High on Yourself* he deemed, with trademark hyperbole, "The Woodstock of the 1980s."

I chuckled long and hard the first time I saw a motley assemblage of TV stars and athletes badly group-singing an obscure anti-drug jingle christened one of the major cultural events of the Reagan era.

I laughed just as long and just as hard every subsequent time I came to the part in *The Kid Stays in the Picture* where Evans favorably compares a half-forgotten "Just Say No" anthem to a generation-defining concert from the 1960s.

I derived so much joy from Evans' delusion that he'd created the "Woodstock of the 1980s," whether society acknowledged it or not, that I never went through the bother of actually watching the special.

Then I was doing a podcast with my friend Alonso Duralde about *The Kid Stays in the Picture* and a surreal weekend I spent at the home of its subject and he mentioned that *Get High on Yourself* was on YouTube and was every bit as gloriously insane as it seems.

Evans' magical Rolodex and legendary charm attracted some of the biggest names in sports and entertainment, megastars like Paul Newman, Henry Winkler, Mark Hamill *and* Dorothy Hamill, Earvin "Magic" Johnson, Julius "Dr. J" Irving, and Bob Hope, but the biggest star is the Kid Who Stayed in the Picture, the Prince of Paramount himself, Mr. Robert Evans.

Henry Winkler jokes that the reason he's there is because, "Bob Evans extorted money from my family," before gushing, "Bob Evans loves to say that there were more celebrities in one place for free than he could have ever gotten for one of his films, or all of his films combined."

Possible murderer Robert Wagner, meanwhile, picks up a phone and, with a stiffness seldom seen outside of athlete cameos on *Arli$$*, woodenly insists, "Evans, if it has to do with kids, you got me!"

A comeback-hungry Evans brought together the biggest stars in the world in one studio with telegenic kids so that they could deliver the straight dope that drugs like marijuana and cocaine had no place in 1980s pop culture or the entertainment industry.

The *Kid Stays in the Picture* icon was too much of a hedonist to evangelize on behalf of something as dreary as boring old sobriety, so he offers a very 1980s substitute. Instead of getting high on illicit substances, Evans and his celebrity friends admonish children to get high on their own abilities, on their creativity, optimism, and irrepressible energy.

The legendary narcissist invites children and adults alike to get high on their own egos, to pursue the natural exhilaration that comes with spectacular achievement. After all, what drug high could possibly compare to winning a gold medal in the Olympics, flying to the moon, or producing the Woodstock of the 1980s?

To that end the special randomly inserts quick shots of Caitlyn Jenner at the Olympics, a NASA ship landing on the moon, and for reasons I cannot begin to fathom, an image of John Wayne smiling alongside footage of celebrities and singers.

Like so much anti-drug propaganda, *Get High on Yourself* feels like the product of people who were high on illegal drugs. Everything about it feels redolent of cocaine abuse or the "pink cloud" of ecstasy that sometimes accompanies the early stages of sobriety.

Only someone seemingly on powerful stimulants would be delusional enough to imagine that a clamorous anti-drug ditty written by a composer of commercial jingles merited not just a thirty-second or minute-long commercial or even a music video, but an entire HOUR of hopelessly padded prime-time television.

The special's grandiosity and messianic sense of purpose feel cocaine induced, as does the live-wire energy and jittery excitement of everyone involved.

Evans promises that *Get High on Yourself* is no mere song or special, but rather a "new spirit" sweeping the nation. From the vantage point of 2021, that "new spirit" feels suspiciously drug induced.

The producer of *Chinatown* set out to save the children and his career simultaneously by showing himself in action putting together a star-packed spectacle the likes of which the world had never known.

A producer's job is not without complications. For example, Bob Hope threatens to pull a no-show until he learns he'll be standing next to Cheryl Tiegs. All it takes is the promise of being within groping distance of a genuine *Sports Illustrated* sex symbol to get Hope to spend a few hours in the company of the super-famous scoring major media attention and good publicity.

Get High on Yourself provides an opportunity for impressionable children to learn, straight from noted pill enthusiast Burt Reynolds himself, that, despite what the entire history of television comedy might suggest, smoking marijuana and writing comedy simply do not mix. That is, of course, unless the audience for the jokes from stoned writers was also totally baked, which was pretty much the case from roughly 1968 to 1986.

Get High on Yourself should end after a half hour, once the title song has been performed by movie stars, athletes, musicians, and adoring children.

But, like the cocaine addict it so often resembles, *Get High on Yourself* is just too goddamn wired and amped-up to go home quietly, so it lingers on inexplicably for another half hour.

For reasons known only to Evans, we segue directly from a haggard-looking drug casualty talking about shooting heroin alongside a friend who died of an overdose in front of him to a raucous concert hall where a bare-chested, long-haired Ted Nugent, the Motor City Madman himself, is holding court, looking like a greasy hippie outlaw messiah.

Nugent treats the audience in the club and at home to a free-associative beatnik ramble about how he doesn't need drugs or alcohol. "I like to get myself beyond your wildest dreams, do you know what I'm talking about?" Nugent boasts with a lascivious gleam in his eyes that betrays that what he has in mind involves a school bus full of underage groupies and murdering animals.

Nugent relays how some show-business phonies asked him to participate in a special about getting high on yourself involving a song that he plays on a small boom box.

The right-wing lunatic mugs wildly while the clamorous ditty at the special's core plays with an expression that suggests he thinks it's some Up With People, "It's a Small World After All," Donnie and Marie horseshit that he wants nothing to do with.

Before Nugent performs his version of "Get High on Yourself," he first ostentatiously wipes his ass with it, then hurls it onto the floor so he can take a massive dump on Evans' muddled good intentions.

Strangely, Evans kept Nugent's lengthy, profoundly disrespectful segment in the special all the same, which makes me wonder what exactly he was smoking when he put this thing together.

Nugent illustrates that even the sappiest song can be turned into a bona fide rocker in the right hands. Nugent gives "Get High on Yourself" a dirty, nasty, primal "Johnny B. Goode"/"Roadrunner" feel that unexpectedly saves it from its overly caffeinated cheerfulness.

In Nugent's hands, "Get High on Yourself" fucking rocks to such an extent that Nugent's swagger completely obscures the message of the lyrics.

Nugent's seedy presence alone renders *Get High on Yourself*, ostensibly an anti-drug special for children, inappropriate for family audiences. What's the point of having the clean-cut likes of Henry Winkler on hand when you're going to turn over the show for eight minutes to a disgusting dude with a vibe that suggests he'll fuck your sister, then your mother, then your dead grandmother, then go hunting black people for sport?

It's too bad they couldn't get someone more wholesome than Nugent for the rock and roller slot, like GG Allin or one of the members of Motley Crüe who didn't kill anybody.

In an equally misguided move, the R&B super-group The Clarke/Duke Project plays a soulful cover of The Beatles' classic pro-drug song "With a Little Help from My Friends" alongside Leif Garrett and some country crooners.

Here's the thing about a famous drug song like "With a Little Help from My Friends": you can't turn it into a non-drug song, or even an anti-drug song, just by saying that it's no longer a drug song.

"With a Little Help from My Friends" is not just any Beatles song: it's one of the druggiest songs on an album that boldly declared that the Beatles were on drugs, and loved drugs, and if you loved the Beatles, you should love drugs the way they do.

"With a Little Help from My Friends" is from *Sgt. Pepper's Lonely Hearts Club Band*, which could just as easily be titled *Holy Shit the Beatles Are on Drugs Now*. There's LSD in that album's DNA. You can no sooner effectively spin "With a Little Help from My Friends" as an anti-drug song than you can convincingly portray "Lucy in the Sky with Diamonds" as an ode to a woman who is an astronaut and a jeweler.

If you're going to include a drug song like "With a Little Help from My Friends" in an ostensible anti-drug special, you should at least change the lyrics, so that someone one like Leif Garrett, who would soon be better known for getting high with his friends than his fading music career, isn't literally singing about getting blazed with his stoner buddies.

Having watched *Get High on Yourself* twice now I finally understand what Evans meant by "Woodstock of the 1980s." Just as Woodstock featured many different kinds of performers, from Sha Na Na Na to Jimi Hendrix, and kids, and drugs, *Get High on Yourself* similarly involves drugs and kids and performers from across the pop music spectrum, the most talented of whom are invariably African American.

Unfortunately, the brilliant, engaged black musicians who can not only sing but sing beautifully, in sharp contrast to folk like Henry Winkler, Mark Hamill, and Paul Newman, fill secondary roles so that the special can fawn over its Caucasian stars in a way that anticipates the disastrous original cut of Evans' then-upcoming musical *The Cotton Club*.

Get High on Yourself established an unfortunate template for wildly ineffective, star-studded anti-drug propaganda that served the outsized egos of celebrities but did nothing to actually fight the plague of drug addiction. It represents an early incarnation of a simplistic, hypocritical "Just Say No" mindset that inspired kids like me to just say yes.

Despite Evans' bold assertion that *Get High on Yourself* captured the zeitgeist like little before or since, Evans' wobbly exercise in star-fucking masquerading as charity seems to have left only the faintest of footprints.

What Evans described as the Woodstock of the 1980s does not show up on the Internet Movie Database, nor does it have a Wikipedia entry. It's not available for purchase or rental on Blu-Ray or DVD.

That's too bad because this feels less like an actual special than a five-minute video for a mediocre song sung poorly by amateurs with forty minutes of the random nonsense that fills DVD special features: interviews and behind-the-scenes footage and outtakes and famous people poorly faking spontaneity and excitement.

In *The Kid Stays in the Picture, Get High on Yourself* feels like a minor footnote to Evans' drug arrest and thwarted comeback.

Having experienced an entire hour of its rambling, wildly inessential nonsense, I now find that earlier judgment impossibly generous.

CARTOON
ALL-STARS TO THE RESCUE
(1990)

If you're not a Gen Xer, it's easy to forget what a huge deal the star-studded animated anti-drug special *Cartoon All-Stars to the Rescue* was at the time of its release. It was the "We Are the World" of anti-drug propaganda, a massive enterprise that brought together popular cartoon characters from across the pop culture spectrum for the sake of a worthy cause.

Cartoon All-Stars to the Rescue is also, not coincidentally, the *Reefer Madness* of synergistic animated specials, a lumbering anti-drug manifesto that transforms children's favorite wacky, lovable cartoon characters into angry, glowering moralists.

Here's the thing about cartoon characters: they're assholes. They're essentially children in the bodies of anthropomorphic animals. Like children, they're only concerned with their own desires. You think Alvin of Alvin & the Chipmunks fame cares if your kid tries weed? That selfish fucker doesn't care about anything other than himself.

Alternately, consider ALF. That intergalactic piece of shit eats cats. You think he's intimidated by drug laws?

What about Garfield? It's canon that he doesn't care about anything other than lasagna and sleep. Lastly, Slimer is an otherworldly ghoul, a creature of pure id from the darkest recesses of the spirit world. Is he really going to squeal, "Drugs bad news!"?

Yet this special asks us to believe that these animated narcissists are emotionally invested in the sobriety of a random teenager.

The special begins with a hand reaching into the room of a blonde girl named Corey to purloin her piggy bank. This violation of innocence is so horrific that it causes various cartoon characters to come to life to act as spiritual mentors to the piggy bank thief, Corey's brother, a marijuana- and beer-crazed superfreak named Michael.

These emissaries from the world of children's entertainment are on hand to prevent Michael from making that inevitable small hop from trying marijuana to crack addiction.

Oh, but it all began so innocently! A mere two years earlier, an insufferable Michael goes up to some kids blazing sweet kind bud and demands, "You guys cruising for lung cancer or what?"

They explain that they're getting high—on the pot— and Michael instantly transforms from an insufferable Goody Two-shoes to a cosmic cowboy and begins a nightmare descent into marijuana addiction.

Before ALF and Baby Kermit can begin lecturing Michael on the evils of marijuana, these cartoon characters first suss out the nature of Michael's problem. Simon, the insufferable brains of Alvin & the Chipmunks, offers, "I hate to suggest this, but my guess would be marijuana, an unlawful substance used to experience artificial highs."

The first time a cartoon character for babies mentions marijuana it engenders intense cognitive dissonance. The cognitive dissonance never stops. It never stops being bizarre and wrong that tacky cartoon characters created to sell toys are suddenly behaving like professional interventionists.

Michael is followed everywhere by Smoke, the living personification of drugs voiced by the great George C. Scott.

Michael is surprisingly blasé about cartoon characters coming to life and lecturing him on personal responsibility, but I guess when you're high all the time it just seems natural for Bugs Bunny to show up with a time machine.

Cartoon All-Stars to the Rescue marked the first time Mel Blanc did not voice Bugs Bunny or Daffy Duck. That seems appropriate, since the characters here feel hopelessly ersatz, pod-people versions of beloved pop culture institutions who behave nothing like the real thing.

Bugs Bunny is an inveterate anarchist. He's not a grim foot soldier in the war on drugs. He's not supposed to say things like, "What's up, Doc, is your life, if you don't cut it out."

When the grouchy alternate universe version of Bugs Bunny churlishly asks Michael, "What's this, a joint? What's the big attraction?" I wanted him to answer, "Well, it does make watching Bugs Bunny cartoons more enjoyable. There's that."

Everybody here seems to be channeling Nancy Reagan, even when doing so involves behaving crazily out of character.

Later in the special, for example, Michael, Smoke, Baby Miss Piggy, and Baby Kermit embark on a roller coaster ride through Michael's weed-frazzled mind. While the roller coaster grows increasingly more nightmarish, Kermit lectures his human friend, "You see, Michael, drugs can take you up and make you feel okay for a while. But for every up, there's a down, and the bigger the up, the steeper the down. You get used to a thrill ride like this pretty fast, and pretty soon, they're not even a thrill anymore! Then you gotta take drugs just to feel normal!"

A monologue like that would seem natural coming from an acid casualty in their fifties or sixties visiting schools to talk about reefer. It's less convincing coming from a character who is the following:

1. A fictional cartoon character.

2. A frog

3. A baby

4. At a developmental stage in which he's still constantly shitting himself

5. Almost assuredly illiterate

6. Suspiciously knowledgeable about the effects of long-term soft drug use for an illiterate cartoon baby frog.

Then again, everyone is fascinating off-brand here. In this alternate universe, ALF isn't a wacky, cat-eating alien; he's a scold who sternly informs our hapless doper, "Drugs aren't your pal, pal. They're the enemy, storming the battlements, trying to take control!"

"Something tells me we're not in cartoon territory anymore!" ALF "quips" early in the special. He's kidding on the square, as *Cartoon All-Stars to the Rescue* illustrates indelibly that lighthearted cartoon goofballs do not belong in the world of fear-mongering anti-drug propaganda, just as fear-mongering anti-drug propaganda does not belong in the carefree world of lighthearted Saturday morning cartoons.

Forget *The Avengers: Endgame*. *Cartoon All-Stars to the Rescue* is the biggest crossover ever. It's also possibly the worst.

THE EPISODE OF DONAHUE WHERE PETER CRISS CONFRONTED HIS ALCOHOLIC HOMELESS IMPOSTOR (1991)

The greatest hour in the long, unfortunate history of trashy talk shows occurred in 1991, when famously debauched longtime Kiss drummer Peter Criss used *The Phil Donahue Show* to confront Chris Dickinson. Dickinson was a homeless alcoholic notorious for impersonating the self-destructive superstar to score five hundred dollars in cash and a three-night stay in a motel from the unscrupulous tabloid *Star*.

What happened is this: the impostor is Chris, not Criss. The real Criss is pissed and feels dissed and knows something is amiss and can't believe he has to put up with this.

Donahue is enraged on Criss' behalf. He feels duty bound to defend Criss' honor. He's particularly apoplectic that a substance abuser like Chris is pretending to be Criss because, as Donahue cluelessly thunders of one of the most notorious drug addicts in rock history, "He doesn't even drink coffee!"

Chris is in the hot seat. By his own account, he's a homeless alcoholic who has spent 90 percent of his time in a drunken haze. Yet somewhat disconcertingly Chris still looks healthier than Criss, who, in Donahue's mind at least, has been living the life of a monk for a decade since leaving Kiss, raising a family, writing his memoirs, and composing songs for his next solo album. Criss eventually published that memoir decades later and it is a masterpiece of sleaze and degradation on par with Motley Crüe's *The Dirt*.

Then, one day, something interrupted the Zen calm of the drummer's post-Kiss lifestyle when people at his beloved mother's funeral started asking him about being what *Star* describes as a "hopeless alcoholic leading a pathetic life on the streets." They were wrong: the real Peter Criss was a hopeless alcoholic leading a pathetic life of luxury.

Having an impostor to blame for his misfortune represented a change of pace for Criss, who was accustomed to destroying his own life.

Dickinson is visibly uncomfortable as an indignant Donahue explodes with manufactured outrage at his crimes.

Donahue then introduces, via satellite, an affable, strangely familiar-looking goofball with an intense, jet-black power-mullet and an ingratiating smile he refers to as "Thomas." Donahue might refer to this young man as Thomas, but you and I know him by a different name: Tom Arnold. Yep, as just one of the many too-crazy-for-fiction elements of this episode, Roseanne and Tom Arnold were so concerned about Criss that they went to skid row to look for him.

Arnold is a minor player in the sordid melodrama, but he comes off more like a spectator overjoyed to have a front-row seat to one of the craziest hours in television history. You know the famous GIF of Michael Jackson eating popcorn from the *Thriller* music video? That's Tom Arnold on *Donahue*.

Alongside Chris and Tom Arnold, the audience is also introduced to Cheryl Ann Thompson, an actress who claims to have had a drunken five-month-long romantic relationship with Criss in 1981. Thompson talked to Chris for five hours over the phone to confirm that he was the real Peter Criss, but when she picked him up at the airport, she was aghast at being confronted with a blatant impostor.

Thompson describes Chris as, "disgusting. He was enough to make anyone throw up." Yet, she and her mother graciously allowed him to live in their home for a month despite this sad gentleman's vomit-inducing disgustingness. Thompson says she felt sorry for him, but also that he seemed like a pretty chill guy, despite being a raging alcoholic.

Criss ribs Chris by asking, in his thick New York accent, "How you doing? Why couldn't you impersonate the Lone Ranger, or Tonto or something like that? You really gave me a rocky time."

The rock icon then proceeds to forgive Chris, blaming *Star* for manipulating a desperate alcoholic. Criss, Donahue, the guests, and the audience don't just go easy on Chris: they give him a free pass. They like him. They sympathize with him. They see him as a victim of an unscrupulous tabloid and dishonest schemers. The crowd has so much sympathy for Chris that the host has to remind the audience, "He did acknowledge he was Peter Criss. Let's not have any telethons for the man!"

Chris' appearance on the show is a massive bait and switch. We're promised the drama and conflict of an outraged rock star tearing into the drunken, lying impostor who fucked up his life at the worst possible time, when he was still reeling from his mother's death.

Criss, honestly, doesn't seem to have too much of a problem with the sad-eyed vagrant pretending to be him for tabloid fame and walking-around money. He does, however, have a huge problem with Thompson, whom he accuses of calling his home constantly and badgering him and his child.

We were promised the real Peter Criss versus a fake Peter Criss. Instead, the episode ends up being about a fake girlfriend and a fake relationship that might not actually have been fake. Criss rages against Thompson for being a sketchy opportunist lying about having had a romantic relationship with him for fifteen minutes of fame.

Thompson could not be more indignant. "I," she proclaims defensively, "am an established actress, Peter!" Despite her claims to have appeared on *Matlock* and *Simon & Simon,* Thompson's greatest performance is undoubtedly as conniver who possibly had sex with Peter Criss.

Thompson does not have physical evidence to back up her claims. There are no photos, love letters, or other mementos, although if a pair of alcoholics were getting blackout drunk and fucking in 1981, and one party was married, I'm guessing they wouldn't be too keen on documenting their fling for posterity.

Arnold doesn't have much to do on the show. Like Chris, he mostly just sits there and takes in the surreal spectacle until he announces at a particularly dramatic moment that Thompson and her mother asked him and his wife for ten thousand dollars. The pressure is relentless, but Thompson refuses to crack.

Things just keep flying farther and farther off the rails. Late in the episode a man named Clifford Blessing calls in and contributes to the assault on Thompson's story by describing her as a compulsive liar.

A clearly rattled Thompson then announces very theatrically, "Clifford Blessing is a homosexual," as if that had any bearing on anything.

I can't help but wonder what happened to Chris. I hope he got the help he needed and turned his life around. As for Criss, he was replaced by an impostor of sorts when Kiss drummer Eric Singer began performing wearing Criss' Catman makeup after Criss was repeatedly kicked out of the band for being self-destructive and unprofessional even by the exceedingly lenient standards of 1970s rock and roll.

It's safe to assume that Singer got more than five hundred dollars and three nights in a motel for essentially stealing Criss' persona, but you never know. I wouldn't put it past Gene Simmons or Paul Stanley to lowball Singer that way. Besides, if Singer puts up too much of a fuss, they can always just replace him with a cheap impersonator. They've certainly done it before.

BAYWATCH NIGHTS
SEASON ONE
(1995-1996)

Despite devoting a sizable chunk of my life to documenting the insanity of *Baywatch Nights'* supernatural second season for this book, I had no intention of watching any of its first season, let alone covering it.

Why would I? Compared to "*Baywatch* is *The X-Files* now, David Hasselhoff is David Duchovny and they're fighting monsters every week," turning a lifeguard adventure show into a cheesy 1980s-style interracial detective romp is comparatively predictable and sane.

But, as it so often does, curiosity got the best of me, and I resolved to watch and write about one episode of *Baywatch Nights*. I was instantly hooked. Before it made the regrettable choice to go spooky, *Baywatch Nights* was a masterpiece of accidental but utterly inspired self-parody.

If you were to slap the words "Adult Swim Presents" on the opening credits of "Pursuit," the first episode to air, geeks and hipsters would declare it the most brilliant exercise in gleefully postmodern television satire this side of *Lookwell* and *Heat Vision and Jack*.

Hasselhoff would receive the best reviews of his career for the light touch he brings to this boldly stupid new vision of life for iconic lifeguard Mitch Buchannon, a winking self-awareness that suggests he knows just how ridiculous everything around him is and is having a goddamn blast.

How did a show whose star happily slathered on white face-paint to play an undercover mime, performed show tunes in drag while wearing a bulletproof vest, and joined his partner in donning chicken-themed fast-food get-ups turn into a science-fiction downer that refused to acknowledge even the possibility that there might be something silly about David Hasselhoff fighting mummies, vampires, unfrozen viking warriors, space aliens, and an evil CD-Rom game?

In its second season, *Baywatch Nights* wasn't just a very different show: it was the antithesis of its first season. A show that didn't take anything seriously, particularly itself, somehow morphed into a science-fiction monstrosity that took *everything* seriously, no matter how ridiculous.

Among its many fascinating miscalculations, the second season of *Baywatch Nights* made the fatal mistake of not letting David Hasselhoff be David Hasselhoff.

The infinitely superior first season, in sharp contrast, empowers Hasselhoff to be himself to the nth degree. Like Adam West, Bruce Campbell, or William Shatner, David Hasselhoff is a personality more than an actor.

Hasselhoff doesn't disappear into roles. Instead, roles disappear inside the *Knight Rider* star's impossibly vast, hammy persona.

In *Baywatch Nights*, Hasselhoff's partners are Garner (Gregory Alan Williams), a black guy; and Ryan (Angie Harmon), a sexy, no-nonsense lady, but tonally and thematically they should be played by *The Simpsons'* Troy McClure and Joe Camel.

That's because *Baywatch Nights* is essentially a straight-faced version of Chief Wiggum P.I. from the legendary "The Simpsons Spin-Off Showcase" episode of *The Simpsons*—that is, if anything in *Baywatch Nights* can be deemed straight-faced.

Only instead of Springfield's most inept crime fighter relocating to New Orleans and setting up shop as a private investigator, hotshot lifeguard Mitch is moonlighting as an overworked, underpaid gumshoe handling Malibu's sexiest, tackiest crimes.

If Joe Camel were a television producer instead of a disturbingly phallic, unnecessarily sexual cigarette spokesperson for small children, *Baywatch Nights* is a show he would create. *Baywatch Nights* is the television equivalent of a Camel print ad of camels relaxing at a club where the blues is hot, the jazz is cool, and the taboo sex between Joe Camel and human women is hotter for transgressing every law governing the co-fraternization of man and beast.

Baywatch is less a television show than a Man Cave in television form that contains everything Hasselhoff loves in one place: hot tunes, cold drinks, designer duds, sports cars, beautiful babes, and light action executed with a wink and a goofy smile.

When *Baywatch Nights* debuted, Hasselhoff was bored with *Baywatch*, and producers were eager to hold onto him before he bolted his billon-dollar baby to become an A-list movie star with a shelf full of Academy Awards, so they gave him carte blanche to do whatever he wanted with a spin-off.

The problem, from a commercial standpoint at least, was that *Baywatch Nights* was created to please Hasselhoff rather than audiences who might understandably be confused as to why the lifeguard show with all the boobs was now a detective show.

In "Pursuit," *Baywatch Nights*' premiere, Hasselhoff addresses the audience directly to explain how *Baywatch* became *Baywatch Nights* in the most exquisitely half-assed manner imaginable.

Oozing Troy McClure smarminess, Hasselhoff confides in us, his friends in the audience, "You know some people think the beach closes after the sun goes down. Uh uh. That's when it *really* starts to heat up. *Especially* if you're a PI. Now I know what you're thinking: Mitch is a lifeguard. What does he know about being a PI? Well, they both involve rescuing people.

It turns out my best friend Garner went partners in a bankrupt detective agency with a beautiful brunette PI (Angie Harmon as Ryan) who left New York for the California sun and adventure. What can I say? When someone yells 'help' I jump in with both feet! And I hope you do too as we introduce a new series of private eye adventures called *Baywatch Nights*! Sit back and ENJOY the ride."

You'd think it would be impossible to sustain that level of camp good-badness for an entire episode, let alone an entire season, but *Baywatch Nights* accomplishes that feat with twenty-two episodes of pure kitsch bliss.

In the beginning music was central to Hasselhoff's vision. Hasselhoff had been hanging out at the House of Blues when *Baywatch Nights* was being conceived and was infected with its conception of the blues as corny music for lame white people rather than as a raw, authentic expression of black pain.

Baywatch Nights was the most mid-1990s show possible, but it's so deliriously retro that it also feels like a spectacular symphony of silliness that could have aired in 1985 or 1975.

If *Baywatch Nights* had aired in the mid-1980s, right after *Knight Rider,* then its curious conviction that drag and hip-hop were both crazy fads on their way out would make more sense.

In an episode where Hasselhoff wears a bulletproof vest under a slinky dress while going undercover to catch a killer of drag queens, one-hit wonder Skee-Lo auditions to perform at Lou Raymond's (Lou Rawls) club Nights with a spirited performance of "I Wish."

Listening to Skee-Lo, Ryan sports an expression that conveys, "I've never heard of music where people 'talk' rather than sing before, but I kind of like it! It's fun!"

The club owner with the million dollar voice is less impressed, however. He doesn't even let Skee-Lo finish the only song he would ever be known for. Instead, he brusquely cuts him off and coldly admonishes him to listen to some "Muddy and some T-Bone" before befouling his sacred stage with his infernal "rap" claptrap again.

Skee-Lo sports an appropriately ashamed expression that just as incontrovertibly says, "I'm sorry for wasting your time, Mr. Raymond, Sir. I'll learn a real instrument so I can play real music and will forget about all of this 'Hippety Hop nonsense."

Maybe Skee-Lo should have sought out one of the show's many white child blues prodigies so that a twelve-year-old white moppet from Australia could teach him to play black music with authenticity and conviction.

Late in "Blues Boy," the aforementioned white orphan is playing a lonesome tune; the music is so powerful that it inspires Proustian reveries for Mitch, Garner, and Ryan.

Over a sultry, sexy, wildly inappropriate groove, Ryan thinks back to frolicking with her naval officer dad in his dress whites with an expression that is disturbingly, unmistakably sensual.

The look on Harmon's face says so much more than it's supposed to. It's supposed to convey, "I love my dad." Instead, it insists, "I know he's my father and all but, *damn*, did the man look good in a uniform! No wonder I have daddy issues and lust after a man twenty years older than me!"

I don't want to single Harmon out for criticism because she is a revelation here: funny, smart, sexy in an incongruously grown-up, understated fashion and able to make her character's intense attraction to Mitch less icky than it should be.

Anyone who can hold onto their dignity in a scene where they try to convince their macho black male partner to dress up like Whoopi Goldberg to go undercover at a drag show is destined for bigger and better things.

Ryan is SO unbelievably attracted to Mitch that it becomes a problem. Sure, he's played by an actor literally old enough to be her father, on his third hit television show, but how is she supposed to look at her divorced, forty-three-year-old single father coworker and not want to jump his bones, consequences be damned?

She's not alone! *Baywatch Nights'* first episode finds Mitch succumbing to the sexual advances of a femme fatale played by guest star Carol Alt. The sex symbol's seduction techniques include a private swimsuit fashion show for the character played by *Baywatch Nights'* star, co-creator, and executive producer.

This establishes a sturdy template: an impossibly beautiful sexpot will throw herself at Mitch in a cynical attempt to draw attention away from her crimes. Mitch will submit but look very sad at the end when she's led away in handcuffs, leaving him to drink away his pain at Nights and nobly resist Ryan's sexual advances.

In "Just a Gigolo" Mitch starts charging beautiful women for his sexual favors by going undercover as a male prostitute.

The first credit that comes up at the end of every episode is Hasselhoff's for Executive Producer, something that plays unintentionally like a self-deprecating running joke.

OF COURSE David Hasselhoff would be behind a show where David Hasselhoff drives a cool car, wears designer suits, hangs out in a cool blues club with his buddy Lou Rawls, catches bad guys, and entertains scores of gorgeous, scantily clad women.

The first season of *Baywatch Nights* is a glorious, glorified midlife crisis. It's pure wish-fulfillment, the entertainment answer to a long ponytail, sports car, and much younger girlfriend.

Watching *Baywatch Nights*, I felt like it was created exclusively for me. Whoever cast the show's guest stars seemed to possess a direct line to my subconscious.

The second episode, "Bad Blades,"casts the actor who played J. Peterman on *Seinfeld* as the evil overlord of an international criminal gang made up of the most extreme athlete/criminals in the world and Jason Hervey as a rich rollerblading doofus under his spell.

Nancy Cartwright, Bart Simpson herself, sells carnal fantasies by the minute as the guest star in an episode devoted to the steamy world of phone sex, but, thankfully, Cartwright does not do phone sex as Bart Simpson. It would be very disconcerting hearing THAT voice purr, "Eat my shorts! Oh yeah, eat my shorts, baby! Aye Carumba! I am having a cow right now. I am having a cow SO HARD!"

Michael Winslow pops up randomly as a tech guy with a predilection for elaborate sound effects, and it's always great to see Charles Fleischer, the voice and soul of Roger Rabbit, make an appearance as a weaselly career criminal.

But no *Baywatch Nights* guest makes as indelible an impression as Geraldo Rivera. When I saw the man who opened Al Capone's vault's name in the credits of "Payback," I naturally assumed that he would be playing the same role he plays in everything: pompous, mustachioed boob Geraldo Rivera.

I was delighted to discover just how wrong I was. Rivera doesn't just act in "Payback." He ACTS! He's a thespian giving it his all in the histrionic role of Albert Romero, an old rival of Mitch's who comes to him seeking help when his much younger trophy wife goes missing.

Introduced holding a bucket of Kentucky Fried Chicken and a bouquet of flowers for his missus and then tumbling gracelessly to the floor when he sees she's being held at gunpoint by ancient mobsters, Rivera commits to the role's melodramatic emotions with wildly misplaced conviction.

It's pure soap opera as the FOX "newsman" emotes as if he was promised his own spin-off if he only delivered a big enough performance as a man traumatized to discover that Bobbi, the woman of his dreams, has a seedy past as a kept woman who speaks many languages and has MANY frequent flier miles.

"Bobbi, part of me feels like I don't even *know* you anymore! *Farsi*? *Mandarin*? Nearly a *million* frequent flier miles? *Stripping* in a club?" the diminutive schmuck asks his hot, mysterious wife. He then reassures her, "I would *die* for you baby!" in a manner even Tommy Wiseau might consider a bit much.

Midway through its first season *Baywatch Nights* did what failing shows generally do when it becomes apparent that what they're doing isn't working. They rearrange the proverbial deck chairs on the Titanic in a doomed attempt to stave off disaster.

They apply a cute little band-aid to a gaping chest wound.

The producers understandably figured that what this *Baywatch* by-product needed to bring in ratings was a busty blonde in her twenties who was married to a member of Motley Crüe.

So Donna D'Errico, the then-wife of Nikki Sixx, was added to the cast as Donna Marco, the new owner of Nights and a Baywatch babe in the classic mold, to the point that her character became a lifeguard and joined the cast of *Baywatch* for a few seasons.

D'Errico was joined by another twenty-something hardbody in Eddie Cibrian as hunky photographer Griff Walker, a cocky stud who wants to break into the detective business because in the mixed-up world of *Baywatch Nights* everyone wants to be a PI.

Baywatch Nights understandably assumed that it might be more successful if it had more in common with the most watched television show in the world. The line between *Baywatch Nights* and *Baywatch* began to blur and the shows began to overlap in cast, themes, and settings.

When it came to ratings, being more like *Baywatch* wasn't the boost *Baywatch Nights* desperately needed.

Being *nothing* like *Baywatch* in its second season didn't work either, but thanks to the extraordinary international success of *Baywatch*, Hasselhoff had the power and leverage to make his ridiculous fantasy of the ultimate David Hasselhoff vehicle a preposterous reality for forty-four episodes that must be seen to be believed.

I found *Baywatch Nights* so ridiculously enjoyable that at a certain point my enjoyment crossed the line from ironic to sincere.

I cordially invite all lovers of glorious trash to revisit an old series of private eye adventures called *Baywatch Nights* and ENJOY the ride.

BAYWATCH NIGHTS
SEASON TWO
(1996-1997)

When NBC canceled *Baywatch* after a single season of lackluster ratings and scathing reviews, David Hasselhoff and the show's creators and producers gambled on themselves and hit the jackpot.

After failing as a network drama, *Baywatch* succeeded as a syndicated international ratings dynamo that won Hasselhoff the impressive, nebulous title of "The World's Most Watched Man on Television" from the Guinness Book of World Records in tribute to the astonishing global popularity of *Baywatch*.

When a Baywatch spin-off about the exciting, sexy, music-filled adventures of Hasselhoff's moonlighting lifeguard-turned-shamus Mitch Buchannon called *Baywatch Nights* struggled in its first season, Hasselhoff could be forgiven for imagining that with some tinkering the second season of *Baywatch Nights* could explode in popularity the way Baywatch did upon hitting syndication.

In its infamous second season, *Baywatch Nights* found inspiration in an unlikely place: *The X-Files*, a cult hit that had captured the cultural zeitgeist with its savvy combination of monsters, mysteries, and explosive sexual chemistry.

The kids sure seemed to dig bogeymen and Draculas and Chupacabras and Frankensteins and various other things that go bump in the night. So, in a miscalculation of historic proportions, *Baywatch Nights* decided that, fuck it, monsters were suddenly real and it was now Mitch and Ryan's job to stop them.

Baywatch Nights wasn't just switching genres—it was switching realities. It was morphing unexpectedly from a detective show in which the supernatural does not exist to a horror/science-fiction show where *everything* is supernatural.

It'd be like if *Archie Bunker's Place* decided to stay on the air for one last season by having Archie Bunker fight the Wolfman or if the goofs of *Hogan's Heroes* squared off against the Creature from the Black Lagoon as well as hilariously incompetent Nazis.

If you were to make a list of actors whose personas are so big and so cheesy that it becomes impossible to see them as anything else, Hasselhoff would be near the top.

Yet, the second season of *Baywatch Nights* nevertheless asks us to suspend disbelief and become emotionally invested in the reality of David Hasselhoff playing a lifeguard by day and monster hunter by night.

When does he sleep? Who knows? He's such an Ubermensch that after a long day of saving lives and a long night of fighting EVIL, all he needs is a fifteen-minute nap and then he's up and raring to go.

Mitch is also a father, something that is referenced only once in passing, so that we don't think less of this god among men just because he's too busy fighting mummy curses to help his son with his homework.

Baywatch Nights made the fatal mistake of assuming that *The X-Files* was successful due to its most easily replicable elements, that it was a hit because the public demanded murder, mysteries, monsters, and male-female leads with a "will they or won't they" dynamic.

The reality is that *The X-Files* was a pop phenomenon because everybody wanted to fuck David Duchovny and Gillian Anderson, be David Duchovny and Gillian Anderson, or some combination of the two. The monsters and world-building didn't hurt, but it was fundamentally about sex, and sex, weirdly enough, is one of the many things that this uniquely off-brand *Baywatch* variation is lacking.

To the extent that a show as surreally lazy and cynical as *Baywatch Nights* in its second season exudes any effort at all, it tries way too hard to be *The X-Files*. It fails in every conceivable way. This isn't a show inspired by *The X-Files*; it's twenty-two episodes of *Baywatch* cosplaying as *The X-Files* in a homemade costume its indulgent mom made for it.

Instead of Duchovny with his offbeat sexuality and quirky deadpan humor, we're stuck with the perversely asexual, avuncular Hasselhoff in dad jeans and denim jackets straight out of the Jay Leno Collection at Sears.

In place of Gillian Anderson's icy cool and smoldering sensuality we have Angie Harmon as Mitch's partner and love interest Ryan.

Harmon warms up over the course of the season but initially seems less like a foil for our hero than an exposition-delivering robot who unpacks reams of information in a husky monotone.

The future star of *Rizzoli & Isles* has the looks to play Dana Scully by a different name. She has the voice. She has the presence. She has the icy, intimidating sexuality. What she fatally lacks, however, is the material.

Baywatch Nights limply tries to re-create *The X-Files'* dense world-building exclusively through the character of Diamont Teague (Dorian Gregory), the mysterious, shadowy puppet master who hires Mitch and Ryan to explore the world of the eerie and unexplainable.

Who is Teague working for? To what end? Is he a government agent? Is he a space alien? The answers to this, and every other question involving *Baywatch Nights'* final season, are "who knows?" and "who cares?"

The success of *Baywatch* made Hasselhoff the top paid actor in syndication when he launched *Baywatch Nights*. That meant that most of the show's budget went toward an element guaranteed to keep it from being scary—the living personification of kitsch in a lead role behind the scenes as well as in front of the camera—to the expense of all the things that *would* make it scary, like production values, makeup, creature design, and veteran writers and producers with experience in horror.

The primary weapon in *Baywatch Nights'* arsenal of scares is darkness. It subscribes to the notion that if scene after scene is shrouded in near-total blackness, then audiences won't be able to see how cheap everything is.

Baywatch Nights leans way too hard on the audience's ability to create terror out of nothing at all. It will show a dimly lit wall being pounded on, accompanied by a monstrous howl, then leave it to the audience to imagine the unthinkable horror that must lurk behind the wall, just beyond our sight.

"Dimly lit" is *Baywatch Nights'* entire aesthetic. In an episode that anticipates Peter Hyams' famously shitty adaptation of *A Sound of Thunder*, Mitch and Ryan journey to an alternate dimension future that, unsurprisingly, looks like a few dark rooms in an empty building.

Baywatch Nights doesn't just suffer from production values on par with Roger Corman productions from the mid-1990s; it suffers from a paucity of imagination as well. It doles out scare sequences stingily. It knows that it has nothing, creatively, so it rations out that nothing carefully.

Within the dark universe of the show Ryan is a true believer in all things spooky. Mitch, however, is a skeptic despite a staggering amount of evidence that we are not alone.

Late in the season Ryan brings up the terrifyingly real possibility that what they might be dealing with is a mummy and a mummy's curse. Mitch scoffs at the idea as patently absurd. A mummy? In Malibu in 1996? Why, the sheer notion is preposterous!

Or at least it would be preposterous if Mitch and Ryan did not literally deal with a monster every bit as absurd as an ancient Egyptian ghoul running amok in the middle of the Clinton era every episode.

In a rare bit of humor, Mitch dismisses the notion of a modern-day mummy as *Abbott and Costello Meet Frankenstein* foolishness, as if *Baywatch Nights* were not fundamentally *Lifeguard Mitch Meets Lady Dracula and the Wolfman and the Evil CD-Rom Game and The Sinister Green Ooze.*

For *Baywatch Nights*' second season, no premise is too stupid to be taken seriously. An episode where Vikings frozen in the middle of a blood feud are unfrozen a thousand years later and immediately start flipping around like Olympic gymnasts as they reignite their war of wills in a weird new world, for example, is begging for tongue-in-cheek treatment.

It would seemingly be impossible to do a straight-faced version of a story as goofy as "unfrozen, thousand year-old Vikings renew conflict in contemporary Malibu," but *Baywatch Nights* accomplishes the impossible by using this storyline to explore Mitch's sense of honor.

In addition to being the world's greatest lifeguard and a shockingly effective paranormal investigator, Mitch is an expert on Vikings. He knows their rituals and traditions and, in a line delivered without a hint of irony, says that he feels a deep affinity for Viking culture because he would have been a Viking if he'd lived in Viking times.

What are lifeguards/paranormal investigators, ultimately, if not the Vikings of contemporary society?

On a similar note, when Mitch is possessed by a demon it would seemingly be a perfect time to go crazy with delirious self-parody. That's not how Hasselhoff plays it. From the misplaced conviction he brings to his performance, you would think Hasselhoff was trying to become the first actor to win a Nobel Prize for a single episode of syndicated television.

Baywatch Nights never stops giving Hasselhoff unique acting challenges he is uniquely ill-equipped to tackle. The deadly yet noble unfrozen Viking warriors aren't the only aberration for which Mitch feels a deep affinity.

An early episode shamelessly rips off *Species* through the character of a sexy woman created by a mad scientist who is at once dangerous and naive, an innocent and an inhuman abomination. Oh, and it's also established repeatedly that unlike most hot women, she is also amphibious. So even though she's part-frog Mitch is still torn between wanting to protect her from harm because that is his sacred calling and wanting to make sweet love to her because she's hot.

Baywatch Nights seems to think it's easy to do horror. It's right in that it's easy to do horror badly, but it is VERY difficult to do horror right.

Horror is a craft. Horror is an art. Horror is a world onto itself. The same is true of science fiction. In its fascinatingly dreadful endurance test of a second season, *Baywatch Night* is artless and devoid of craft in a way that betrayed that its creators neither understood nor respected the genres it was throwing together in a lame attempt to stay on the air.

In the right hands and the wrong hands, twenty-two hours of entertainment can be an eternity. It's one thing to know that a second season of *Baywatch Nights* exists and somehow spawned four more episodes than *Freaks and Geeks* in its entirety. It's another to binge all twenty-two episodes in the space of a few days, as I did for this book.

Over the course of just a single season, *Baywatch Nights* resorted to episodes about an EVIL CD-Rom game; spooky unfrozen Vikings; and multiple episodes about possession, one of which involves a serial killer who infects people with his EVIL blood.

Pitches that would have gotten writers committed a season earlier, like Mitch getting struck by lightning, then forming a telekinetic bond with an alien child at the mercy of an extraterrestrial cult, got the green light for a season that's nothing but insane ideas terribly executed.

As with *The X-Files*, the monster-of-the-week shenanigans are supposed to build to a glorious crescendo as the various strains intertwine and connect with the long-simmering sexual tension between the leads.

Baywatch Nights ends with Mitch kissing Ryan after tearfully confessing his love for her. With a weirdly misplaced look of achievement, Teague then slinks confidently back into the shadows, his work done.

This suggests that the goal of this enigmatic, powerful figure with limitless resources was to get two attractive straight white people to admit that they *like* like each other, and not just as friends.

The expression on Teague's face subtly but unmistakably conveys, "Now that I've gotten these coworkers to smooch, I can shut down the shadowy, covert operation I work for and walk proudly into the sunset, my destiny fulfilled."

This makes Teague seem less like a master of the universe than a glorified matchmaker, one who understands that the path to true love is twisty, complicated, and littered with Lady Draculas, mummy's curses, and space aliens.

It was the beginning of what would undoubtedly have been a romance for the ages had the show survived. Instead, it was an ending as well as a beginning.

Before *Baywatch Nights* debuted Hasselhoff adorably imagined that his future lay in detective heroics and movie stardom. It took the show's failure to make him realize that the only role the public would ever accept Hasselhoff in, other than hunky lifeguard Mitch Buchannon and Michael Knight, was David Hasselhoff.

To that end, in the years following *Baywatch Nights'* cancellation, Hasselhoff has played a version of himself in *Dear God, The Big Tease, Welcome to Hollywood, The New Guy, Dodgeball: A True Underdog Story, A Dirty Shame, The Spongebob Squarepants Movie, Kickin' It Old School, Hop, Piranha 3DD, Keith Lemon: The Film, Stretch, Ted 2,* and *Killing Hasselhoff,* a whole movie devoted to giving its titular star the business.

He's played characters not named David Hasselhoff much less frequently. Winking, grinning self-parody is seemingly all Hasselhoff does these days, but when it comes to sheer perversity, nothing he has done can compete with the unintentional self-parody of the second season of *Baywatch Nights.*

Hasselhoff's biggest success spawned his greatest failure. Hasselhoff was able to crawl back to his cash cow, which remained extraordinarily popular, but his career never quite recovered from the enduring humiliation of *Baywatch Nights.*

Hasselhoff now invites the world to laugh at him, but the voluminous laughter that greeted his attempts to crossbreed his billion-dollar baby with *The X-Files* was strictly of the unintentional and mocking variety.

SHASTA MCNASTY
(1999-2000)

As the decadent 1990s approached the millennium, pop culture de-evolved into a glittering Sodom and Gomorrah forever tempting the fury of an Old Testament God with its extravagant stupidity.

A new network called UPN led the charge with shows whose names would become synonymous with television schlock, titles like *The Secret Diary of Desmond Pfeiffer, Homeboys from Outer Space, Chains of Love* (a reality romance competition that got its name from contestants literally being chained together), and *Shasta McNasty.*

Shasta McNasty quietly changed its name to *Shasta* as part of an elaborate retooling late in its first and only season, but it was too little, too late. A show people knew only for having an iconically stupid name continued to be half-remembered solely for its title.

There's a lot about *Shasta McNasty* that is boldly postmodern. Style-wise it's ahead of the curve in being a fast-paced, one-camera sitcom with a fourth wall–breaking anti-hero that's full of cutaways, pop culture references, and parody. *Shasta McNasty* does not have a laugh track. Unfortunately, it does not have laughs either.

Yet there's nothing at all meta about *Shasta McNasty*'s awfulness. It's targeted exclusively not at men or even guys, but bros. Bros are like men and guys except that they're dumb assholes whose existence revolves around trying to trick attractive women into showing them their boobs. There's nothing wrong about trying to look at boobs. It is a noble, even heroic pursuit, but it seldom leads to sublime comedy.

In *Shasta McNasty* the bros in question are the titular rap-rock trio. There's leader Scott (Carmine Giovinazzo), a smart-ass who communicates directly with the audience through fourth wall–shattering asides, and Randy (Dale Godboldo), an African American the show is not too "politically correct" to depict as a criminal and thief with a penchant for spinning wild tales in order to get into women's pants.

Jake Busey rounds out the toxic trio as dumbass doofus Dennis. Dennis likes boobs. Scott and Randy like boobs as well, but Dennis likes boobs to such an extent that it's his defining characteristic. But he has other interests as well. He also loves lingerie, since it showcases boobs at their most alluring, but what Dennis REALLY loves are lesbians.

Bear in mind, Dennis isn't into bisexual women because he'd like to have a threesome with two women. He doesn't seem to know that bisexuality even exists, so he's not angling for a ménage à trois.

Instead, Dennis believes that lesbians are magical creatures who will either let heterosexual men participate in their sex lives despite being, by definition, not sexually attracted to bros, or give straight men a lifetime of sexual excitement through their mere existence.

Lesbians only exist in *Shasta McNasty* as figures of sexual fantasy and punchlines. This is true of its odious pilot, which depicts our ostensible anti-heroes/actual villains less as horny bros than as sex criminals, scumbag dipshit Monkees for a shitty new era.

The pilot finds Shasta McNasty happily videotaping their sexy neighbor having sex with her boyfriend. But it's not enough to simply record this poor woman having sex surreptitiously and then masturbate to the images.

When the bros discover that the woman whose sex life they're secretly taping is being cheated on, they decide to spring into action. They sneak into the poor woman's apartment and plant underwear in it so that the beauty will be so distraught by her boyfriend's infidelity that she'll have rebound sex with Scott in appreciation for lending her a shoulder to cry on.

Scott is established as both the brains and the conscience of the group, in that he is a horrible person but does not appear to be a total sociopath. He is, however, very much into playing sick mind games with a stranger for the sake of getting laid.

The trio's psychotic ruse ultimately proves *too* successful in convincing the unnamed mystery woman (early online It Girl Cindy Margolis) that men are unfaithful dogs because while she did opt for rebound sex after learning about her boyfriend's infidelity, it's with a woman.

THIS is how *Shasta McNasty* introduced its characters to the American people, although there is also a very long sequence in which Scott beats up an angry, violent parrot that threatens to "pop a cap" in his ass and calls him a jerk-off repeatedly.

In the next episode, *Shasta McNasty*'s charmless lummoxes have a dog named Dinner that they "liberated" from a Korean butcher who gave him the name because, unless a white man had intervened, the canine was going to be his meal for the evening.

We never see poor Dinner again. He's not in the background of shots. He doesn't play a role in subsequent episodes despite Americans loving dogs above all things, including their children. No, Dinner was only onscreen for the sake of a racist joke. Even the dogs in *Shasta McNasty* deserve better.

The Dinner joke sets the bar awfully high for offensiveness, but *Shasta McNasty* soars over it continually over the course of its twenty-two-episode run.

The next episode, "Little Dude," begins with a bona fide SLUR in its introduction. It opens by once again breaking the fourth wall and having *Three's Company's* Richard Kline say that no little people were harmed in the making of that week's episode.

But Kline does not use the phrase "little people." Instead, he uses two more anachronistic, less sensitive terms to describe little people, the more offensive of which begins with M. This phrase wasn't considered AS offensive in 1999 as it is today, but it was nevertheless understood to be cruel and out of date, as evidenced by guest star Verne Troyer kicking Kline and telling him that "little people" is the correct term.

It's far from the only time *Shasta McNasty* is deliberately offensive, only to wink away the ugliness by positing it as a bad-taste gag.

In "Chubby Chick," for example, Scott tells his housemates that if they want to score they should try to make it with anorexic chicks, since women with issues around eating have low self-esteem and a need for validation the bros can exploit for sex.

When they happily acquiesce, Scott breaks the fourth wall to tell us he was only joking, but that doesn't negate that the rest of the episode is about how women with issues around eating have low self-esteem and a need for validation that can be exploited for sex.

However, instead of Dennis unethically exploiting the insecurities of women who are unhealthily thin, he hits on a woman in an overeating support group with a mind toward convincing her to lose weight, so that he will be able to find her sexually desirable.

A night of ecstatic lovemaking changes Dennis' mind. He goes from finding overweight women repulsive to fetishizing them as sexual dynamos who "try harder" than their slender peers.

Dennis decides that his happiness is dependent on tricking his new lover into remaining overweight, so that she won't have the confidence to leave him. With a ghoulish grin on that giant gourd of his, Dennis lovingly feeds his oblivious new sex partner fattening food and drinks that she wrongly thinks are low calorie.

Shasta McNasty can't conceive of straight men being attracted to someone that size, or the size of semi-regular Verne Troyer, as anything other than a weird kink or opportunistic way to game the system.

In meta framing segments an offscreen, an upper-crust narrator lists items taller than Troyer, including a medium-sized pizza and seven rolls of toilet paper. Comparing a human being to rolls of Charmin is injurious to the human soul on an individual and collective level.

That's true of most of Troyer's role here. Little people actors through the decades have often had to make an impossible choice between positive onscreen representation and working regularly.

With *Shasta McNasty*, Troyer opted to work, to do the best he could with a role that's essentially a sentient site gag whose height and physical appearance are constantly being referenced in mocking ways.

Too often, that's the price of visibility: the cost Troyer, hot off the *Austin Powers* sequels, paid for being one of the only little people on television in a regular role when *Shasta McNasty* aired was a part that was entirely predicated on his height.

UPN seemed to realize, along with everyone else, what a DOA dud they had with *Shasta McNasty*. They decided that the way to save a show widely mocked for being called *Shasta McNasty* involved removing "McNasty" from the title.

The show got less McNasty in other ways as well. A raunchy jiggle fest that began as a glorified twenty-two-minute Axe Body Spray commercial took a hard turn into *Friends* territory when a kinder, gentler Scott became the center of a love triangle between the cute, nonthreatening girl next door and his ex-girlfriend.

Early in the show's ill-fated run, Randy quips that they're Shasta McNasty, not Shasta McNice. That wasn't true at the end. Turning *Shasta McNasty* into a bland romance centered around the bar that Verne owns and operates didn't save the show, but it did make it less egregiously terrible. It also made it less memorable.

Through its spectacular incompetence, *Shasta McNasty* ended up accomplishing something wonderful. The show's toxic buzz and terrible ratings spelled doom for the program cursed to follow it, the animated adaptation of Scott Adams' *Dilbert*.

Adams dubbed *Shasta McNasty* "the worst TV show ever made" and held it responsible for the cancellation of *Dilbert*, though he later argued that his show was canceled for being "white."

We'll never ultimately know whether *Dilbert* was canceled due to the lingering stink of *Shasta McNasty* or the plague of diversity causing people like Scott Adams to not be as wealthy and successful as they obviously deserve to be.

What I do know is that thinking about Adams learning that the success or failure of the *Dilbert* cartoon would be inextricably intertwined with the fate of *Shasta McNasty* makes me happy.

Shasta McNasty is the tacky ghost that haunts the failure of Adams' big shot at Jim Davis/James L. Brooks money and multimedia fame. When Adams dies and his life flashes before him, there's at least a slight chance that it will contain at least a fleeting glimpse of *Shasta McNasty*, possibly of Verne Troyer wearing a giant sombrero designed to hold tortilla chips and salsa.

That possibility alone justifies the show's otherwise indefensible existence.

EMERIL
(2001)

If you've ever lain awake wondering why the sitcom where Emeril Lagasse played himself was not a television dynamo on par with *Seinfeld, Friends,* or *The Sopranos,* answers can be found on Wikipedia.

A section on the show's Wikipedia page claims, "NBC had high hopes for (*Emeril*), as it was created by (Linda) Bloodworth-Thomason, however, the show was savaged by many critics, one calling it a train wreck. Lagasse was said to be hesitant to participate in the project. The show was in the middle of filming when the September 11 terrorist attacks occurred; the show was scheduled to premiere on September 18, a week after the attacks, but was delayed by a week. Despite this, the opening sequence still featured the World Trade Center towers standing. The show was never able to find much of an audience and the sitcom quietly went off the air by November 2001."

There are a lot of crazy conspiracy theories surrounding the Thomasons' best friends the Clintons. But Pizzagate is reasonable compared to the conspiracy theory that one of the things the terror attacks of 9/11 took from the American people was the opportunity to see Emeril Lagasse evolve as an actor.

Bin Laden didn't just change American life forever: he also sadistically snatched away Lagasse's opportunity to develop his instrument as a thespian.

But *Emeril* had problems beyond airing in the gloomy aftermath of the 9/11 attacks. For starters, it starred a rank amateur with no talent as an actor and also was terrible. *Emeril*'s original pilot was so poorly received that the show was extensively retooled before it made it to air. Robin Riker, Chris Elliott's foil in *Get a Life*, was unceremoniously dropped as Emeril's improbably hot wife in favor of the even more attractive Mary Page Keller. Robert Urich was added to the cast as Lagasse's horndog agent sidekick, and the focus shifted from Emeril's struggles to balance work, family life, and massive fame to the workplace almost exclusively.

You would think that giving a dude his own sitcom built around his world when he has no background as an actor would be a big enough ego boost for Lagasse. You would be wrong. The never-aired pilot episode of *Emeril* never stops reminding us what a wonderful guy Emeril is.

The flattery begins with Emeril returning to his hit show from a trip to his hometown of New Orleans, where he is mobbed like a one-man Beatles of cooking.

Then this family man goes from a studio where he's worshipped to his fake family. To the accompaniment of heartstrings-tugging piano, Emeril lovingly tucks in his pretend sleeping children. This incarnation of *Emeril* didn't just expect audiences to laugh at Emeril Lagasse: it wanted us to be moved by him as well.

I then made an even more horrifying discovery. Since Emeril's next stop is to the bedroom and he tells his wife, "All I want to do is get in bed and wrap myself around you, and, well, maybe that's not all, babe," delivered with a lascivious gleam, we're then forced to think of Emeril as a sexual creature as well. This is one of many bridges too far.

Emeril says of his fuck style and insatiable flesh cannoli, "That happens to be my other specialty besides cooking," but he's not going to be treating his wife to marathon sex sessions, on her birthday or any other day, if he keeps coming home at midnight every evening, giving his family the short shrift in favor of his career.

Emeril ends up making it up to his wife by cooking her an elaborate meal on his show and sputtering about his love for her in a rambling monologue about how you gotta do nice things for the ladies, stating with tongue-wagging insouciance, "I know feminists pooh pooh (treating wives nicely on their birthday), but I'm telling you guys, chicks, they dig this stuff!"

I'm not sure where Emeril picked up the idea that feminists hate men being nice to their wives. I suppose he's arguing that traditional romance has fallen out of favor with third-wave feminists, but if you have any doubts about the kind of man the fake Emeril Lagasse is they should be cleared up when he ends the episode by taking a pay cut AND giving raises to every member of his staff out of his own pocket.

What fake nobility! Emeril was worried that the pressure of his astonishing success as the king of cooking shows would tear him away from a family we would almost never see again, so he engages in an epic act of self-sacrifice.

In the pilot and episodes that followed, Emeril was at once the star attraction and a straight man overshadowed by more dynamic performers. Unfortunately, these slick professionals are stuck playing retrograde stereotypes that were antiquated even at the time of the show's release.

Sherri Shepherd plays the show-within-a-show's brash and opinionated location manager, Melva LeBlanc. In one of her first lines, Melva motivates her coworkers by screaming, "There are two ways you do not want to see me, and that's naked and mad! So, get in gear before I get to stripping and whipping! What YOU looking at?"

These lines somehow made it into *both* versions of the pilot while much else was cut for either not fitting the new conception of the show or not meeting *Emeril*'s standards.

Melva's threat to expose her naked body fits in snugly with the show's creepy obsession with the bodies of its female cast members. In "Fat," the first episode that aired, Emeril becomes so excited by the prospect of winning a hundred-thousand-dollar prize for being the show on his network whose cast and crew collectively lose the most weight that he has everyone who works with him, even his agent, go on a diet so that they can win a contest that in real life would be both illegal and unethical.

In another appallingly tone-deaf episode, Emeril tires of hearing Melva and the even brassier, even more man-hungry Cassandra (Lisa Ann Walter) complain about not having boyfriends, so he cooks up a scheme where he'll make a gourmet meal for men willing to date Emeril's coworkers even though they are louder and larger than society deems acceptable.

Poor Shepherd is better than dialogue like, "Black people, we don't like *The Sopranos*. We don't go for all that drama about honor and betrayal. Somebody does something to somebody in my neighborhood, we just say, 'Fool!' or settle it with a good bitch slap. Or, we take to the next level, which is Jerry Springer!"

I'm not really sure what Urich is doing here beyond some of the worst work of his career.

Urich lends the show testosterone, star power, and a deceptive air of professionalism, but he's stuck playing a knockoff of the creep John Larroquette played brilliantly on *Night Court*. Urich's Jerry McKenney is the show's resident misogynist, a womanizer who favors the gang with bon mots like, "Unfortunately, I committed myself to a cocktail party for those Barbi Twins. You know, they wrote that book about the pain of bulimia. And they have really huge breasts. So, they're being honored."

Emeril offers a perversely retrograde Battle of the Sexes pitting a trio of Bush League wannabe designing women in Melva; Cassandra; and flighty southern-fried eccentric B. D. Benson (Carrie Preston), the show-within-a-show's food dresser, against chauvinist pig Jerry and the saintly Lagasse.

Emeril only lasted seven episodes before NBC pulled the plug on a show that was simultaneously half-baked and overcooked.

Some might say that 9/11 was responsible for the show's demise. Those people are insane. The truth is that *Emeril* never should have made it beyond the "terrible idea" phase, but thanks to the magic of YouTube, anyone morbidly interested in one of the most misconceived television shows of all time can feast, and feast heartily, on this overflowing buffet of idiocy.

ADRIEN BRODY INTRODUCES SEAN PAUL IN CHARACTER ON THE MAY 10, 2003, EPISODE OF SATURDAY NIGHT LIVE

Saturday Night Live has played such a central role in my life that if I had a time machine, I would use it to keep Andy Dick from introducing Brynn Hartman to cocaine. Then, if I had time, I would go back and kill Hitler.

I'd want to prevent the Holocaust, of course, but I'd also want to ensure many more decades of Phil Hartman hilarity. Hey, we all have our priorities.

For as long as I can remember *Saturday Night Live* has occupied a place of supreme importance for me and my generation. I grew up on *Saturday Night Live*. It played a huge role in shaping my comic sensibility and how I see myself and the world.

Yet, for all my love for *Saturday Night Live* at its best, no single moment has gotten under my skin and penetrated my psyche like that exquisitely uncomfortable nadir when, on May 10, 2003, host Adrien Brody hijacked the show to introduce musical guest Sean Paul in character as an amped-up rude boy with a clumsily improvised blur of mostly incomprehensible patois.

In a dreadlock wig and dirty undershirt, Brody comes bounding onto the stage, a hurricane of nervous energy. Even before he opens his mouth it's clear that something is terribly wrong.

The wig is a giveaway, as is the expression on the Academy Award–winning actor's face. It's the terrified, excited look of someone who is about to take a HUGE chance, on live TV, where there are no second takes and everything he does will go down in comedy history.

Before he starts nervously sputtering vaguely Rastafarian-sounding gibberish, Brody has the look of a man who does not know whether the pool he is about to dive into is empty or not.

Brody doesn't just risk looking foolish or not getting laughs: he risks dying. He risks obliterating himself on live television in a way that people will talk about for decades to come.

But Brody can't go back. He's too far gone. Sure, he could limit the shtick to a wig and an unintelligible accent, but he's onstage on *Saturday Night Live* with an opportunity to do *his* comedy *his* way, so he goes for it.

Besides, what are they going to do? Have a security guard tackle him? Send Lorne onstage to give him a public scolding? By the time anyone even figures out what he's doing it'll be over, and the focus will be on Sean Paul.

Brody's fidgety body language and facial expressions betray no small amount of existential terror. Powered by a potent combination of arrogance and fear, Brody talks so quickly that it's difficult to understand him.

"Ya mon," Brody slurs repeatedly as the crowd hoots and hollers, egging him on the same way a class of unruly students would encourage the misbehavior of the class clown.

The audience knows instantly that Brody will get into a *lot* of trouble for breaking the rules of this most rigid and rule-bound of comedy institutions. They fucking love it.

"We got original rude boy Sean Paul here, ya know?" Brody eventually gets around to sputtering.

Having exhausted the comic possibilities of saying "ya mon" in a matter of seconds, Brody then turns his attention to the word "respect" and starts riffing manically on it, mumbling, "Me respect, me neck spect, me uncle spect, me auntie spect."

Brody mistakenly seems to think that the audience is hooting and hollering because they think he's funny. He doesn't realize that the studio audience is cheering for the same reason NASCAR fans root for crashes: because it's a fascinating shit show they can't take their eyes off—a five-car pileup commemorated for posterity on live TV.

Every second seems to last an eternity as Brody continues to toss out every Jamaican-sounding phrase he can think of, from "big up Jamaican massive" to "big up Kingston massive" before returning to his beloved "ya mons" and promising that the whole family was in the house.

The whole routine is over in about forty seconds, but it seems much longer, for it is that rarest of wonders: a genuinely spontaneous moment on *Saturday Night Live*.

There is a system in place specifically to ensure that moments like Brody's outburst do not happen. There is an awful, terrible magic to the moment, a cringe-inducing fascination, a level of miscalculation that is nothing less than mesmerizing.

To call Brody's Rastafarian-spoofing antics satire would be obscenely generous. Even categorizing it as humor seems a stretch. There's no target, no point of view, no satirical thesis, only a childish conviction that the way that those reggae guys talk is funny, and that there are big healing laughs to be won from someone outside the culture cartoonishly imitating them.

Brody might have thought that he was honoring Sean Paul by giving him an in-character introduction.

Instead, Brody upstaged Sean Paul. Brody's introduction ensured that audiences would spend the entirety of Sean Paul's second song wondering what just happened and whether it's possible for Lorne Michaels to fire someone who doesn't actually work for him.

After breaking Michaels' iron-clad rule against improvisation and ad-libbing, Brody instantly made the list of people banned from *Saturday Night Live*.

In his early roles, Brody consistently illustrated taste, intelligence, and solid judgment. That taste, intelligence, and judgment abandons him, however, when he indulges an unfortunate weakness for broad comedy.

Roughly a decade after Brody became the youngest man ever to win the Academy Award for Best Actor, he lent his time, energy, and name to the 2013 sketch comedy film *InAPPropriate Comedy*.

When Brody decided to use his artistry to breathe life into the character of flamboyantly gay Dirty Harry parody Flirty Harry, he was not an unknown. He wasn't a teenager. He wasn't a kid.

By that point Brody had won an Academy Award. He'd been directed by Spike Lee, Terence Malick, Roman Polanski, Steven Soderbergh, Francis Ford Coppola, Barry

Levinson, Peter Jackson, and Wes Anderson, with whom he would collaborate repeatedly.

The voice inside Brody that insisted that the world MUST meet his wacky white Rastafarian character angrily demanded that he *choose* to be associated with *InAPPropriate Comedy.*

InAPPropriate Comedy is so convinced that gay equals funny that it doesn't bother with jokes. Or logic. Instead of "Go ahead, make my day," Brody's *Flirty* Harry instead substitutes, "Go ahead, make me *gay*," when he's already so cartoonishly gay that his in-your-face sexuality reduces the movie to giggle fits.

For six endless minutes Brody rasps lascivious dialogue like,

"I told you before, I am not gonna wait around for a bunch of other dicks. Not when I have an opening to take those guys from the rear."

"Yeah. I don't think you understand. Those boys were packing heat. I mean, as soon as I came, those assholes opened up. Yeah, opened up and started spraying everywhere."

"So I went in. Yeah, I went in deep, balls to the wall, but I unloaded into both of those assholes. And it felt good."

While Flirty Harry talks dirty his fellow cops look on with visceral disgust, as if the mere idea of gay sex makes them want to projectile vomit in horror.

The most embarrassing aspect of Brody's role in *InAPPropriate Comedy* is that he's given an additional dialogue credit for it. That means that Brody didn't just play Flirty Harry; he helped create the character as well, using the same improvisational muscles that once gave birth to his Rastafarian character on *Saturday Night Live.*

There's something fascinatingly personal about Brody's ill-fated *Saturday Night Live* improvisation and performance as Flirty Harry. Watching Brody die a horrible death onscreen I feel like I'm seeing something weird within him that should be repressed at all costs.

Watching Brody in both of these roles, I felt as though I was seeing the real Adrien Brody, one whose desire to make people laugh is as poignant as it is innately doomed.

Michaels had ample reason to be apoplectic over Brody's shenanigans. It's not that Brody's Rasta routine was too racist and unfunny to make it onto the show. Instead, Brody was unlucky in that his brand of Caribbean minstrelsy was racist in a manner that Lorne Michaels did not condone.

But if Michaels had ample reason to rue the day he ever agreed to book Brody as a host, he has reason to be grateful as well.

Since Brody so clearly went rogue with his Sean Paul introduction no one could blame the dreadfulness of his shtick on the man in charge.

For perhaps the final time, audiences found themselves appreciating the relative racial sensitivity and quality control Michaels brings to the show.

STRIPPERELLA
(2003)

When Stan Lee died at ninety-five, the world mourned a giant, but the prolific creator was decades removed from his prime.

In his final years Lee's job, and one he did masterfully, was to serve as the public face and avuncular soul and spirit of Marvel; the pop icon served as a mascot whose familiar visage could be seen briefly in pretty much every Marvel movie post–*Iron Man*.

Lee's destiny toward the end was not to create new characters but rather to be Stan the Man, the human personification of comic books as a medium.

Lee brought his superpowers of self-promotion to *Stripperella*, a smutty, non-Marvel Spike TV collaboration with Pamela Anderson about a stripper/secret-agent/kinda-superhero-maybe that ran for one season in 2003, a few years before 2007's *Iron Man* ushered in the current Age of Marvel. *Stripperella* has subsequently been mostly forgotten, a smutty joke that didn't quite land.

During its brief, unmourned existence, Lee sold the hell out of *Stripperella*. In full-on pitchman mode, he gave a public whose needs he understood on a deep level the hard sell on the character and the TV show. Lee promised the animated Anderson vehicle would be a multimedia dynamo, complete with a comic book spin-off and merchandise and a feature film adaptation.

On paper at least the show had a certain vulgar charm, appealing as it did to both the public's enduring love of campy secret agent shenanigans and enormous breasts. It was going to be Adam West's *Batman*, but with big boobs and rampant T&A.

And the nudity! Such nudity you've never seen on basic cable before, in such volumes that it becomes distracting, even off-putting! Such nudity that it will make you say, "Wait, are they allowed to show naked boobs on basic cable?"

When I was a teenager, the notion of nudity being gratuitous would have struck me as preposterous. The nonessential display of naked breasts wasn't a creative fault to me back then. It was the essence of life. It was the raison d'être of human civilization, the reason movies were made, songs were sung, why human art proceeded beyond the cave-painting phase.

My adolescence was, alas, a long time ago. Consequently, I spent much of *Stripperella* irritated by its endless parade of animated T&A. Has anything ever been made funnier by the addition of enormous naked breasts? These naked nipples were pixilated in the episodes that aired on Spike TV, which adds an additional level of pointlessness to the endeavor. What's the point of showing naked breasts when you can't actually show naked breasts?

You've got to at least give the show credit for truth in advertising. True, it was pitched as a Stan Lee superhero show and it is more of a secret agent show, but *Stripperella* more than lives up to the "stripper" part of its title. If you are a fan of animated stripping, then this is the show for you.

Anderson, who also serves as a creative consultant, voices Erotica Jones, a humble stripper who leads a glamorous and dangerous secret life as the titular crime fighter Agent 69 (that's funny because it's a sex number!). Jones toils in the employ of a clandestine agency that fights evil in the form of a series of campy supervillains.

Erotica/Stripperella is consistently and predictably the least entertaining aspect of the show. The farther removed from her, the funnier any individual element is liable to be. That's partially because she's cursed with playing straight woman to grotesque bad guys and bumbling, leering comic relief. But that's also because there isn't much to the character.

You know you've attained a curious form of fame when "you as a super hero" becomes a palatable commercial conceit. *Stripperella* is essentially Pamela Anderson as a superhero. Stripperella has Anderson's bombshell dimensions, sex kitten purr, fierce animal rights convictions, and famous weakness for bad boys.

Alas, Pamela Anderson in a campy, self-aware comedy would be more of a draw if that didn't pretty much describe everything she's done, from *VIP* to *Stacked* to *Barb Wire* to her supporting turn in the dreadful *Baywatch* movie.

The brain trust behind *Stripperella* seems to have realized just how dramatically the soft-core, peep show element of the show clashes with its superhero and sitcom elements. Halfway through its run the animation style changed dramatically along with the tone. The characters became softer, rounder, more cartoonish, and less pornographic. The change suited the show, as did scaling back the "erotic" elements. However, the material remained just as uninspired.

Stripperella is deliberately offensive. Some of its attacks on propriety feel like the product of the dire period post–*There's Something About Mary* when opportunistic lowbrow filmmakers competed in a race to the bottom to dream up the most stomach-churningly tasteless comedic tableaus, mostly just punishing moviegoers in the process. This is most apparent in Agent 14, a coworker of Stripperella's who wears a protective helmet and is "comically" mentally challenged. He's a "special" agent in more than one sense of the word.

In keeping with the rest of Lee's oeuvre, *Stripperella* is a fourth wall–busting postmodern extravaganza that is continually winking at the audience and celebrating its artifice and acknowledging the groaning clichés of the medium in ways that grow progressively less funny as the series progresses.

What's frustrating about *Stripperella* is that there are flashes of real comic invention, even wit, throughout: take, for example, a bad guy named Cheapo who looks and acts like a thrift-store Joker, pulls off literal penny ante crimes like knocking off "Take a penny, Leave a penny" trays and wishing wells before stealing the world's largest Cubic Zirconia.

The sheer randomness of *Stripperella* can be fun. Deep into a dreadful episode dominated by double entendres involving a "Dr. Clitoris" whose island is bushy, wet, and down under and also covered with crabs, we briefly survey an out-of-control party at the strip club that features not just Kid Rock and Pamela Anderson but also a 1980s-era "Cheech" Marin, a middle-aged James Brown, and a drunken monkey throwing beer bottles back and forth with "Weird Al" Yankovic.

There's funny stuff in the margins of *Stripperella*, but the grand gestalt stubbornly does not work. Instead of ratcheting up the tawdry, pandering sexuality of comic books to comic and satirical extremes, *Stripperella* ramps them up to levels it imagines are sexy and titillating, but just ends up undermining comedy that was already shaky.

According to Wikipedia, "In 2003, ex-stripper Janet Clover, a.k.a. 'Jazz', a.k.a. 'Stripperella', filed a lawsuit in the Daytona Beach, Florida circuit court against Viacom, Stan Lee, and Pamela Anderson, claiming she is Stripperella's true creator and Stan Lee stole her idea when she discussed it during a lap dance. Clover filed the original suit herself without an attorney as she said she couldn't afford the $6,000 lawyer fee."

For people who subscribe to the popular conception of Lee as a sleazy, selfish idea thief who shamelessly ripped off Jack Kirby and Steve Ditko, among others, the image of Stan the Man getting his latest idea not just from a professional sex worker but *during* an actual lap dance is irresistible. It almost doesn't matter to these folks whether it's true or not. It sure *seems* like it could be true.

Wikipedia goes on to dryly propose that the bad publicity from the lawsuit "as well as creative differences led to the show's demise," but I'm not sure the show could have succeeded under any circumstances.

The show was pitched as Stan Lee's return to creation, but while the show's vulgarity, campiness, broad humor, winking postmodernism, and superhero milieu all make this feel like a bona fide Stan Lee production, the raunch and mean-spiritedness feels weirdly off-brand for the Marvel maven.

An unmistakable childlike innocence informs so much of Lee's art and life, but *Stripperella* is smutty and self-consciously naughty in a decidedly adolescent fashion.

When Lee put his energy and name behind *Stripperella* he could not have imagined how dramatic the decade and a half ahead of him would be. He could not have foreseen how massive his creations would become, how they would take over pop culture and become a multi-billion-dollar multimedia juggernaut with Dr. Octopus–like tentacles spreading everywhere. He also could not have imagined that in his final years he'd be the subject of dark whispers of elder abuse and exploitation.

Lee's life was a roaring, epic, two-fisted melodrama full of highs and lows. *Stripperella* was not one of the highs, but there are moments that suggest the sly marvel that could have been if the superhero spoof weren't so self-defeatingly intent on being "sexy" at the cost of all else.

ALF'S HIT TALK SHOW
(2004)

I don't have much in the way of happy childhood memories. I consequently will always treasure the "*ALF* parties" I used to have with my dad where we'd microwave burritos and then watch *ALF* reruns together. My life at that point was traumatic and terrifyingly uncertain, so I gravitated to silly escapism that promised not to tax my frazzled brain. *ALF* filled that role perfectly.

I subsequently have an even fiercer nostalgic attachment to that dumb show than most members of my generation. The mere sight of ALF's furry visage is enough to inspire a Proustian reverie. When I see a clip of ALF hollering exuberantly, "I kill ME!" it speaks to something deep in my soul.

However, I was only vaguely aware that in 2004 the wisecracking, cat-munching alien from the planet Melmac scored his own short-lived talk show on TV Land that went by the painfully ironic title *ALF's Hit Talk Show*. It lasted only seven episodes.

I have now watched all the episodes of *ALF's Hit Talk Show* available on YouTube, and I'm still not entirely sure that this is a real show rather than a drug-induced hallucination. And after watching Ed McMahon awkwardly banter with ALF as the host's jovial sidekick, I still can't believe that they got the *Tonight Show* legend to do their dumb show.

As a commercial pitchman and Johnny Carson sidekick, McMahon was an honest hack. He genuinely seemed happy and excited to be paid large amounts of money to endorse products and laugh at Johnny Carson's jokes.

This, however, marks the rare, possibly unprecedented instance wherein McMahon seems to be feeling guilty about the money he's being paid to pretend to find the jokes of a 250-year-old E. T. funny.

I couldn't believe they got television's most legendary TV sidekick to appear in this shlock. Judging by McMahon's facial expressions, neither can he. McMahon's empty, hollow laughter silently but powerfully asks questions like, "What am I doing here?" "Why did I think this was a good idea?" and finally, "This is a mistake, right? I can leave at some point? I'm not locked into this, am I?"

McMahon's presence here is at once *ALF's Hit Talk Show*'s most impressive and saddest element. Having McMahon on the couch alongside a Hawaiian shirt–clad ALF should confer instant credibility. It'd be like a third-rate Public Enemy knockoff group landing not just a Flavor Flav–like hype man, but Flavor Flav himself.

Not even having Johnny Carson's sidekick fill the same role here can make *ALF's Hit Talk Show* seem like an actual talk show. Having ALF host a painfully conventional, hacky third-rate late-night talk show is an Adult Swim idea, but instead of Adult Swim execution we get something that feels like *The Rick Dees Show* or *The Pat Sajak Show*, only with a wisecracking space alien doing bits and interviewing guests, and, god help us, regularly singing duets, as opposed to a toothy DJ or alcoholic, right-wing game show host.

Thankfully, McMahon has a satisfying arc here. After looking visibly uncomfortable for the show's first few episodes, at a certain point the light goes out in McMahon's eyes and he stops caring. He obviously must have come to the realization that his legacy as history's most successful TV sidekick is secure no matter how transparently he sleepwalks through the final few episodes of *ALF's Hit Talk Show*.

This is a talk show Titanic. Can't fault the musicians for getting a few notes wrong in the watery final hours.

The ALF puppet isn't capable of distinct facial expressions, let alone selling material like, "Shouldn't *Diff'rent Strokes* have been a hospital drama?"

On his eponymous sitcom, ALF was always a wisenheimer, but *ALF's Hit Talk Show* reimagines its host as an open-mic comic from outer space, a surprisingly low-energy funnyman with gags like one about how Michael Jackson was ordered to show his face in court but "he's having trouble finding it."

I do not envy Bryan Cranston, whose ability to seem legitimately excited at the opportunity to promote his sitcom *Malcolm in the Middle* to an alien puppet represents an acting triumph on par with anything he did on *Breaking Bad*.

Cranston is one of a number of guests who seem way too excited to be sharing the screen with a tacky fictional alien cut-up. An ancient Merv Griffin shows up to awkwardly exchange banter and jokes with ALF, hovering over him like a human Macy's Day balloon, before doing a duet with ALF. A duet!

ALF's Hit Talk Show is best understood not as an official television show sequel to *ALF* so much as an official piece of ALF-branded product, no different than a poorly assembled stuffed ALF doll or a glow-in-the-dark poster.

In the sixth and penultimate episode of *ALF's Hit Talk Show*, ALF answers a question about relationships from guest Tom Green by casually inquiring whether it constitutes "dating" if you pay for it. The 250-year-old space alien seems a little abashed, but make no mistake: in this mildly ribald ad-lib, Paul Fusco, creator and performer of ALF, is establishing beyond a shadow of a doubt that in this particular iteration, ALF pays for sex.

Let that marinate in your mind a little. ALF fucks sex workers. That is canon in ALF mythology because Paul Fusco thought that one-liner belonged in the broadcast version of an officially licensed ALF product.

By the end, it was clear that neither alien nor sidekick gave even a single, solitary fuck. That's why you could slip a casual "ALF pays for sex" joke into a family-friendly oddity seemingly aimed at the two to twelve demographic and the sixty-five and older crowd and no one in between, and not have it cut as wildly inappropriate.

ALF's Hit Talk Show somehow managed to make it past the script stage, and the pilot stage, and the production stage without anyone having any idea what they were doing.

There's something weirdly hypnotic about seeing something so horrifically misconceived go down in flames. So if you are curious as to just how bad, how weird, and how off a late-night talk show hosted by ALF could be, I encourage you to check out *ALF's Hit Talk Show* even if it ultimately fucked my pleasant childhood memories of long-ago "ALF Parties" just as aggressively as ALF fucked all those sex workers.

THE "YOUR LITTLE BROTHER IS STANDING IN THE MIDDLE OF AFGHANISTAN!" SCENE FROM STUDIO 60 ON THE SUNSET STRIP (OCTOBER 23, 2006)

When *Studio 60 on the Sunset Strip* and *30 Rock* premiered, the consensus seemed to be that the Tina Fey–created workplace comedy about the zany goings-on at a *Saturday Night Live*–like sketch show stumbled out of the gate while Aaron Sorkin's much-hyped drama soared.

When the shows ended their respective runs, history had rendered a much different verdict. *30 Rock* was rightly hailed as one of the best and most influential television comedies of all time, a whip-smart show-biz satire that forever changed the look and feel and pace of sitcoms, while *Studio 60 on the Sunset Strip* went down as one of television's most spectacular disasters.

Studio 60 on the Sunset Strip began and ended its brief, unfortunate tenure while I was employed as a staff writer for the entertainment section of *The Onion*. I was, therefore, in a privileged place to judge the accuracy of its portrayal of the art and craft of comedy.

But you do not need to be immersed in the world of funny people for Sorkin's melodrama to ring hilariously false. You don't have to know comedy writers to know that they don't talk and act like the characters in the show because *nobody* talks or acts like the satirical saints of *Studio 60 on the Sunset Strip*.

Even the wonkiest bullshit detector would be able to detect that Sorkin's breathlessly preachy, didactic exploration of the society-saving power of mediocre sketch comedy was bogus.

But comedians and comedy writers were particularly fascinated by how desperately Sorkin tried to capture their milieu and how miserably he failed.

Sorkin was a television and film veteran with a gift for writing snappy, rapid-fire banter. Yet, he somehow labored under the delusion that funny people are mostly concerned with proving their moral righteousness and lecturing each other and the ignorant masses.

Sorkin approached an innately irreverent sphere from a place of near-religious reverence. Comedy wasn't just important to Sorkin. It was sacred. It was church. It was religion. It was certainly nothing to laugh about.

It takes a writer and creator of Sorkin's extraordinary talent to create something as transcendently misconceived as *Studio 60 on the Sunset Strip*.

Of the many iconic moments of unintentional hilarity to be found in *Studio 60 on the Sunset Strip* none is more infamous than the scene from "The Wrap Party" where Tom Jeter (Nate Corddry), a cast member of the titular show-within-a-show, leads parents with a strong, stoic "American Gothic" vibe on a tour of the historic studio where his show is filmed. The painfully earnest young man hopes to impress them with his success and the show's rich tradition, only to have his father respond to his son's prissy assertion that they were "standing in the middle of the Paris Opera House of American television" by sarcastically yelling, "Well that's swell, Tom, but your little brother is standing in the middle of Afghanistan!"

By that point it has already been established that Tom's parents don't know who Abbott and Costello are and have never heard their "Who's on First" routine. Yet that somehow does not keep their insufferable boob of a son from talking about the Paris Opera House as if it were a reference with deep meaning to them.

The "Your little brother is standing in the middle of Afghanistan!" line embodies everything that made *Studio 60* both mesmerizingly terrible and weirdly irresistible in one eminently quotable exchange.

When it comes to unintentional laughter, "The Wrap Party" offers an embarrassment of riches. I'm focusing on the Tom and his parents plotline here, but "The Wrap Party" is also the episode where Eli Wallach shows up as a senile old writer to teach everyone about how the blacklist was bad. It's also the episode where D. L. Hughley's character goes to a comedy club to see a black comedian he's interested in as a potential writer and is so horrified to be in the presence of sub-par humor that he looks like God won't stop punching him in the dick.

We open with Tom understandably anxious that he won't be able to impress his parents with his job MAKING LOTS OF MONEY BEING ON A HIT TELEVISION SHOW because, as he tells his colleague Simon Stiles (Hughley), "They don't know what I do for a living."

Tom's motormouth flibbertigibbet mom and scowling, stoic dad do not seem to have ever met a black person before, either. When Tom introduces his folks to his black cast-mate, his mother gushes that she shouldn't be saying anything, but when they saw that James Bond movie she thinks Dad got a bit of a crush on Halle Berry.

When Tom responds with mortification at the idea that his black colleague has a personal connection to Halle Berry just because they're both black, Simon is quick to judge him harshly, scolding of the man's glowering, unpleasant, possibly racist papa, "He works for a living. Don't be an ass."

It's a line that reflects Sorkin's disingenuously bifurcated take on Tom's parents and common people in general. The suspiciously oblivious *Studio 60* cast member's mom and dad are simultaneously one-dimensional, mean-spirited caricatures of folks from the flyover states and the simple, God-fearing men and women who make our nation great.

Sorkin is like an oily politician in that regard, perpetually waxing poetic about the greatness of a common man he looks down on from a place of unearned superiority.

Tom's parents know nothing about comedy history, but that's okay in Sorkin's book because he probably works with his hands and she probably belongs to the PTA or something and, consequently, they are real Americans we should respect and value.

Every bit of trivia Tom lovingly recites is met with blank faces of non-recognition from salt of the earth philistines who wouldn't know the difference between commedia dell'arte and the Blue Collar Comedy Tour. Tom's parents seem simultaneously bored, confused, and unimpressed by everything he's saying, but that doesn't keep him from prattling on all the same, as if an hour in he'll start talking about Ernie Kovacs, and a look of recognition and surprise will unexpectedly dance across his parents' now-impressed faces.

As the thundering climax of his tour through his workplace's storied past Tom attempts to dazzle his folks with a bit of information he's certain will astound even comedy-hating half-wits like the people who raised him: it was in this very building that a comedy duo named Abbott and Costello recorded a routine called "Who's on First?"

Not only are Tom's folks implausibly unfamiliar with Abbott and Costello but they're vaguely insulted by the notion that they should know about a piece of Americana as deeply woven into our national fabric as *Citizen Kane* or Gershwin's "Rhapsody in Blue."

In dialogue that betrays just how often Sorkin forgets how human beings think, talk, and behave, he has Pops grouse of "'Who's on First,' you say that like it's famous," and Mom insist, "Honey, Dad and I don't watch Comedy Central."

Funny people know how to read the room and their audiences. Yet, learning that his parents are unfamiliar with one of the most famous routines in comedy history doesn't keep Tom from continuing with his lengthy spiel about comedy that's all roughly ten thousand times more obscure than "Who's on First?"

When Tom's mother has the audacity to refer to the noble art form of Tom and his colleagues as "skits," he can no longer hold his tongue or conceal his rage.

Voice quivering with wildly misplaced outrage, Tom snaps, "We don't do skits, Mom! Skits are when the football players dress up as the cheerleaders and think it's wit. Sketches are when some of the best minds in comedy come together and put on a national television show watched and talked about by millions of people!"

Equally overflowing with unearned self-righteousness, Daddy hisses, "Don't you talk to your mother like that!" This leads directly to the most deliriously, deliciously insane moment in an epic boondoggle full of them, the aforementioned exchange wherein Tom angrily spits back, "I'm trying to tell you you're standing in the middle of the Paris Opera House of American television!" and Dad hollers defiantly in return, "Well, that's swell, Tom, but your little brother is standing in the middle of Afghanistan!"

It's a line that stops the scene and the episode cold, an absolute humdinger of a doozy that exists because seemingly no one was willing to say no to Sorkin or tell him that he'd lapsed irrevocably and entertainingly into self-parody.

Tom's pop may look down on his son for being a rich, famous millionaire entertainer instead of a real man like his soldier brother, but he discovers there are upsides to wealth, fame, and power, like Tom being able to send body armor to his sibling and his fellow soldiers (real, patriotic, hardworking Americans, Sorkin would condescendingly and half-heartedly insist) to use.

This at least has historical precedence, as John Belushi famously armed several Navy SEALs Teams personally out of his *Saturday Night Live* salary during the late 1970s. The "Bluto Brigade" was known and respected everywhere.

Sorkin is such an insufferable centrist that he has Tom use his personal fortune to send supplies to his brother and his fellow soldiers in Afghanistan. Motherfucker is helping out THE PENTAGON while uplifting the soul of a nation with his artistry.

Tom's story does not end with the most notorious dialogue in all of *Studio 60*. With cloying sentimentality, Sorkin attempts to engineer a fragile peace between these warring caricatures of huffy show-business arrogance and middle-American ignorance.

When his parents get into their car and prepare to drive back home, Tom asks his dad if he has a turntable. The man grouchily insists that he doesn't need one of them newfangled CD players.

Confident that introducing his father to the concept of "comedy" can only bring them together, Tom gives his father an LP of "Who's on First?"

In a wholly unearned burst of treacle, Tom tearfully tells his comedy-oblivious old man, "I love you, Dad, and whether you like it or not, you taught me everything I know."

It's supposed to be a tear-jerking moment of connection between two very different men whose stubborn pride drives them apart even as they share the bond of blood and history and tradition.

Most of what Tom seems to know involves granular knowledge of comedy history from vaudeville to the present. If his father did, indeed, teach him that, he seems to have been stricken with amnesia in the interim.

The Tom and his parent's plotline from "The Wrap Party" reminds me of *Loqueesha* in its stubborn insistence that comedy has the power to change society and uplift the human spirit.

Comedy does, of course, have the power to change society and uplift the human spirit, but Saville's and Sorkin's delusional conviction that their own brand of didactic, brutally unfunny comedy can achieve miracles doesn't just undercut their arguments: it destroys them.

When Preston Sturges used *Sullivan's Travels* to articulate the lifesaving, life-affirming power of comedy and escapism, the film was his best argument. Sturges didn't just assert that comedy is important and that comedy matters: he illustrated it as well.

With *Studio 60 on the Sunset Strip*, Sorkin set out to create nothing less than the Paris Opera House of American television, an enduring tribute to the righteous satirical warriors who make us laugh while speaking truth to power.

Instead, Sorkin created a laughingstock for the ages. We've never stopped laughing derisively at Sorkin and his epic folly. We never will. In that sense the series has endured, albeit not in the manner its creator intended.

H8R
(2011)

CW's notorious *H8R* wasn't just an unusually sleazy and unethical reality show, that sleaziest and least ethical of television genres: it represented a nadir for humanity as a whole.

After watching the four episodes of *H8R* that aired before God finally struck it down in righteous anger, I felt like I needed a long bath or all-day shower to ever feel clean again. That's only partially because the final segment of the show I watched involved a seemingly strong-willed "hater" conceding that, actually, *Girls Gone Wild* guru Joe Francis is a good dude if you get to know him a little.

H8R provided a forum for a dude like Joe Francis, whom his "hater" earlier called a "reputation rapist," to prove that, despite literally all available evidence, he's a nice guy and not the misogynistic, rage-filled sociopath he appears to be.

Furthermore, the show's format doesn't require him to pretend to be nice, or rather "nice," for more than what appears to be ten minutes.

The concept of *H8R* is to allow reality show stars like Snooki, Jake from *The Bachelor*, Kim Kardashian, and

Scott Disick, whose images have been hopelessly distorted via their roles on highly scripted, manipulatively edited, fundamentally dishonest reality shows, an opportunity to reveal their authentic selves by appearing in a highly scripted, manipulatively edited, fundamentally dishonest reality show.

It's the revenge of the undeservedly rich, powerful, and famous over the non-rich, powerless, and anonymous nobodies who dislike them, sometimes for petty, racist, and sexist reasons and sometimes because they're a sociopathic soft-core pornographer who made a fortune destroying lives and single-handedly making our culture sleazier and more awful.

The idea is for misunderstood celebrities like *The Bachelor*'s Jake Pavelka, Kim Kardashian, Snooki, and some guy from *Dancing with the Stars* to get a chance to reveal their true selves, but in reality the series is a bizarre exercise in fake-nice-bullying and passive-aggressive generosity.

There's an aggressive, even hostile element to the celebs' sometimes lazy, sometimes frenzied attempts to win over the nobodies talking smack about them online—an underlying sense of, "Oh, so you think I'm a piece of shit, huh? Well, I'm going to use what appears to be the horrifically swollen budget of this nationally televised reality show to treat you to such an extravagant, expensive day of visually compelling bonding that you will look like a huge asshole if you say you still hate me at the end."

H8R stacks the deck in favor of celebrities, yet most come off as huge assholes all the same, sometimes in wonderfully quotable ways. As a parade of jackassery, *H8R* is one for the ages. It's full of moments I will treasure until my dying day. In one particularly inspired interchange, broodingly handsome *Dancing with the Stars* stud Maksim Chmerkovskiy favors "hater" Rebecca, a basic blonde single gal who melts into a puddle of lust at his touch, with what

I imagine is one of his stock lines, about how he's so intense about his art that he pretty much lives in his dance studio.

When Rebecca replies that she doesn't see a bed in the studio, the palpably irritated dancer growls, "It's a metaphor," in a voice dripping with condescension. He doesn't come right out and say, "Of course I don't actually live here, you fucking moron," but his tone of voice and body language convey that message all the same. If *H8R* were to have become a *Jersey Shore*–like guilty pleasure, "It's a metaphor" might have ended up on a T-shirt, possibly sold on the Jersey Shore Boardwalk.

I was also enamored of *The Bachelor* villain Jake Pavelka trying to convince his hater, punky-haired, sassy twenty-year-old Danielle, of his bona fides as a secretly awesome human being with arguments that include, "Morally, I'm GREAT." I love how he doesn't soft-pedal the amazingness of his morals. He's not saying he's morally sound, or that morals are important to him, or that he thinks of himself as a moral person. No, one of the many assholes from *The Bachelor* straight up says that when it comes to the entire complex field of morality, he is straight up *killing it,* bro, like he kills it at the gym to get those washboard abs.

But *H8R* isn't just a singularly misguided exploration of fame, anger, and jealousy: it's also the world's most needlessly complicated hidden camera prank show. Instead of simply having the "hater" audition to be on a show where they'd spend a day with a celebrity they hate to see if the celebrity would be able to win them over, *H8R* goes to ridiculous lengths to get the "hater" to talk shit about the celebrity in public before their artificial meeting, and then to have some, but not all, of the celebrities really play into their images by being as obnoxious as possible in public.

To cite a typically convoluted setup, an episode featuring Kim Kardashian hater Deena begins with the already unnecessary complication of Deena thinking that she's auditioning for a pop culture television show other than *H8R*. That's where the taped footage of her talking shit about Kim Kardashian comes from. Then, in an equally pointless twist, Deena is led to believe that she'll be participating in a yoga video, but when she's doing yoga, out comes Kim Kardashian to confront her.

After all that setup Deena spends a pleasant idyll painting and talking with Kim Kardashian and is moved almost instantly from sour judgment to what appears to be a low-level crush. Kardashian has beauty and star power on her side, of course, but like every female celeb on the show, she's able to silence her haters with the old "I do a lot of charity work" line.

You can hate on Snooki all you'd like, but by doing so you're disrespecting her work with burn victims. Got something against burn victims? Or orphans that are adopted, like Snooki was? I thought not. It sounds like maybe you have a problem with hate.

All of this artifice serves no purpose beyond padding out the clock, but host Mario Lopez exhibits such palpable joy over every step of his dumb charade that you would imagine that he was a trickster god like Loki manipulating the affairs of foolish mortals from afar, not a lightweight jackass doing a joke-free TMZ version of *Candid Camera*.

But why would a show all about how, actually, maybe it's Joe Francis and Scott Disick who are cool and good and *you* who are wrong for not liking them begin by having Disick and Francis make-pretend to be even more horrible than usual for the sake of Lopez's hidden cameras?

I have no idea. Throughout *H8R* it feels like the show and its awful celebs are "negging" both the audience and the haters. It's as if they're being so intentionally obnoxious off the bat that when they reveal a softer, more ingratiating side, haters and the audience are going to be so grateful that they'll accept the feeblest of evidence as proof of a hated celebrity's fundamental goodness.

Kourtney Kardashian ex Scott Disick is the focus of the show's most riveting and revealing segment. Like all the segments involving dudes, it begins with a requisite display of boozy, bleary self-parody. In this case, Disick, who looks like a Madame Tussaud wax figure of *American Psycho*'s Patrick Bateman come to life, acts like even more of a creep than usual before Lopez pops up to explain the show's premise.

Disick, seemingly, has his work cut out for him with Dayla, a beautiful black spitfire who objects to Disick for many reasons, merited and otherwise. He does not impress her with a ride in his yellow Lamborghini, but when he turns on the charm and faux vulnerability during a bowling date/heart-to-heart she warms up and says that she's made the evolution from hater to lover.

Disick has "won" this pointless game, but he cannot live with that win. He asks a now-charmed Dayla if she has haters and when she guilelessly replies that she doesn't, he turns on her.

Disick can't believe that his hater has never been hated on. His voice rising with anger, Disick, embracing his villainy, seethes, "I think of her as less than nothing at this point. So, it was a fun experience to see if I could turn a hater around and she turned me around and now I hate the hater. The hater has been hated."

It's as if the producers coached Disick and said, "That was great, but now can you say it in a way that makes it seem probable that you've murdered women in a coke-filled rage? Thanks."

As human drama, *H8R* is fascinating and revealing. As television, it's consistently appalling, all but baiting audiences to hate everything about it.

Christ, part of Joe Francis' pitch to his hater Peggy as to why he's not the arrogant sleazebag she thinks he is involves pointing out that Michael Bay lives in his neighborhood.

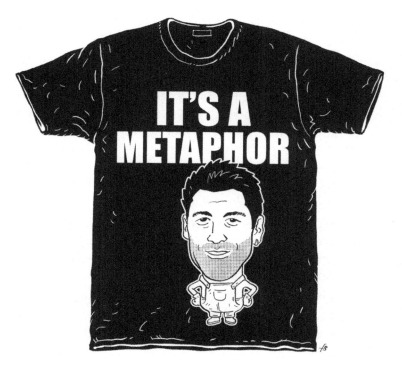

With a mocking edge, Francis introduces his hater to the bikini-clad women in his mansion, all of whom are being carefully stage-managed in the manner of Stalin parading foreign journalists before towns made up to look like socialist utopias.

Francis taunts, "This is my new friend, Peggy. She thinks you're being exploited," and insists, with coked-up self-delusion, "I'm a woman lover. I empower women!" and "Materialism is not important to me." Somehow, this seemingly tough-as-nails defender of the dignity of underaged woman is won over by Francis' argument that he can't be a misogynist because he has three sisters and *Girls Gone Wild* has what I imagine is a legally mandated "remorse policy," allowing girls to nix an appearance on one of its products if they choose to opt out within a certain time frame.

All it takes for the hater to go from fretting of Francis' mansion, "All I see is lost souls and tears," to drinking champagne and smiling with Joe is eye contact and a little one-on-one seduction.

On one level, Francis' "victory" is appalling and infuriating. On another, it's not terribly surprising. Everything Francis has is the product of his ability to talk women into doing things they shouldn't do. Why shouldn't that apply to a hater as well as a drunken eighteen-year-old pondering whether to make a swap of her top and dignity in exchange for *Girls Gone Wild* booty shorts?

That this woman could look into Joe Francis' cold, dead shark eyes and see a good man who will be devoting the years ahead to empowering women and personal growth betrays the fundamental dishonesty at the show's core.

In *H8R*, we aren't seeing a hated celebrity's authentic self for the first time: we're seeing an awkward photo op fused with the world's most misconceived hidden camera prank show.

It's fascinating and poignantly pathetic how little of *H8R*'s ambitions were realized. According to a 2011 article in the *Hollywood Reporter,* "The CW's new reality series *H8R*, which pairs celebrities with the everyday people who hate them, has a wish list that includes Sarah Palin, Lady Gaga, Mel Gibson, Arnold Schwarzenegger and Anthony Weiner, to name a few."

The article goes on to say, "Producers, which include Lisa Gregorisch-Dempsey and Mike Fleiss, have booked more than 20 celebrities so far, including Kim Kardashian, Kat Von D, Eva Longoria and former San Francisco Giants slugger Barry Bonds and have offers out to more."

Oh, and you might be familiar with Mike Fleiss' cousin, Heidi. They're involved in similar lines of work, but Heidi's a little more honest about it.

Alas, *H8R* was apparently beneath the dignity of even Sarah Palin, but Levi Johnston did unnecessarily continue his lifelong project of humiliating himself by taping an unaired segment on the show. There was talk that CW would burn off these episodes after the show was quickly canceled, but that never happened. That's probably for the best for everyone involved, and for television as a medium. And Western civilization. And humanity.

H8R was designed to illustrate that the distance, ignorance, and selective knowledge that fuels hating celebrities would dissipate in the warmth of time spent together and candid conversation about who the celebrities *really* are. Instead, it just ended up proving that, most of the time, the haters are right.

STAN LEE'S MIGHTY 7
(2014)

Stan Lee's high-profile cameos in Marvel movies are distracting by design. They're supposed to briefly hulk-smash the fourth wall and remind us of the history behind the super heroics. Lee's cameos were a very effective form of branding that linked every Marvel film to every other Marvel movie not just through a shared universe but through the iconic presence of a man who embodied comic books as a medium. Lee's cameos were fan service, a tip of the hat to the comic book world that inspired many of our biggest and most beloved blockbusters.

Stan Lee's bit parts in Marvel movies are inherently tangential. The lovable face and voice of Marvel pops up for a minute or so, we're all reminded of our love for the man and the world he created, and then we get on to more pressing matters.

Stan Lee's job as a thespian was to take audiences out of whatever movie he graced with his cheeseball presence and into a winking world of meta-textual self-promotion. If Lee's presence in the periphery of Marvel movies intentionally takes us out of those movies ever so briefly then how distracting would Lee be in a lead role?

That's the question posed by 2014's *Stan Lee's Mighty 7*. It's a bizarre vanity project from the simultaneously sad and triumphant final decade of Lee's life and career. At the very end of his epic life Lee was at once the face of one of the biggest, most successful, and ubiquitous brands in pop culture and a desperate hustler chasing after non-Marvel projects that could only tarnish his legacy.

Stan Lee was Marvel's biggest star, a monolith so vast he blocked out the sun and overshadowed his fellow creators, not all of whom had positive things to say about him.

So, there's a certain warped logic in the late self-promoter finding inspiration for his big new superhero team from looking in the mirror and deciding that, dammit, it was finally Stan Lee's time to shine—not just as a creator, writer, and cameo king but as a heroic main character. After all those years of toiling in obscurity, wasn't it time Lee finally had a taste of the limelight?

Who could possibly begrudge the creator of every superhero a late-in-life showcase as a voice artist and animated personality? Hence, *Stan Lee's Mighty 7* was born.

The animated pilot, the first part of a proposed trilogy that did not come to fruition, opens with a suspiciously young and vigorous-looking Stan Lee driving in the desert, looking for inspiration after pitching new superhero ideas to Archie Comics (real-life publisher of Stan Lee Comics) and getting rejected.

In *Stan Lee's Mighty 7* Stan Lee is, of course, Stan Lee, but for legal reasons he can't reference any of his Marvel characters, so while he refers to himself as the man behind many "legendary superheroes," the only credit he drops is his reality show *Who Wants to Be a Superhero?*

Stan Lee plays a fictionalized version of himself here but it's a strangely off-brand iteration, with his Marvel pedigree replaced by clumsy plugs for the decidedly lesser productions of POW! Entertainment, Lee's production company, which possessed just as much dignity as its name would suggest, exclamation point and all.

"Come on, brain! Get off your keister! Inspire me!" Lee challenges himself before receiving inspiration from an unlikely source: an alien ship containing five space fugitives and two space marshals. There is, for example, Lady Lightning (Mayim Bialik), of whom Lee quips, "You are one *fast* woman! And I mean that in a good way."

Lee's encounter with a world beyond even his own famously fertile imagination inspires a comic book pitch undeniable enough to impress even the snobs over at Archie: the first-ever reality superhero comics!

Drawing upon his extensive history and expertise in myth-making, Lee decides these powerful aliens need to pivot ever so slightly into super-heroism. To that end, he gives them all shitty new superhero names. Notorious sex cannibal Armie Hammer becomes terminally bland leader Strong Arm. Christian Slater does an unconvincing tough guy routine as bad boy Lazer Lord, a laser-shooting poor man's Wolverine while Flea is cast as Roller Man, a portly, bespectacled Poindexter type who can roll up in a ball and launch himself purposefully at targets.

Stan Lee's Mighty 7's voice cast is surprisingly star-studded. This extends to James Belushi as one of the main villains, a power-mad military madman with a cybernetic robot arm who wants to wipe out the Mighty 7 and Michael

Ironside as Xanar, an evil lizard man from a race at war with the aliens of the Mighty 7.

This sixty-six-minute Hub Network pilot is powered by a decidedly Stan Lee combination of shameless self-promotion and corny self-deprecation. The Stan Lee here is a wisecracking ham who delivers his lines with the rat-a-tat rhythms of a Borsht Belt comic who isn't shy about making lawyer jokes.

The vaudevillian shtick comes fast and furious from the Marvel magnate. "I'm Stan Lee. Hey, don't hold that against me!" the octogenarian quips by way of introduction, following it up with an admonition that people either follow him because of his legendary comic creations—or because he owes them money! Hi-yo!

Lee spends much of his time onscreen imploring his protégés to sign their contracts, so he can start exploiting them legally through the sale of a comic book based on their real-life antics.

Mighty 7 fleshes out its world with flashbacks revealing how its five prisoners ended up in space jail for their space crimes. These ostensible criminals all had good reasons to do what they did; though it would be giving this dopey-ass superhero nonsense entirely too much credit to pretend that it traffics in moral ambiguity.

In matters of roughly equal proportions, the bad boys and girls of the Mighty 7 save the world from evil aliens, and Stan Lee is finally able to achieve a little success in the comic book world when he sells his "real life superheroes" idea to Archie Comics.

The movie ends by teasing a sequel that was supposed to be followed by yet another sequel and then a TV series on top of video games and merchandise and clothes and Lunchables. That didn't happen, obviously, and while *Stan Lee's Mighty 7* is slicker and more professional than you might imagine, that doesn't feel like any great loss.

It could be worse. Around the time he was developing *Stan Lee's Mighty 7*, Lee was trying to transform another larger-than-life American icon into a superhero in the form of *The Governator*, an aborted vehicle for Arnold Schwarzenegger. Wikipedia describes this unrealized venture as featuring "a fictionalized Schwarzenegger who after stepping down from his role as Governor of California became a superhero in order to fight crime. His real-life family and Brentwood home would have fictional counterparts with the home having an Arnold Cave under it as a base of operations. To assist in crime fighting, the cave would have high tech vehicles, super suits, gym, and a group of sidekicks. One sidekick is his cyber security expert, Zeke Muckerberg, a teenage computer genius. The Governator would go up against G.I.R.L.I.E. Men

(Gangsters Imposters Racketeers Liars & Irredeemable Ex-cons), his recurring super-villains. A recurring character shown in the trailer is an investigative reporter, voiced by Larry King."

Yes, the end is oftentimes not pretty or dignified when it comes to the lives of great creators, and while *Mighty 7* is probably less embarrassing than *The Governator* (which was shuttered when news broke that the action hero had impregnated his housekeeper) or another never-to-be-realized late-in-life Lee project that would have transformed Ringo Starr into a superhero, it's still many professional rungs below where Marvel Films was operating at the time.

If nothing else, *Stan Lee's Mighty 7* underlines the uncanny commonalities between Lee and Robert Evans, another inveterate self-promoter and show-business character with an unmistakable voice and cadence who attained a secondary fame late in life as a larger-than-life personality who embodied the heart and soul of his industry.

It speaks to the faith the entertainment industry had in Lee that a multimedia product line was planned around him and his dynamic personality and public persona when he was in his late eighties. Then again, as corny as *Stan Lee's Mighty 7* might be, and it's mighty corny, it's nice just to hear his voice again.

THE WORST OF
FILM

PLAN 9 FROM OUTER SPACE
(1957)

It's hard to overstate the role *Plan 9 from Outer Space* and its eccentric creator have played in the birth and evolution of bad movie culture.

When the Medved brothers dubbed *Plan 9 from Outer Space* the worst movie ever made in their influential 1980 book, *The Golden Turkey Awards,* and Wood the worst director, it introduced a bold new dynamic: trash aficionados wanting to see a movie specifically *because* it's terrible, not despite being terrible. The enduring cult of *Plan 9* is rooted in the transparently false but irresistible notion that it's not just a bad movie, but literally the *worst* movie ever made. *Plan 9* was the original best worst movie.

At this point I have seen *Ed Wood* so many times that it starts to feel like *Plan 9 from Outer Space* is lifting scenes wholesale from Tim Burton's cult classic rather than the other way around.

This begins with Criswell's opening narration, which is delivered directly to the camera in a state of barely controlled hysteria: "Greetings, my friend. We are all interested in the future, for that is where you and I are going to spend the rest of our lives. And remember my friend, future events such as these will affect you in the future. You are interested in the unknown, the mysterious, the unexplainable. That is why you are here.

"And now, for the first time, we are bringing to you the full story of what happened on that fateful day. We are bringing you all the evidence, based only on the secret testimony of the miserable souls who survived this terrifying ordeal. The incidents, the places. My friend, we cannot keep this a secret any longer. Let us punish the guilty. Let us reward the innocent. My friend, can your heart stand the shocking facts about grave robbers from outer space?"

As a writer, one of the worst things you can do is repeat yourself. If you're going to use the same words, for the love of god, space them out a little. Consequently, I can't tell you how much malevolent joy it brought me that over the course of just two sentences and thirty-two words Criswell repeats the word "future" three times.

This opening monologue beautifully embodies the cracked poetry of Wood's feverish overwriting. Wood could not write, or tell a story, or make a coherent film, but the joy he takes in his nonexistent gifts is irresistible and infectious. The world would be a better place if everyone who was as bad at what they do as Wood took such pride and pleasure in their job.

Criswell's opening narration uses a lot of words to tell us almost nothing except that the laughable travesty we're about to watch happens in the future, albeit a future that looks and feels exactly like the present, and is rooted in "evidence," "testimony," and "incidents."

Criswell's narration continues just as floridly when the action shifts to a funeral where a melancholy figure known only as the "Old Man," played by special guest star Bela Lugosi, is burying a beloved wife played by proto-Elvira Vampira.

The Old Man's wife isn't content to stay in the ground, however. For it seems a highly developed race of aliens have developed the technology to bring corpses back to life.

At first the aliens' intentions are not quite so sinister, but when their attempts to seek a meeting with the governments of the world, so they can share their incredible secrets, are rebuffed they resort to plan B, or Plan 9, as it were. Plan 9 involves resurrecting the dead to create an army of zombies who will march on the capitals of Earth and overtake humanity.

It's a terrible plan, particularly since the aliens seem intent on bringing the dead back to life individually and with great effort. At the rate they're creating zombies, it would probably take them a few thousand years to animate enough corpses for an unstoppable army of the undead. Hell, it'd probably take a couple of years just to assemble a softball team worth of reanimated corpses.

The grave robbers from outer space *really* did not think things through. No wonder all their previous plans failed. As they are only too happy to point out, their technology is far superior to that of stupid earthlings, but their plan-making is rudimentary at best.

John "Bunny" Breckinridge hilariously plays The Ruler, the leader of the aliens, less as an all-powerful otherworldly being bent on world domination than as a harried middle manager frustrated that his latest project is falling apart due to poor design and execution.

As *Ed Wood* hilariously chronicled, a big part of what makes *Plan 9 from Outer Space* so unintentionally funny is that Wood chose to replace Lugosi, who was too busy being dead to finish shooting, with a body double who looks nothing like Lugosi, and was also markedly taller than the *Dracula* star.

That would not be a problem if the reanimated corpse of the Old Man, who holds a cape over his face to ineptly try to hide the fact that he's being played by a moonlighting chiropractor and not one of the great icons of horror cinema, did not have so much screen time.

There is a reason zombie movies generally involve terrifying packs of the undead stalking the living. As *Plan 9* establishes, there is nothing particularly scary about a single zombie shambling toward humans slowly enough to give them more than enough time to get away safely.

Yet, due to budget constraints and total incompetence, Wood limited himself to three zombies: the Old Man; his

Old, Dead Lady; and finally Inspector Daniel Clay (Tor Johnson), a detective who meets a bad end in the spooky graveyard where much of the film takes place.

For the role of a sharp detective skilled at getting to the bottom of things, Wood adorably chose a hulking Swedish professional wrestler so unintelligible that he talks like he has a mouth full of borscht. That's less of a problem when he becomes a zombie.

The aliens, in their zeal to destroy humanity and teach humanity lessons, fly their saucers over Washington, DC, and the West Coast. The "flying saucers" were not paper plates or hubcaps, as commonly thought, but rather a commercially available UFO model kit, complete with a little green man inside.

Plan 9 is so wonderfully threadbare and homemade that it's downright startling when Wood shifts from the ingratiatingly inept footage he shot to stock footage of massive guns shooting down UFOs or a plane soaring through the sky.

Plan 9 looks like it cost about a dollar, yet Wood chose a style of film—special effects–intensive science fiction about a war between aliens and earthlings—that requires a sizable budget and a skilled battalion of craftsman to do adequately, let alone well.

Wood had none of these things and, yet, he went for it anyway. Like his creative progeny Tommy Wiseau and Neil Breen, Wood wasn't about to let the fact that he couldn't do anything keep him from attempting to do everything.

Plan 9 even has a message: as a disappointed Ruler informs the stupid earthlings, the real purpose of the alien's visit is to keep human beings from creating and then using weapons so powerful that they destroy the whole universe, not just their own stupid planet.

Criswell returns at the very end to jab an accusatory finger in the direction of audience members unconvinced that space aliens are real based on the verisimilitude-rich motion picture they just experienced.

Did you forget the part where he said it was all based on sworn testimony? Did you? You can't just make stuff up and say that it's based on sworn testimony. That would be dishonest.

Criswell closes the film by imploring, "We once laughed at the horseless carriage, the airplane, the telephone, the electric light, vitamins, radio, and even television. And now some of us laugh at outer space. God help us in the future!"

The writing in *Plan 9* is wildly entertaining. It's eminently quotable. It's colorful. It's iconic. It's flavorful and unique. It has stood the test of time. It reflects the wonderfully warped personality of its creator so purely that it's like a cinematic X-ray of his tortured, joyous soul.

These are all qualities we associate with great writing, so why is *Plan 9* considered not only not great but the worst movie of all time?

Probably because "worst of all time" is less criticism than high praise. *Plan 9* is so crazy, audacious, and eminently re-watchable that it deservedly dwells in the realm of superlatives.

For better or worse, the future that Ed Wood forces us to contemplate *repeatedly* would evolve in ways the preeminent trash culture icon never could have imagined.

Wood couldn't have anticipated just how many people would end up seeing and loving *Plan 9 from Outer Space*. In his wildest dreams he couldn't have foreseen the huge role it would play in bad movie culture.

From the vantage point of 2021, *Plan 9 from Outer Space* looks like the Big Bang that led to podcasts like *The Flop House, How Did This Get Made?* and *We Hate Movies*; television shows like *Mystery Science Theater 3000*; and my career.

It's impossible to separate Ed Wood from *Plan 9 from Outer Space*. Its idiosyncrasies are his idiosyncrasies, its wonderful madness his own.

Plan 9 is Wood's triumph, the one we will remember him for, and a movie that thoroughly earns its place high atop the pantheon of movies so transcendently bad they single-handedly make the world a better place.

MANOS:
THE HANDS OF FATE
(1966)

Manos: The Hands of Fate's reputation precedes it. As with so many terrible movies that have endured, the story behind the film is every bit as fascinating and unlikely as the film itself.

This will not come as a surprise to anyone who has seen *Manos: The Hands of Fate*, but writer, director, and star Harold P. Warren did not come from a filmmaking background. Before he made an accidental bid for cult immortality, Warren made his living selling fertilizer and insurance.

As a fertilizer salesman, he literally sold shit for a living. As a life insurance salesman, he also pretty much sold shit. He understandably figured he would be able to sell shit to moviegoers as well.

The movie is the product of a bet between shit salesman Harold P. Warren and prolific television and film writer Stirling Silliphant, whose credits include *In the Heat of the Night*, *Village of the Damned*, and *The Towering Inferno*.

Warren bet the Academy Award winner that he could make a feature-length motion picture despite having zero experience in the filmmaking business.

Now, if there is one quality that unites all of humankind, beyond admiration for the actor Paul Rudd, it's a stubborn if wholly insupportable conviction that if they really put their mind to it, *anyone* could make a good movie.

How hard can it be? You just make up a story, think of some dumb stuff for your characters to say, tell the phony actors in your film where to stand, and BOOM, the next thing you know you're onstage at the Academy Awards accepting the Best Screenplay award like that phony Silliphant fellow.

That's clearly how Warren saw filmmaking. He set out to prove that despite what professionals like Silliphant might think, it was super-easy to make movies. Anyone could do it! Instead, he ended up proving the opposite point.

Manos: The Hands of Fate is often bandied about as the worst movie of all time. On IMDB, it currently holds down the number three spot on the reader-voted list of the worst films. However, even this rating is generous, as *Manos: The Hands of Fate* is less a singularly terrible motion picture than a hilarious and unexpectedly poignant attempt at making a movie.

Warren failed miserably in his attempt to create an actual film, yet succeeded in creating something much more perverse, an exploitation cheapie that's closer to outsider art than the B-movies Roger Corman's production company was cranking out at the time.

Warren doesn't just write and direct ineptly; he also stars as Michael, a Perry Como–looking Shleprock who gets hopelessly lost while driving one day with his dog; his smoking-hot wife (Diane Mahree as Margaret); and their daughter, Debbie (Jackey Neyman Jones).

Adding to the amateur hour vibe: in the early going, characters routinely look at the camera with a pained expression that silently but powerfully conveys: "Get me out of here!" and "Why did I agree to do this?"

The lost and desperate family ends up seeking refuge in a creepy domicile where they encounter Torgo (John Reynolds), who looks like a cross between Vincent van Gogh and Dr. Frankenstein's sidekick/helper Igor.

Everything about Torgo angrily screams, "Go away! Flee while you still can! There is nothing here for you, but death and insanity. Nothing but ruin awaits you in this most cursed of hellholes!"

The huge and ever-growing cult of *Manos: The Hands of Fate* is largely the cult of Torgo. Reynolds is so twitchy and mannered that it seems like he broke every bone and is blackout drunk every moment onscreen. That's not that far from the truth.

In actuality, Reynolds was apparently blasted off his mind on LSD throughout filming, which makes sense because watching Reynolds act on LSD is liable to make you feel like you're on LSD yourself and in the midst of a trip so intense that it makes you feel like your own grasp on reality is disintegrating.

Torgo's essence is ineffably disturbing. The only way Torgo could more overtly convey menace would be if he was introduced covered in blood and talking proudly about someone he just murdered. Instead, he manages to convey the sense that he has killed before and will happily kill again through body language and facial twitching.

If Michael were not the single stupidest human being in the history of the universe, as soon as Torgo screams that someone known only as "The Master" doesn't like children, he would have taken the hint and skedaddled.

Instead, Michael behaves as if The Master is like the night manager of a Holiday Inn and if he just flashes a credit card, he'll be shown a nice room with a queen-sized bed near the ice machine with color television and air conditioning.

Yorgo's whole vibe is, "I'm going to murder you and your family and then drink your blood." Michael's response is essentially, "That's cool. We'll have to get off to an early start tomorrow to make up for the time we lost today. Do you offer free continental breakfast?"

Nobody moves like Torgo. That's probably a good thing. Thanks to LSD, Reynolds' face never stops moving either. Like everyone in the film his acting is silent-film broad. Since the whole disaster was post-dubbed, actors couldn't really use their voices to express emotion, so everything has to be conveyed visually, through over-the-top mugging.

At a certain point *Manos'* focus shifts from Torgo and the family to The Master (Tom Neyman), a mustachioed fiend who upon being resurrected almost immediately gets into a spat with his six wives.

Sure, the guy may call himself The Master but, upon his return to the land of the living, he falls snugly into the role of henpecked husband.

His wives, they won't stop jibber-jabbering! They're making him crazy with all their womanly squabbling! It isn't long until The Master sports an expression that says, "Oy vey, women, amirite? Always with the talking! And the fighting! Even if you're evil incarnate, you can't get a word in edgewise!"

The film's not-so-secret message is that if you think one wife is a headache, imagine having six!

Manos: The Hands of Fate is about a figure of supreme evil, a demonic force of supernatural menace whose wives give him the business something awful. *Manos: The Hands of Fate* is the *Rosemary's Baby*/Lockhorns hybrid we never knew we needed.

Manos, incidentally, is an evil Satanic deity to whom The Master and his wives pledge obeisance. The Master and his wives all have different ideas on how to best serve Manos, however. Some of the wives take a strong stance against sacrificing a girl child on the logic that she will grow up to be a woman.

Others take a more positive view of sacrificing the girl, so that they can better serve Manos and The Master.

The wives settle their philosophical differences the only way they know how: through a three-on-three catfight that takes up much of the film's sixty-nine-minute runtime.

As for Torgo, he's just a dick. For a craven supplicant, Torgo is a huge asshole to The Master. Yes, The Master sentences him to death, but Torgo has it coming.

In its third act *Manos: The Hands of Fate* becomes a struggle for survival with the family trying to stay alive and The Master trying to take Mike's wife and daughter as new wives, because the old ones are *really* getting on his nerves, what with their incessant chatter about, "You're selfish in bed," and, "This compound isn't big enough for all of us," and, "Wouldn't you love to hear the pitter-patter of the feet of little Masters??!?!"

To watch *Manos: The Hands of Fate* is to step outside the realm of competent filmmaking and sanity and embrace the free-floating madness of a production that's jarringly off in every conceivable way. At times, *Manos* attains the queasy power of a waking nightmare.

Manos: The Hands of Fate lives up to its reputation as the worst of the worst, but also the best kind of worst. It's so bad it's great, a one-of-a-kind abomination overflowing with quotable lines and unforgettable aspects. The film features, for example, a pair of teenagers necking and getting drunk in a car who keep popping up for no reason at all, as well as a score that sounds like Warren kidnapped a few of Herb Alpert's Tijuana Brass and forced them to provide jazzy accompaniment for his amateur exercise in entertaining incompetence.

Watching and loving and marveling at the existence and afterlife of *Manos: The Hands of Fate,* I had a thought. This cosmic joke of a motion picture, which should never have been made, should lead to more movies.

After all, *Plan 9 from Outer Space* led to *Ed Wood. Troll 2* spawned the wonderful documentary *Best Worst Movie.* The making of *The Room* led to the dynamite show-business comedy *The Disaster Artist.* The wonderfully terrible films of Rudy Ray Moore became the subject of the terrific Eddie Murphy comeback vehicle *Dolemite Is My Name.*

So why not make a narrative film or feature-length documentary based on the too-strange-for-fiction production of *Manos: The Hands of Fate*? The juicy role of John Reynolds, the doomed actor who so unforgettably breathed life into Torgo, then took his own life before the world could appreciate his unique gifts, could win the right actor an Academy Award.

The worst movie in the world could very easily lead to wild critical acclaim, boffo box-office and Oscar glory. If Harold P. Warren could make his cinematic dreams happen despite a complete lack of qualifications, there's no reason dedicated Hollywood professionals with actual talent couldn't turn the behind-the-scenes insanity of this preeminent "so bad it's good" camp classic into a rapturously funny ode to show-business ambition at its most exquisitely misguided.

ROBOCOP III
(1993)

Some franchises are blessed to have budgets that expand exponentially alongside box-office grosses. Not *Robocop*. By *Robocop 3*, which was filmed in 1991 but went unreleased until 1993 due to Orion's bankruptcy, the franchise was in serious cost-cutting mode.

The series was learning to do without. By the second sequel original Robocop Peter Weller was gone, replaced by the less expensive Robert John Burke.

Robocop 3 did not have Peter Weller. It didn't have a big budget, or an adequate budget either.

The costumes in *Robocop 3* are so cheap that it looks like the production team saved money by buying off-brand Halloween costumes with names like "Compu-Crime-Fighter" off the rack from a Party City on November 1. The choice to make the good guys hobos feels similarly pragmatic: you save money dressing your cast in rags.

Robocop 3 didn't have Peter Weller. Or Paul Verhoeven, director of the classic first film. Nor did it have the unexpectedly high-powered team behind *Robocop 2: Empire Strikes Back*'s Irvin Kershner directing a script from comic book god Frank Miller and Walon Green, whose credits include *The Wild Bunch* and *Sorcerer*.

Robocop 3 didn't have a big enough budget or a rating that would allow it to indulge in the gleeful ultra-violence that had thus far defined the series.

The second sequel to *Robocop* had an ace up its sleeve, however. It had something the other two *Robocop* films desperately lacked, something that would single-handedly elevate it to unexpectedly great heights, literally and figuratively.

Robocop 3 had something wonderfully, exquisitely American, as American as mom, apple pie, and school shootings: a jet-pack.

A jet-pack!

In the great timeline of important historical events involving the Robocop franchise, the day some genius thought, "Fuck it: Robocop's got a jet-pack now!" ranks right up there with the seminal moment the Robocop statue was unveiled in Detroit, finally giving residents of the city a reason to feel civic pride and hope for the future.

Who needs Peter Weller when you've got a jet-pack? Who needs profanity or excessive violence or an R rating? Who needs a halfway decent budget when you've got a jet-pack?

Even without the climactic reveal of Robocop's jet-pack, *Robocop 3* would still qualify as a staggeringly bizarre motion picture, a weirdly populist cartoon satire that centers on the fantasy that Robocop, a police officer, robot-man, and famous white heterosexual male, would be down for the revolutionary struggle rather than a shiny cog in The Man's Machine.

In *Robocop 3*, even the police are on the side of the oppressed masses. Forget the whole robot-cop thing: that is the film's truly fantastical element. The cops in *Robocop 3* all climactically quit in protest rather than be used by an evil corporation to evict poor revolutionaries locked in a righteous class war against an evil privatized police force.

"COMPU-CRIME-FIGHTER"

ADULT
Size Costume

Robocop's improbable radicalization begins when he makes a judgment call in the line of duty, much to the horror of corporate scum Jeffrey Fleck (Bradley Whitford in one of his first big weasel roles), who casually insists that Dr. Marie Lazarus (Jill Hennessy) eliminate everything human about the crime-fighting cyborg, reducing him to a cold, inhuman machine.

The heroic Dr. Lazarus disobeys the command. Instead of becoming all machine, Robocop grows increasingly human after he falls in with a renegade band of impoverished rebels lousy with heavyweight character actors like C.C.H. Pounder, Daniel von Bargen, and Stephen Root, who are being evicted from their homes by mercenaries known as "Rehabs."

In yet another exquisitely off-brand moment for this most bonkers of *Robocop* sequels, Robocop consoles a child on the death of her parents, even stroking her hair paternally, the way a police android built by an evil corporation would.

The true villain of the *Robocop* franchise is capitalism. In *Robocop 3*, the gluttonous demi-oligarchs of Omni Consumer Products are supplanted by an even more evil and decidedly more Japanese hyper-capitalist cabal: the Kanemitsu Corporation.

Cowriter/director Fred Dekker, whose impressive résumé includes two cult hits, *Night of the Creeps* and *The Monster Squad,* and some standout episodes of *Tales from the Crypt,* was enamored of Hong Kong cinema and wanted to give the film a John Woo feel.

Dekker's admirable ambitions unfortunately and unsurprisingly lead to less than noble results. *Robocop 3* is very much a product of its time in portraying the Japanese as a malevolent economic force out to crush the United States.

Oh, and you know what else the Kanemitsu Corporation has? Ninja Terminators. That's right: in addition to Robocop in the Weather Underground AND a nifty jet-pack, *Robocop 3* has Ninja Terminators in the form of the Otomo, a cyborg with the skills and preternatural reflexes of a robo-samurai.

Robocop 3 did not have the budget for Ninja Terminators. It did not have the creative resources for Ninja Terminators. But the filmmakers threw caution to the wind and created Ninja Terminators anyway. That's the spirit that makes America great: Ninja Terminators and Robocop in a jet-pack. To ask for more out of any one film, indeed, out of any one franchise, would be unbecomingly selfish.

JAR JAR BINKS IN THE PHANTOM MENACE (1999)

It's funny the things that stick out in your mind. For whatever reason, I have a vivid memory of the first time I heard about Jar Jar Binks. It was in an *Entertainment Weekly* article about *The Phantom Menace*, and Liam Neeson was predicting that a silly talking space frog named Jar Jar Binks voiced by Ahmed Best would be a standout among the film's cast, a fan favorite that audiences wouldn't be able to stop talking about.

In a Monkey's Paw scenario, Neeson's words came true in the darkest possible sense. Jar Jar Binks did stand out from the rest of the cast in that he was inevitably singled out as a fatal flaw that single-handedly sunk an already dodgy enterprise.

Over two decades later, we still haven't stopped talking about Jar Jar. We've never stopped wondering what George Lucas was thinking when he sprung Jar Jar upon a world that only ever wanted to love the director and his creations.

Jar Jar Binks isn't just hated the way unpopular characters are hated. He's hated the way monsters, real and otherwise, are hated. He's hated the way Adolf Hitler is hated. Jar Jar Binks is hated with a ferocity that has abated over the years only because it would be impossible to sustain that level of rage permanently.

Jar Jar's job was created to entertain the younglings with his unique brand of outer space minstrelsy, so that a three-movie saga about how a plucky little eight-year-old hero becomes the most evil man in the universe would not be too grim.

That's a tall order. Remove Jar Jar from the equation and *The Phantom Menace* becomes a much darker film about the inevitability of evil, and the ways in which good intentions and pragmatism sometimes lead to the worst possible outcomes.

A good indication of just how achingly dull *The Phantom Menace* can be without Jar Jar's excessively energetic presence to enliven it is provided by the prequel's opening crawl.

When the words, "A long time ago in a galaxy far, far away . . ." were followed by: "Turmoil has engulfed the Galactic Republic. The taxation of trade routes to outlying star systems is in dispute," the formerly tumescent fanboy penises made rock-hard in anticipation of not just a kick-ass new movie, but a spiritual event by John Williams' rousing main title theme, not only wilted but actually receded back into their bodies, never to emerge again.

"Turmoil has engulfed the Galactic Republic" is acceptable enough, but "The taxation of trade routes to outlying star systems is in dispute" all too effectively conveys the film's perversely dry tone, which is closer to Outer Space C-SPAN than swashbuckling space adventure.

Gungan Jar Jar makes his much-ballyhooed appearance about ten minutes into the film when Liam Neeson's Qui-Gon Jinn saves his life. In both the broad outline and specifics, Jar Jar resembles a racist caricature of an African villager or Caribbean islander from a colonialist-minded serial. In a world of adults, he's a simpleminded child in a man's body, a bungler with a heart of gold.

Jar Jar speaks in such a heavy dialect that it can be hard to understand what he's saying. But instead of "Yassuh" and "Nosuh," we get "Mesa" and "Yousa." Jar Jar's defining characteristic might just be his cowardice, followed closely by his predilection for buffoonery. He's a clown, but he's also comically inept. Jar Jar's race is seen as inferior by people who speak the Queen's English. Despite these shortcomings, the Gungans pride themselves on being fierce warriors.

Jar Jar Binks is rescued from oblivion by a white savior. In appreciation, Jar Jar pledges to be Qui-Gon Jinn's servant, but that role shifts to one closer to slave when Qui-Gon Jinn saves Jar Jar a second time when he's about to be punished by his fellow Gungans.

Thankfully Qui-Gon Jinn proves a benevolent master, unlike Watto, the grotesque anti-Semitic caricature who owns Anakin Skywalker (Jake Lloyd). Qui-Gon Jinn helps this simple, backward soul achieve things he could never have imagined had he never left his backward home planet.

When Jar Jar Binks enters the proceedings, he's like the shot of adrenaline to Uma Thurman's chest in *Pulp Fiction*. A perversely sleepy story that takes its tone from Jedi masters so Zen they barely seem awake develops not just a pulse, but a manic, nervous, jittery energy.

Jar Jar Binks is a goddamned train wreck. He is voracious and insatiable in his demand for attention. Jar Jar Binks is also the most compelling and alive element of *The Phantom Menace*. In a mind-numbing, nap-inducing spectacle where no one seems to have much of a personality, Jar Jar Binks has entirely too much personality.

There's an energy to Jar Jar, a vulgarity, a raucous sense of life that almost makes it possible to forgive that everything he brings to the movie is not only terrible but egregiously wrong.

The Phantom Menace makes it apparent that George Lucas spent the twenty-two years between *Star Wars* and *The Phantom Menace* losing touch with how people talk, think, and behave. It is a movie born not out of lived experience but out of compulsive consumption of old movies.

Lucas was among the most retro of the major American filmmakers of the 1970s. While the rest of Hollywood was snorting cocaine off the breasts of sex workers like real artists, Lucas was looking back at his teenaged years with *American Graffiti,* the sci-fi movies and comic books of the 1930s and '40s with *Star Wars,* and old adventure serials with *Raiders of the Lost Ark.*

As the millennium ended, Lucas was still drawing inspirations from old movies, rather than an outside world that seemed to scare him. It's not surprising, therefore, that his first film as a director in over two decades traffics extensively in antiquated racist stereotypes.

There is no such thing as benign racism. By its very nature, racism is malignant. But there are gradations of racism. There's the harsh, brutal racism of Nazis, the KKK, and the Alt-Right. There's also a softer version that angrily insists that a moderate amount of racism and bigotry is not only acceptable but necessary for society to function.

White people love soft racism because it replaces an honest, deeply challenging, and unflattering narrative of institutionalized anti-black racism with a dishonest, but more flattering, fantasy of endless Caucasian benevolence.

The anger directed toward *The Force Awakens* and *The Last Jedi* is primarily a backlash against what fanboys see as the tyranny of identity politics and diversity. But it is also undoubtedly rooted in nostalgia for the kinds of stereotypes *The Phantom Menace* recycles without examining or critiquing.

It wasn't the racism of Jar Jar Binks that bothered fans as much as the stupidity. By the time George Lucas' space saga roared back to life in 1999, Star Wars fandom had become a secular religion. Jar Jar Binks exposed that Lucas' beloved epic was not a New Testament for our times but rather silly space nonsense for children.

Lucas himself got to the core of this dissatisfaction when he said: "(The *Star Wars*) movies are for children, but they don't want to admit that. . . . There is a small group of fans that do not like comic sidekicks. They want the films to be tough like *The Terminator,* and they get very upset and opinionated about anything that has anything to do with being childlike."

It's a tribute to how seriously fans take *Star Wars* that the very idea of Jar Jar struck them as heresy.

Still, in a world where *Nancy* became the hippest comic strip and characters like The Flintstones, Scooby-Doo, and Snagglepuss have all been reimagined for gritty, critically acclaimed adult comics/graphic novels, I'd like to think we haven't seen the last of Jar Jar yet.

Jar Jar Binks did not cut it as a comic sidekick or lowbrow comic relief. But he might be perfect for tragedy. That'd be appropriate, since everything about his sad, brief life as the most unpopular would-be fan favorite of all time is tragic, including the fact that Michael Jackson desperately wanted to play the character. It's probably for the best that that did not happen because, let's face it, Jackson as Jar Jar might be a little embarrassing.

THE TURTLE CLUB SEQUENCE IN MASTER OF DISGUISE (2002)

According to pop culture legend, if not necessarily the historical record, on September 11, 2001, something happened that changed American life forever. It was a momentous day whose impact was so profound that American history can usefully be divided into two categories: pre and post.

Everyone knows where they were when this historic event occurred. It is burned indelibly into the cultural memory, in our collective consciousness.

I'm speaking, of course, about how Dana Carvey ostensibly launched a devastatingly successful attack on our collective funny bone by filming, on September 11, 2001, the legendary Turtle Club sequence in *Master of Disguise.*

It turns out that the Turtle Club sequence was *not*, in fact, filmed on that fateful day. The auspicious event occurred a few weeks later, but why let something like the truth get in the way of a story so juicy and perfect?

To be a true *Master of Disguise* super-fan is to forever be asking yourself, "Am I not turtley enough for the Turtle Club?"

That is the question our hero Pistachio Disguisey (Carvey), the titular master of disguise, uses to righteously confront a Turtle Club doorman played by Brandon Molale when he asks Pistachio and his sidekick Jennifer Parker (Jennifer Esposito), "Can I help you? Are you a member of the Turtle Club?"

Before they enter the Turtle Club, Pistachio's mortified friend tells her compatriot, "I don't mean to keep harping, but the name the Turtle Club, you know, is just a name. I think you're taking it a little too literally."

Pistachio *is* taking the name of the Turtle Club *way* too literally in that he thinks that it means that in order to get in you need to look like a turtle, act like a turtle, and possibly be a turtle, in addition to communicating how a turtle might if it acquired the gift of human speech yet retained the same level of subhuman intelligence.

Pistachio mumble-stutters, "turtle, turtle," over the course of the scene in a viscerally unnerving whimper. "He's dreamt of this place since he was a child. Do you think we could go in for a moment? We'll be out in five minutes. Please?" Jennifer implores flirtatiously, using her womanly charms to convince a man who should know better to let what appears to be a mentally ill mutated turtle-man into the club when his ONE JOB involves keeping the Pistachio Disguiseys of the world out.

Even before he enters the club, Pistachio is the center of attention. Everyone understandably seems to be wondering what's going on with the mutated turtle-man with his hideously deformed back squeezed uncomfortably into a green suit making unsettling eye contact with strangers and blurting with deeply unsettling hostility, "Turtle! Not turtle. TURTLE! Not turtle."

Pistachio strides purposefully through the crowd, determining, on a patron-by-patron basis, whether the people he encounters are human beings like everyone since the beginning of time, or human beings who are also, inexplicably, weird turtle-human hybrids like himself.

Pistachio keeps blurting out the word "turtle" throughout the scene for no discernible reason. It's as if the word is a safety blanket, the only thing that can possibly get his mind off the unspeakable horrors of the terrorist attacks of 9/11 that must have hit the *Saturday Night Live* alum close to home, literally and figuratively.

Carvey, though the character of Pistachio, perseverates ceaselessly; it is as if he cannot help himself, as if the only thing that makes sense in a world gone mad involves compulsively mumbling the word "turtle."

At a certain point, the weird but implicit aggression of Pistachio's shtick becomes explicit.

"What if HARM found its way to you? Terrible, terrible, TERRIBLE harm!?!" Pistachio threatens his tormentors in a weirdly milquetoast fashion, fidgeting in a manner that's supposed to be intimidating. "Would that change your mind? Perhaps it's time to go into my shell."

"Shell time coming!" Pistachio promises as his bald, bespectacled head, tiny in comparison to the enormity of his human-sized turtle shell, begins to retract into his body.

Pistachio walks away with Jennifer, at which point a cocky businessman asks Jennifer, "Hey baby, can I buy you a drink, and maybe some POND water for your friend?"

At first Pistachio pretends to be amused, but the businessman's cruel barb brings out the maniac in Pistachio, an angry, turtle-like man of violence overcome with incoherent aggression and murderous rage.

The insult sets off something ugly and cruel in Pistachio. He retracts his head into his giant turtle torso-shell-body. The men foolishly come over to investigate, at which point Pistachio's turtle head pops out. He bites off a man's nose, then spits it back out so smoothly that the appendage reattaches to his face instantly.

Then, because we have entered a world of pure madness where logic has no power and chaos reigns, Pistachio spins around on the ground on the giant turtle shell–like apparatus inside his outsized green suit.

And then, friends, it's over. The whole sequence lasts a mere 147 seconds. That's less than two and a half minutes.

In the shadow of 9/11, Dana Carvey articulated our collective fears when he said "turtle" and then just kept saying it. Carvey was like all of us in the dark aftermath of the terrorist attacks on the World Trade Center and Pentagon. He was overwhelmed. He was confused. He was scared. He was unsure of what had just happened and what the undoubtedly far-reaching consequences might be. He was desperately in need of consolation and comfort in a world seemingly careening into madness. Lastly, Carvey was wearing a bizarre turtle-man costume and mumbling the word "turtle" obsessively.

So, while national history was made in a very dark way on September 11, 2001, cinematic history was made a few weeks later in a life-affirmingly stupid manner. The astonishingly, eminently re-watchable idiocy of the Turtle Club scene in *Master of Disguise* stands as an essential rebuke to the awful solemnity of 9/11, to the idea that we would never laugh again, that irony was dead, and we would have to be earnest forevermore, or we would be dishonoring the memories of the fallen.

By filming "The Turtle Club" scene first when filming resumed, Carvey was telling Osama bin Laden and his whole disreputable lot that not only would we laugh again after 9/11 but we'd laugh at stupider, more juvenile nonsense than ever before, and we would *never* feel guilty for laughing.

And you know what? We've kept that promise. We've stayed dumb and superficial, and that, ultimately, is how we have survived, individually and collectively.

THE TEST
(2012)

A trailer for an upcoming low-budget independent film recently went viral in the worst possible way. The film is *Loqueesha*, the brainchild of writer, director, and producer Jeremy Saville, who also stars as a straight white man who pretends to be a sassy black woman on the radio to help pay for his son's private school tuition and becomes a sensation for "her" down-home wisdom.

This widely shared, universally mocked trailer prompted questions. Questions like: What the fuck? No, seriously, what the fuck? What could have convinced this doofus that minstrelsy on that level was acceptable, ever, but particularly in 2019, when we, as a culture, are a curious, combustible combination of wanton, proudly xenophobic cruelty and cultural hypersensitivity?

Who was Jeremy Saville? What hole did he crawl out of? I checked out *Loqueesha*'s joke-free but aphorism-rich Twitter feed, which began in 2012, but has produced exactly ten tweets.

It is not coincidental that 2012 was also the year that Saville's feature film writing, directing, producing, and starring debut *The Test* was released.

The astonishing thing about *The Test* is that it may actually be more offensive than *Loqueesha*. I do not make that claim lightly.

The morally repellent premise of *The Test* is that Nathan, the wan charisma vacuum Saville plays, is so terrified that his impossibly attractive, loving fiancée Julia (Kelly Sullivan) will somehow prove herself unworthy of a soggy, sentient loaf of Wonder Bread like himself that he subjects her to a series of humiliating "tests" with the help of his scuzzy buddies.

The titular parade of mental cruelty is the brainchild not of lovestruck Nathan but rather his friends Todd (Stephen Frejek) and Ron (Danso Gordon). Todd is the film's preeminent misogynist, a dead-eyed sociopath who looks like Kevin Corrigan's sinister, Mexican, nonunion twin.

Because he's been hurt in the past, Todd seems personally offended by monogamy, commitment, relationships, healthy relationships, unhealthy relationships, and women as a gender.

When Nathan tells his buddies that he's marrying a beautiful woman ridiculously out of his league, Todd becomes enraged. He tells his friend of his possible future, "I don't want to see you wind up one of those weekend dads, picking up your kid at the ex's while some other dude is diddling her on your dime."

The ugly, unexamined core of *The Test*'s misogyny is a fear that a sexually desirable woman who marries a schmuck will happily trade up at the first opportunity, that all women are inherently distrustful, only as faithful as their options.

Ron and Todd propose a series of tests. Ron, the film's only black character, only half-jokingly proposes that he and Todd kidnap Julia, shoot her full of truth serum, and "smack her around a little" to see if she's worthy of marrying Nathan.

If he had a soul or scruples, Nathan would tell his friends to go fuck themselves. Instead, Nathan initially gets upset at his friends, but when he gets home and Julia tells him about friends of theirs who are getting divorced after just a year of marriage, Nathan freaks out.

The mere existence of divorce within his friend circle is enough to make Nathan lose any trust he has in the woman he has chosen to spend his life with. He opts in on Ron and Todd's campaign of psychological torture and devotes the rest of the film to being cruel toward Julia in increasingly extreme ways.

The first test is to determine Julia's fidelity. The misogynists pay a handsome actor to pretend to be a dashing millionaire who shamelessly hits on Julia while she waits for Nathan during a dinner date, flattering her relentlessly and offering her a vision of life untethered to a man who dresses like a Sears middle manager from the 1980s.

Julia resists, but that's not enough. Next, Nathan pretends to have lost his job for insider trading. It's not enough that Julia didn't take the bait and rejected someone who possesses the looks, charm, and non-loathsomeness her fiancé lacks. No, Nathan needs to know that Julia will stick with him even if he's homeless or an ex-convict.

This is a big one for Julia, because much of her dialogue involves gushing about how much she likes spending money, how much she likes spending Nathan's money, and how excited she is to spend 150,000 dollars on a lavish wedding, complete with a small orchestra.

The target of these cruel experiments is understandably upset by the thought of her life partner being a white-collar criminal and spending years in jail. Yet, she sticks with him all the same. The first two tests are sadistic, but at least they have a certain logic.

The next test, however, veers away from logic and sanity and into a free-form madness that suggests what *The Room* might feel like if it were a gimmicky romantic comedy written by a deeply stupid Neil LaBute.

The degenerates then arrange for Julia to be fired from her job to test whether the multiple stressors of her wealthy fiancé losing his job and possibly going to jail, followed by losing her own job, would be so great that she would do something to prove herself unworthy of Nathan.

Julia's male boss is happy to help by firing and then rehiring her in accordance with Nathan's wishes, because he's Todd's frat brother, thrice divorced, and dudes in this movie are *always* happy to set everything aside to help a fellow man, even a complete stranger, psychologically torment an oblivious woman.

Nathan gets so paranoid and extreme in his abuse of his wife-to-be that his crazed zeal begins to freak out even the psychotic woman haters who encourage him to treat his relationship like a cross between *Candid Camera* and a CIA psychological warfare campaign. Nathan has someone pretend to rob him and Julia at home to see whether she will happily volunteer to take a bullet, so that her future husband might live to mistreat women another day.

That's somehow *still* not enough. So, Nathan pretends to be in a coma to see whether Julia will stick by him when he's just barely hanging on for dear life.

Impossibly, even that is not enough for Nathan, so he feigns amnesia and spends whole weeks pretending to be a brain-damaged man-child with no idea who Julia is to, again, prove that she's not the kind of superficial, gold-digging hussy who would leave a man if there was a chance he would never regain his memory and would spend the rest of his days a brain-damaged stranger.

The Test seems to understand that its protagonist goes too far. Yet, the film labors under the delusion that its protagonist is doing bad things for the right reasons and that underneath all his psychotic criminal behavior lies a good heart.

The Test rewards Nathan for his flagrant misbehavior with a gala wedding. But just when it seems like the creep's impossibly cruel scheme will succeed, Julia conveniently overhears Ron describing the plan in elaborate detail to another dude.

Nathan receives his richly deserved comeuppance. Julia angrily confronts him, and he loses all status in society. Yet, the movie unconscionably chooses to give him a happy ending when Julia, after pining desperately for Nathan for six solid months from the inside of a bottle of red wine, tells him that she's going on a date at their favorite restaurant with the handsome actor from the first test. Nathan interrupts the date by showing up and threatening suicide. Julia then realizes that she truly loves this awful man, and because she got back at Nathan by flaunting her date with the actor, she is as bad as he is, if not worse.

In one of the film's concluding insults to women, its characters, and humanity, Nathan plays the "I'll kill myself if you don't love me" card, an incredibly manipulative ploy that the movie sees as a gesture of mad love and not an abusive thing to do to someone you only ever seem to treat with unfathomable cruelty.

These crazy kids get their fantasy wedding, and we're left with a feeling so ugly and empty it's borderline indescribable.

It's cruel of Saville to spare his audience the crowd-pleasing, cathartic release of a city bus rolling over his character's skull, pulverizing his brain, and reducing him to a bloody spot on the pavement in favor of the least deserved happy ending in film history.

Despite spending the last eighty-five minutes torturing and manipulating a woman infinitely better than he deserves, Nathan is forgiven and Julia agrees to spend the rest of her life with him because, in her reasoning, she got mad that her fiancé was a sociopath and told him she'd be going on a date at a restaurant they used to frequent.

Julia tells Nathan, "I failed your test. I'm worse than you," before professing her love for the man who has subjected her to the trials of Job out of petty insecurity.

Those are not equal transgressions. What Nathan and Julia do to each other are not equally bad. What Nathan does is beyond forgiveness. He deserves to be banished from society. She got a little pissy because she found out she'd been devoting her life to the worst man in the world. We're talking a jaywalking violation versus serial killing.

After the BBC's Jimmy Savile's crimes were uncovered and he was posthumously canceled, a horrified world assured itself, "At least the Saville name can't possibly be disgraced any further." Little did the public know how much lower the Saville name could sink.

Loqueesha may look impossibly bad to people who haven't seen *The Test*. For anyone cursed to have suffered through Saville's directorial debut, however, its awfulness looks not just plausible but inevitable.

THE SCENE IN HYDE PARK ON THE HUDSON WHERE FDR GETS A HAND JOB FROM HIS COUSIN (2012)

The job of a pop culture writer like myself is to remember. I am a professional rememberer. It is my duty to remember not just for my own sake but for society. I have taken it upon myself to remember the great failures of our last century or so, primarily but not entirely cinematic in nature, for my long-running column My World of Flops.

I was first given the estimable and enviable task of writing a book helping us remember "Weird Al" Yankovic in his magnificence and glory for the 2012 coffee-table book *Weird Al: The Book*, which I wrote with Al as well as for him. I then gave myself the gig of remembering the American pop parodist's entire recorded oeuvre on a song-by-song basis for the Weird Accordion to Al column and book.

But mostly I see my job, no, my sacred obligation as an artist, thinker, and man, as reminding people that a movie exists where Franklin Delano Roosevelt receives a hand job from a distant cousin. The movie, I hopefully don't have to remind you, is *Hyde Park on Hudson*.

This moment left such an indelible impression on me that I think about it at least once a month. I'm not sure I can say that of any other movie. I adore *The Master* and it got under my skin in a profound and lasting way, but my brain does not randomly and regularly choose to remember a scene from *The Master* the way it does the moment in Roger Michell's crowd-pleasing historical biopic when the man who famously thundered, "The only thing we have to fear is fear itself!" gets his crank yanked to completion by a distant cousin played by the great Laura Linney.

Hyde Park on Hudson is no mere movie. It was made to make an impression, to wow audiences and critics, to win awards like the conceptually similar and thematically overlapping *The King's Speech*. On paper, the movie certainly looks impressive: Bill Murray, our most beloved funnyman, a cult figure who has attained the status of American folk hero for his mysterious and delightful ways, playing Franklin Delano Roosevelt, arguably our greatest and most beloved statesman and leader, in a movie with serious Oscar hopes.

Despite its impressive pedigree, *Hyde Park on Hudson* did not win awards. It was not critically lauded. The critical establishment did not embrace it. The world seems intent on forgetting the movie featuring a scene wherein Franklin Delano Roosevelt is manually stimulated to orgasm by a randy relation.

We have collectively tried our damnedest to forget the seminal moment in *Hyde Park on the Hudson* when the four-term commander in chief gets a hand job from someone whose genes are doing the backstroke in the same pool as his own.

It's precisely because the world is so intent on scrubbing this movie from the historical record that I am intent on reminding every last one of you that there was a screenplay with a scene where a dude gets jerked off by his cousin, and that dude just happened to be FDR, and that screenplay attracted A-list talent like Bill Murray and Laura Linney, and what appears to be a pretty nice budget as well as a theatrical release.

When Bill Murray dies, he will be mourned endlessly and excessively. His legacy will be honored and overrated and religiously celebrated. In my mind (and perhaps only in my mind), part of that legacy will consist of playing FDR in a movie where the legendary American leader, whose heroic leadership helped defeat the Axis Powers in World War II, gets his trouser snake manhandled by a cousin several times removed.

I know that when Murray dies, I'll be thinking of *Groundhog Day* and *Rushmore* and *Caddyshack* and all of the other classics that made him an American icon. But mostly I'll think of his face transfixed in feigned sensual bliss as a distant cousin helps him attain erotic release and escape the horror of blue balls.

So, I implore you all to remember that Bill Murray made a movie where he played FDR getting a hand job from his cousin because the burden of single-handedly keeping that moment alive in the public imagination is, frankly, exhausting. I'd love to share the weight with other dedicated rememberers committed to sharing the glory of this transcendent moment of cinema, so that future generations are not afflicted with the same *Hyde Park on Hudson*-specific amnesia as our own.

ENTOURAGE
(2015)

I am embarrassed to admit this, but I was once an *Entourage* fan. The widely derided HBO hit about four bros broing it up in the bro Utopia of Hollywood was appointment viewing for me for at least a few seasons.

I have a weakness for entertainment about show business. What I initially responded to in *Entourage* was its lightness of touch and its refusal to judge its characters. This was not one of those Hollywood morality tales where someone smokes their first doobie and is sucking off businessmen for crack money in a matter of hours. No, this was a breezy exercise in male lifestyle porn about a couple of ordinary guys enjoying an extraordinary life in the stoned paradise of Southern California. I enjoyed it for what it was, something so flimsy and insubstantial that it almost took more energy to *not* watch it.

I liked that *Entourage* initially depicted life in Hollywood as ridiculous, but also kind of awesome. That was my experience shooting the poorly rated, increasingly reputable AMC movie review panel show *Movie Club with John Ridley* in L.A. in 2004 and 2005.

Then the show stopped being about how show business is ridiculous yet awesome and became about how everything was awesome. And the more awesome the show insisted everything was, the more obnoxious it became.

I eventually realized that I did not like or care about any of the show's characters. It's one thing to not punish partiers with STDs and drug addictions for sleeping around or getting high. It's another to endlessly reward one-dimensional characters with all of heaven's wonders simply for having a penis, being white, and hanging around with an implausibly successful actor.

The 2015 *Entourage* movie wastes no time reminding me why my affection for the show morphed into hatred. The movie never stops justifying its detractors' criticism of it as empty and vacuous, stunningly idiotic, and mind-numbingly superficial. It opens in Ibiza (of course), with the entourage speeding to a yacht where bikini-clad supermodels drink champagne and lounge about decoratively.

As the prophecy foretold, the *Entourage* movie's first line of dialogue is Johnny Drama (Kevin Dillon) talking about how he might have to jerk it before even getting to his brother's floating pleasure palace because he's so horny. That seems fitting since what follows is a masturbatory exercise in self-mythologizing and fan service.

We learn that movie star Vinnie Chase (Adrian Grenier) and his new wife split up on their honeymoon, but don't worry! Nothing bad ever happens to Vinnie, so he still got laid and there are all these supermodels around who totally want to bang him. If anything, he has *too* many beautiful women begging him to put his penis inside them, including Emily Ratajkowski.

Ratajkowski rose to fame as the notorious "video girl" in Robin Thicke's "Blurred Lines." She proved she could act with *Gone Girl*, then proved she could also not act with her work here.

Vinnie isn't the only member of the squad who must fight off the nonstop sexual advances of beautiful women. Vinnie's manager E (Kevin Connolly) finds himself in that enviable position as well.

Would it kill the supermodels, MMA fighters, and actresses of the world to lay off the *Entourage* dudes for even a minute? They're only human, and even that's a stretch. They aren't multi-cocked fuck-beasts like you seem to imagine, and there's only so much of them to go around.

Like *Sex and the City 2*, the *Entourage* movie could be used as a propaganda training film for ISIS. On HBO, the *Entourage* movie was *Sex and the City* for dudes. Like *Sex and the City 2*, *Entourage* sets out to subconsciously punish its audience for enjoying the television shows that inspired them and for living in a world that makes things like *Sex and the City 2* and the movie version of *Entourage* possible.

As played by human mannequin Adrian Grenier, the show's main character, Vinnie Chase, barely seems capable of walking upright and breathing at the same time.

Yet, *Entourage* laughingly asks us to believe that this maroon would be capable of starring in, and directing *Hyde*, an edgy masterpiece and Oscar favorite that, from the brief glimpse we see here, is apparently a 140-minute, one-hundred-million-dollar Apple commercial from 1986 in movie form.

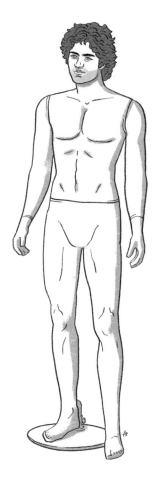

In *Popstar: Never Stop Never Stopping*, narcissistic protagonist Conner4Real keeps someone in his entourage shorter than him to serve as his "Perspective Manipulator." The Perspective Manipulator's sole job is to be in the frame with Conner4Real in pictures to make him look slightly taller by comparison. The *Entourage* movie has its own set of perspective manipulators, designed to make the film, and its characters, seem less terrible by comparison.

To make Vinnie seem less like a beautiful man with a bag of rocks in his head, the movie surrounds him with brother Johnny Drama, whom Kevin Dillon plays not as an unusually stupid human being but rather as an unusually stupid lower primate who's been doing a subpar impersonation of a human being for decades. Vinnie is dumb, but Drama is so much dumber he makes Vinnie seem almost mentally adequate. Johnny Drama is not just dumb for an actor. He's dumb for a mammal.

On HBO, *Entourage* was free to include swearing and naked boobs, but since this is a major motion picture, the naked boobs on display are substantially *more* naked than the naked boobs on the television show.

On a similar note, the *Entourage* franchise is notorious for having incredibly stupid, brotastic fans who live vicariously through the entourage's absurdly blessed lives of bongs, babes, beer, and endless partying with no negative consequences ever.

Entourage and its characters are as dumb as the day is long, so the movie has poor Haley Joel Osment play Travis McCredle, the dim-witted son of a redneck millionaire powerbroker played by Billy Bob Thornton and, remarkably, a character every *Entourage* fan can look down on as their intellectual and cultural inferior.

Of course, you'd have to be *pretty* crude to make the *Entourage* guys look dignified by comparison. Consequently, Osment and the movie really lay the goober routine on thick. Osment stops just short of wearing filthy overalls, rocking a giant Confederate flag belt buckle with his name on it, and toting around a moonshine bottle.

Travis is such an infidel that he is unable to understand Vinnie's masterpiece, a mind-fuck with *sick* visuals and even *sicker* beats about a DJ who's Dr. Jekyll and Mr. Hyde in the future on acid. From what little we see of the film, it looks like a ridiculous parody of a pretentious art movie. Yet, we are angrily discouraged from judging the film-within-a-film's quality for ourselves and encouraged to believe

Vinnie's agent Ari (Jeremy Piven) when he describes it as transcendent.

When Travis complains about the performances of Vinnie and his brother, we're supposed to be apoplectic that this no-nothing rube dares question the artistry of Vinnie Chase, the talent of Johnny Drama, the sound judgment of Vinnie's manager E, and the decision-making of agent turned studio head Ari Gold. Instead, I found myself agreeing with Osment's character that there's no way an "edgy," EDM-fueled dystopian *Dr. Jekyll and Mr. Hyde* update about a rebel DJ starring and directed by Vinnie Chase could be anything other than an epic boondoggle.

Ah, but it turns out the bad guy doesn't actually hate Vinnie's movie. He's just jealous that his hero Vinnie totally scored with this hot girl he wanted to have sex with. There's a weird element of sour, self-pitying meta-commentary in that development. It's as if Osment's character represents all the online *Entourage* haters who pretend to think it's terrible, but really are just jealous because they wish they were living the high life alongside the show's fabulously uncharismatic foursome.

Though the bros of *Entourage* are risking it all on a dream, there is a zero percent chance that that dream won't be realized to a ridiculously hyperbolic extent. Now, to be fair, the movie does not end with Johnny Drama winning the Academy Award. That would be unrealistic. No, it ends with him winning the Golden Globe. After all, you wouldn't want to mess with the verisimilitude that has long been the show's hallmark.

When the *Entourage* bros walk outside, it rains ice cream, hundred-dollar bills, and blow jobs from supermodels.

The outcomes of Harlem Globetrotters games are harder to predict than the path *Entourage* will travel to Bro-vana. Despite being uncharismatic lumps, Vinnie, E, Turtle, and Johnny Drama are like the Harlem Globetrotters of getting laid constantly, sparking doobies, and partying like rock stars.

But I did allude earlier to the film having a plot, so here it is: rebel studio head Ari Gold lays it all on the line out of his unshakable belief in the Kubrick-like artistry of Vinnie Chase. The hick from Texas tries to get Johnny to compromise his creative vision by editing his brother out of the movie, but Vinnie is all, "I am an artist, bro," and then Ari is like, "Vinnie is an artist, bro," and Johnny Drama is all, "My bro Vinnie is an artist, bro," and the movie is all, "Vinnie is an artist, bro."

Oh, and Turtle, the low-energy, low-wattage flunky who spent most of the show getting baked, is now richer than God and has MMA superstar Ronda Rousey pursuing him romantically.

Playing a major supporting role in *Entourage* as Turtle's potential love *and* business interest somehow makes mixed martial arts superstar Ronda Rousey *less* of an actress than she was before. Oh sure, Rousey has some screen time, but what she's doing onscreen isn't exactly acting.

Rousey doesn't just fail to convince us that she's both a superstar fighter and sexually attracted to a man who looks like Turtle: she also fails to convince us that she's a human being. It's as if the celebrities who contribute cameos as themselves are actually super-sophisticated robot clones that look exactly like the individuals whom they are replacing but are unable to communicate emotion.

Then I realized that I was looking at things the wrong way. *Entourage* is not about human beings or reality. It is a science-fiction show about an alternate universe, a computer simulation where every problem, no matter how minor, is immediately and preposterously resolved.

All I know is that I never need to see any of these characters ever again, regardless of the medium.

THE BOOK OF HENRY
(2017)

The Book of Henry is a film of lunatic ambition, a morbidly fascinating, regrettably original train wreck that invariably makes the wrongest choice, and then commits to it with absolute conviction, beginning with its delusional certainty that when it comes to cinematic precocity, no amount can ever be enough.

Thanks to *The Book of Henry*, *Star Trek: The Next Generation*'s Wesley Crusher is no longer the gold standard for insufferably precocious know-it-alls audiences are supposed to admire, yet inspire seething hatred instead.

That dubious title now belongs to Henry Carpenter (Jaeden Lieberher), a pint-sized cross between Rube Goldberg, Warren Buffet, and a less sadistic version of Jigsaw from the *Saw* movies. We're introduced to Henry when he gives a presentation on "My Legacy" that begins, "We can all talk about making our mark, but isn't it all just comfort food to stave off an existential crisis?"

Instead of telling the brat that he needs to get over himself, Henry's teacher looks on adoringly, proud to be in the presence of such a magnificent creature. When she asks him why he wastes his Nobel-level intellect matriculating in a regular school, Henry replies, "Because it's better for my psycho-social development for me to interact with a peer group at a normal school."

Verily, like Jesus among us sinners, Henry is humble enough to move among the common people instead of taking his rightful place as a god. He's also the most aggravatingly mature human being in existence. When his mother rhetorically inquires, "Find me another male of the species who is as grown up as (Henry)," she's not being hyperbolic. Judging by *The Book of Henry*, he's not just the most mature child alive; he's also more mature than every adult as well.

Despite being eleven years old, Henry pays his family's bills, is the primary breadwinner and regularly lectures his mother Susan (Naomi Watts) on finances, maturity, and her friends in ways that are supposed to be cute but instead register as creepily paternalistic and sexist.

Henry is the perfect son, surrogate husband/partner, provider, bookkeeper, and father figure all wrapped up in one precious, precocious package. He's more than a father figure to his own *mother*. He's more like a grandfather figure.

Henry blesses the unworthy mouth breathers at elementary school with his presence and insight, makes a small fortune on the stock market, and treats his mother like a loser friend who is fundamentally good-hearted, but will never get her shit together.

The mom is the child, and the son is the parent. This paradigm is not terribly unusual in chaotic households, but this is patriarchy taken to the next level. It's a version of patriarchy that posits that women shouldn't just be subordinate to their husbands but to their sons as well, particularly if those sons perform every role a husband would, outside of sex.

But Henry has more to worry about than having to raise his silly, sloppy, hopelessly inferior mother. Being a Sherlock Holmes–level crime solver on top of everything else, Henry ascertains that the beautiful dancer next door is being molested by Glenn Sickleman, an evil stepfather played by Dean Norris. We know the police commissioner is a sick man because Henry angrily informs us so, but also because his last name is only two letters away from being Sickman.

Vibrating with righteous fury, Henry busts into the office of his elementary school's black, female principal, refs to her as "Janice," and demands that she get Mr. Sickleman arrested. Otherwise, he insists, she's not living up to her "ethical responsibilities as an educator."

When the principal has the audacity to not treat the angry eleven-year-old boy talking down to her with sufficient reverence, he snottily insists, "Don't condescend to me!"

Considering that Henry spends his time onscreen looking down on humanity, that line reverberates with unintended irony. Henry may be smarter than Einstein. He may know more about money than Alan Greenspan. He may be more compassionate than Jesus. But he is not immortal.

He's too good to live. A world as debased as ours is unworthy of a figure as great as Henry.

Henry has a fatal tumor in his otherwise perfect brain. I half-expected Henry to successfully perform brain surgery on himself, but *The Book of Henry* is a tragedy, as well as an unintentional comedy, so not even Henry is able to do anything about his condition.

A child's early death should not be a crowd-pleasing moment, but in *The Book of Henry* it's deeply satisfying and more than a little hilarious.

Even in death, Henry is overbearing and bossy. Henry died with unfinished business. He needs to murder the next-door neighbor to keep him from molesting his stepdaughter, and he's unfortunately too dead to do so himself.

Thankfully, he has a mother who just doesn't know what to do with herself now that her son is no longer around to give orders. So Henry decides to help his mother process her grief by writing and gifting to her the eponymous Book of Henry, a meticulous step-by-step plan detailing how to kill the police commissioner without getting caught.

Henry has a strong moral compass that tells him that the bad people need to be punished for being bad, and that the best way to punish those bad people is by using his mother as a weapon to kill from beyond the grave. This, to the film, seems like a principled stance. Instead, it feels like Fascism for children with a kooky Rube Goldberg twist.

Director Colin Trevorrow has defended *The Book of Henry* as a precursor to the #MeToo movement, arguing laughably, "I made a film about holding predatory men in positions of power accountable for assault, and that is an uncomfortable subject to talk about. But we are talking about it now and we're listening, and I hope the negative response won't deter other filmmakers from telling these stories, because we need to hear them, both in life and in art."

It is true that *The Book of Henry* is about holding predatory men accountable, but I'm not sure we have much to learn from a juvenile fantasy wherein all problems are solved by a magical dead boy so irritatingly brilliant that he's somehow even more effective in death than he was in life.

Delusional and puffed full of unearned self-importance, *The Book of Henry* closes with Henry lecturing the audience, "Sometimes a good story will remind you of who you want to be," and that is why we are inundated with "stories about good and evil, stories about the triumph of the human spirit, stories about living and dying and how you've got to do one in spite of the other."

The Book of Henry wasn't about to wait for others to affirm its greatness. It closes by delivering an Oscar speech about the "profound" elements at play in a story it clearly believes is about the loftiest subjects imaginable.

The Book of Henry is a terrible movie that thinks it's a timeless masterpiece about the human condition that couldn't be further removed from reality if the characters were Snorks, Wizards, or Noids. It's one for the ages, and not in a good way.

GOTTI
(2018)

There are bad movies and then there's 2018's *Gotti*. The Kevin Connolly–directed late-period John Travolta vehicle about a murderous mob kingpin who was also apparently history's greatest hero was a bona fide bad movie event, a pop culture phenomenon.

The movie's Twitter account went rogue and decided that if critics were going to criticize *Gotti*, then they were going to turn the tables and review the reviewers, criticize the critics, stick it to "The Man" and his stuffy insistence that a movie literally every critic disliked was somehow not good.

The Twitter account tried to promote the fiction that stuffy gatekeepers were trying to keep *Gotti* down, but "the people" wouldn't let them, asking, "Audiences loved Gotti, but critics don't want you to see it. . . . The question is why??? Trust the people and see it for yourself!"

A TV ad went further, taunting, "Audiences loved *Gotti* . . . Critics put out the hit . . . Who Would You Trust More? Yourself or a Troll Behind a Keyboard."

Gotti opens with its title character standing in front of the Brooklyn Bridge addressing the audience directly, like Ray Liotta in *Goodfellas*. Sounding entirely too pleased with himself, Travolta, as a figure I will subsequently refer to as Non Gotti, sneers, "Let me tell you something, New York is the greatest fucking city in the world. My city. I was a kid in these streets. I started in the fucking gutter. I made it to the top. This life ends one of two ways: dead, or you're in jail. I did both."

As Elliott Kalan of *The Flop House* has pointed out, death and jail are not mutually exclusive. You're not going to live forever, whether you're incarcerated or free. There aren't six-hundred-year-old people in jail doing thousand-year sentences. Conviction does not grant you immortality.

Gotti is a shameless *Goodfellas* knockoff that got the film's message backward. The whole point of *Goodfellas* is that the world of organized crime is an amoral cesspool of racists, wife-beaters, and murderers.

Gotti, in sharp contrast, argues that, actually, the mafia is great and, if anything, overly moral, with its codes of conduct and whatnot. In *Gotti*, the mafia is portrayed as a force for good in the universe.

Gotti doesn't dramatize its subject's life so much as it nominates him for sainthood. I'm guessing they went with *Gotti* because it's a brand name for organized crime, but also because the title *World's Greatest Dad* was taken.

We learn just what an amazing father this notorious murderer was in sequences where a dying Gotti talks to his son in prison and explains how he would rather be in excruciating pain every second for the rest of his life than see his son contract as much as a mild headache.

In these sequences, Travolta looks less like an old, fragile man than like an unmasked Darth Vader while his son looks like he was kicked out of Color Me Badd for stealing everyone's hair gel.

But if Travolta's face looks like the makeup artist is testing designs for Skeletor in a *He-Man* reboot, the spirit of Travolta's Gotti remains pure. Oh sure, he murders people, and orders murders, and robs and cheats and steals, but does that necessarily make him a bad person? No, the film argues, it does not.

You know who the *real* bad guys are? Film critics.

Gotti is many things in *Gotti*. He's the don of dons, the boss of bosses. He represents the pure-hearted goodness of the mafia. He's a family man. But more than anything he's just a great guy, a family guy, a stand-up guy. However, just because he devoted his life to crime, a power-mad government treated him like a criminal.

When Non Gotti finally goes away for the long haul after a judge sentences him to five consecutive life sentences plus fifty dollars in court fees, Gotti doesn't seem bummed.

In the kind of acting choice that makes Travolta's turn truly Golden Raspberry–worthy, he musters up a corny grin and says, "The five lifetime bids, that's okay, but the fifty-dollar surcharge, you really know how to stick it to a guy!"

The delight in Travolta's delivery suggests that getting sentenced to die a lonely death in prison is worth it for the hilarious dad joke of complaining about a fifty-dollar court fee.

Gotti intermittently shows us glimpses of the real John Gotti in news footage and screaming newspaper headlines of the time. These montages serve no purpose except to underline how little Travolta resembles the tiny man he is playing so ineptly.

Gotti ends where it begins, with Travolta in front of the Brooklyn Bridge, boasting, "Listen to me, and listen to me good. You're never gonna see another guy like me if you live to be five thousand."

As with the words that opened the film, this line of braggadocio is so self-evidently false that you want to yell at the screen, "What the fuck are you talking about? I have literally seen five thousand guys like you in movies. There are a fuck ton of you in every mafia movie. In fact, I've seen a guy like you named Henry Hill a whole bunch of times in this great movie called *Goodfellas* with which you might be familiar."

Within the context of the movie, Non Gotti's closing boast about being unprecedented in the history of mafia movies feels as unearned as a set-ending mic drop from an open-mic comedian who mumbles incomprehensibly for five minutes then pisses himself out of fear and anxiety.

But if the subject of *Gotti* is not a figure we've never encountered before and will never encounter again, there is nevertheless something special about *Gotti*, which more than lives up to its reputation for being misconceived to a historic extent.

LOQUEESHA
(2019)

When an obscure filmmaker with a low-budget film begins attracting massive attention, it's generally a positive development.

When a sleeper explodes onto the national consciousness, it's usually a cinematic Cinderella story: a dreamer invests her life savings in a labor of love that's bought for millions at Sundance; a wunderkind comes out of nowhere with a film that promises to make them an instant cultural force.

That was not the case with *Loqueesha,* a comedy-drama about Joe (comedian Jeremy Saville, who also wrote and directed), a white bartender who becomes a sensation for pretending to be a crude caricature of a black woman on the radio to pay for private school for his gifted son.

Saville came out of nowhere with a trailer so offensive that it instantly became a viral sensation. The entire internet took turns dunking on *Loqueesha* and its creator/star.

People had a hard time believing that *Loqueesha* was real. Could a movie with such an anachronistic premise really be made and distributed in 2019?

Loqueesha's unfortunate existence engenders intense cognitive dissonance. Could *Loqueesha* possibly be as bad as it looked?

Going into *Loqueesha,* I naively assumed that the film would attempt to undercut the crazed narcissism and racism of its premise by humbling its arrogant protagonist for cynically co-opting blackness.

Instead, *Loqueesha* points an angry finger at an audience that might be inclined to judge its hero. The film argues that when you give advice as society-transforming as Joe does as Loqueesha, your race and gender cease to matter. To suggest otherwise is racist and sexist.

Loqueesha asks who the *real* racist is: critics harping on *Loqueesha* for engaging in audio blackface, or a movie progressive enough to posit that gender and color don't matter if you're a prophet of cornpone wisdom like Joe/Loqueesha?

Loqueesha kicks off with Joe in his natural habitat, a sad bar for alcoholics where he slings drinks as well as advice. "Joe, I've been coming to this bar for 10 years now, and it never ceases to amaze me that you always seem to say the right thing to just the right person," insists a characteristically impressed patron.

Joe's existence is upended when Rachel (Tiara Parker), a gorgeous black woman, strides angrily into the bar and demands "something strong." When our barkeep gives her something called Bottled Rage, she spits back, "What are you trying to do, kill me?"

Joe stridently quips, "No, but from the looks of it, I might be doing you a favor if I was." Joe isn't being presumptuous. He's merely telling this stranger that it might be better if she was dead.

When Rachel says that men are all the same and will do whatever it takes to get what they want (sex), Joe comes at her with serious NOT ALL MEN energy, rattling off the names of some "shitty" dudes, like "Dalai Lama, St. Francis of Assisi, Gandhi."

"Who even knows about Gandhi? He probably lied to his wife too!" Rachel protests. This leads Saville to imitate a cheating Gandhi running around on his wife in a thick Indian accent.

When Rachel complains that her boyfriend has been running around on her and lying, our "hero" informs her, "First of all, you're a fucking idiot."

Then he *really* lays into her, shouting, "I think you want me to sign off on this victim act and find it charming and tell you that you've been wronged, and then you want me to indict half a species based on the actions of a couple of un-evolved and unaccountable members of said species. Okay, a whole lot of un-evolved and unaccountable members, but that doesn't get you off the hook. You want your guy to tame the truth-less tongue, stop indulging him! If you're going to play enabler, you're just as guilty as he is. Actually, you're worse because you're lying to yourself. So, who's got the problem?"

Lest we trust our instincts about Joe's advice being terrible, the beneficiary of this man's white, white-hot rage offers to pay him for his advice because it is so "amazing." Rachel isn't just improbably grateful for the bartender's lecture: she's turned on as well and feels moved by a sense of messianic purpose to elevate Joe to a place of distinction within our culture where his brilliance can help the most people.

After impressing this stranger with his wisdom, Joe's next stop is his emasculating ball-buster of an ex-wife, who informs her ex-hubby that their son is gifted. That's the good news. The bad news is that the gifted school is going to cost thirteen thousand dollars a semester, and being a man, Joe must give her the money for it NOW.

When a sputtering Joe asks if there are scholarships available, the shrew informs him that they're all taken before hissing, "I won't have my son missing out on an opportunity for an excellent life because his father is either too weak, dumb, or lazy to provide for his needs."

Back at the bar, Rachel, the now empowered and confident woman who sought and took Joe's advice, gives him flowers and a flier emblazoned with the words, "WANTED: Radio Talk Show Hosts. Minorities and women encouraged to apply. Contact WRCW Bob or Ken at WRCW at (555) 422-2233."

When Joe demurs that he doesn't talk to people for money, his worshipful acolyte tells him to "share your gift with the world." When Joe continues to hem and haw, she gushes, "The way that you were with me led to transformation and that's a rare ability." Joe has other worries. Actually, he only has one other worry: his evil ex-wife's insistence that he magically make thirteen thousand to twenty-six thousand dollars appear out of thin air, so that she won't consider him a pathetic failure.

We live in a crazy world where both men and women, fathers and mothers, are expected to work and contribute to the expenses of childcare. But in *Loqueesha*, it falls entirely upon Joe to pay for everything.

At Joe's apartment, Rachel leads him through a mock radio show taping, during which Joe, speaking of his future radio star self in the third person, complains that if he's forced to water down his truths for public consumption then "the hard fought wisdom he's accrued by rigorous self-examination and ruthless accountability gets displaced with a self-conscious tick as he strives to satisfy a fickle public opinion."

Joe goes on to explain, "I'm just focused on being a conduit for truth."

Loqueesha takes itself incredibly seriously. It's almost as dramatic as it is comic, or rather "dramatic" and "comic" since it's never genuinely funny or dramatically engaging.

This man who prides himself on "rigorous self-examination and ruthless accountability" never examines himself rigorously enough to feel guilt for his transgressions, and despite his "ruthless accountability" he lets himself completely off the hook for his lies, racism, and misogyny.

Rachel refers to Joe's inability to get his own radio show as a tragedy more than once. A tragedy! A white bartender with no relevant experience not getting his own radio show immediately is not a tragedy. School shootings are tragedies.

The Trail of Tears was a tragedy. Joe not getting his own show barely qualifies as bad luck.

Joe's rationale for doing a radio show as Loqueesha is that as a black woman he'll be able to say things he can't get away with as a white man, that the anonymity of playing a character allows him to confront people with harsh truths they won't accept from him as a white man.

In his first encounter with Rachel, Joe tells her that judging by her attitude, she might be better off dead, calls her "a fucking idiot," then lectures her about how she's responsible for all her problems and how NOT ALL MEN are bad, and it's sexist and wrong to act as if they are.

Joe tells a beautiful woman that she's worse than her cheating boyfriend. If that's the version of Joe that can't fully express himself because of the role straight white men play in society, I can only imagine how he'd behave if he didn't feel so constrained by his gender and race.

When Joe and Rachel get an email from the radio station turning down his show, Joe wearily reconciles himself to a lifetime of being the Deepak Chopra of the drunk at two in the afternoon set.

At home Joe watches *Trash Talk,* a *Jerry Springer*–like show that looks instead like a racist Sega CD game filmed in the bowels of hell wherein two CGI representations of black women hurl insults at each other on a set that consists solely of two uncomfortable looking chairs and two monitors reading "Trash Talkin." It's ostensibly a talk show, but there's no host and no audience, just crude stereotypes from the uncanniest parts of the Uncanny Valley.

Thinking out loud, Joe says, "You go, girl!" He then has his eureka moment, telling himself, "See, that's who needs her own show. That's who they want. See, they want women and minorities. They don't want white guys like me tellin' em what to do. If I was a black woman, I'd be perfect."

A dramatic music cue later, Joe is channeling his inner Madea and playing both sides of a phone conversation between milquetoast white dude Ted and Loqueesha, a sassy advice-giver who seemingly sprung whole cloth from her creator's imagination.

In *Loqueesha*, everyone loves egregious racism. When the radio station's white owners hear "Loqueesha" they don't ask, "My God, who is this asshole doing a clearly fake, unbelievably offensive voice and character?" because they're so blown away by Loqueesha.

"She's brilliant!" gushes the rich old business owner, an opinion shared by everyone who encounters Loqueesha. The owners are so smitten that the radio station SWITCHES FORMATS to talk radio so they can harness the revolutionary power of a white comedian doing a sassy black lady voice.

After his first show, Joe's black engineer sidekick Mason (Dwayne Perkins) congratulates the new radio personality on a show well done and gushes, "I don't know what I'm more impressed by, you as a black woman or your therapy techniques."

Hey, if a fictional black character Saville wrote and paid someone to perform thinks Joe's brilliance as an unlicensed therapist is only matched by his authenticity as a black woman, then Joe's scheme can't possibly be racist, right?

The station is so blown away by Loqueesha's cavalcade of audio minstrelsy that they offer her her own show, sight unseen. She'll be working the late-night shift, from eleven to two, with the caveat that no one can be in the studio with her when she records other than her engineer.

"Loqueesha" invokes the real-life murder of Jennifer Hudson's family as part of her rationale for wanting to be exclusively heard rather than seen. "Did you see the Jennifer Hudson trial? Where her brother-in-law killed her entire family? Well, I got some men out there, if they knew where

I was, would do some nasty ass shit to me, and maybe to you fellas too," Joe as Loqueesha tells the station's white owners, playing to their racist fears that a black woman who speaks in a cartoonish approximation of the cadences of the streets must come from a world of violence.

Exploiting a real-life tragedy to explain why a white man impersonating a black woman over the radio must do so in absolute privacy doesn't even rank as one of *Loqueesha's* top ten most offensive aspects. It's got a lot of competition.

Joe's first show as Loqueesha is an unqualified triumph. Whether "Loqueesha" is telling a nerdy computer programmer, "You need to get yoself some coochie!" or advising a Poindexter dominated by his girlfriend that he needs to stand up for himself and "slap a bitch!" she always says the right thing.

The masses are being entertained by Loqueesha, but they're also learning life lessons. Not just playing but *being* Loqueesha affords Joe the freedom to say provocative things like, "You white people are so afraid to say what's on your mind. What you so afraid of? You the one runnin' thangs! I mean, you slaves to what other people think. After all these years, white people are the slaves! How you like that?"

Saville doesn't just want us to laugh with Loqueesha. He wants us to learn from her as well.

As Loqueesha wisely intones, "There's clearly no gender in the divine nature. It just divided itself up into two for reproductive purposes because we get tired of the same old thing." If there's no gender in the divine nature, can we really get mad at a white man for impersonating a black woman? Isn't that like getting mad at God and the divine nature?

Loqueesha becomes so huge so quickly that Joe and Mason decide to pay a black woman to play the role of Loqueesha for live appearances and publicity photos. You might expect *Loqueesha* to exhibit an iota of racial sensitivity in its depiction of actual black people. You would be wrong.

Any time *Loqueesha* has a choice between being more racist or less racist, it chooses the "more racist" option, in this case by depicting the black candidates for the role of Loqueesha as freak shows.

The first applicant is a ditz who thinks she can "be" Loqueesha without knowing anything about her. The second would-be Loqueesha is a man with a beard and a deep, masculine voice dressed in women's clothing. Joe and Mason are NOT having that! They need a real lady to pretend to be a fake lady! The next contender flatly informs Joe and Mason that she will perform oral sex on both of them for the job.

Just when it seems like Joe and Mason are wasting their time, in comes a seemingly perfect candidate in Renee (Mara Hall). She's a Loqueesha super-fan who looks, talks, and acts the part and, as a nice bonus, thinks Loqueesha is a role model for every black woman. She gets the gig, but don't worry. If anything, she's worse than all the other Loqueesha contenders. She's so narcissistic she thinks she can do Loqueesha as well as an angry, defensive white man and is dressed down repeatedly by Joe for compromising the integrity that makes Loqueesha society's greatest hero.

We know Loqueesha isn't just making people laugh, but *think*, because we're constantly cutting to ecstatic recipients of Loqueesha's gospel of unvarnished truths, nurses who smile with their whole bodies, or a prisoner and prison guard who bond when they become equally smitten with the title character.

All hail Loqueesha! For Loqueesha speaketh only truth. Loqueesha knoweth only righteousness. Foolish are those who transgress against Loqueesha, for Loqueesha will lash out with great anger and vengeance upon those who blaspheme and take false witness against her!

White privilege is being a hokey white dude arrogant enough to make a vanity project where you do a bad Amos and Andy routine that wins you a Michelle Obama level of popularity in the black community.

When Renee, the actress playing Loqueesha in personal appearances, offers to solve Joe's problems by taking over the role permanently, Joe responds, "You do a good job with the personal appearances, but the therapy, that's just not your thing," which is a not-so-coded way of saying, "You're great at being loud and sassy because you're black, but let a white guy handle the smart stuff."

Confronted by dispirited listeners who complain that it's almost like Loqueesha has turned into an entirely different, less Magical person, Renee rages, "You like the Romans who nailed up our Lord and Savior. You a murderous cretin, and I'm God-like."

Renee is not subtle in her villainy. She is demonic, while Loqueesha, the REAL fake Loqueesha, lovingly conceived and performed by Joe, is an angel of tough love.

Loqueesha sees nothing strange or untoward about encouraging audiences to jeer Renee, a real black woman performing the role of Loqueesha, while cheering the white man who created her.

Joe is using antiquated stereotypes for GOOD, to save his son and transform lives. Renee, on the other hand, is using creaky stereotypes for ill, to glorify herself instead of serving humanity.

Loqueesha's perverse message that it takes a straight white man to excel as a proud Nubian princess is driven home when Renee, having humiliated herself and Joe by trying to be as convincing a wise black truth teller as a white bartender, concedes to Joe, "You were a better black woman than I am, okay?" and he does not contradict her.

Vibrating with self-righteousness, Joe scolds a woman egomaniacal enough to imagine she could "be" Loqueesha, "It was never about race or gender or fame or fortune. It was about telling the truth straight from your heart without fear or worry of being wrong or bad. It was holistic healing broadcast from the sky into the hearts and minds of anybody willing to tune in. You turned it into your egomaniacal circus, your platform for your personal power play, and now it's gone!"

Holistic healing broadcast from the sky! Holy fucking shit. That doesn't sound like a radio personality: that sounds like a cult leader.

Joe is VERY angry about someone from another race and gender appropriating a persona that is not their own. Joe is full of rage toward a black woman for having the gall to try to co-opt a character that he stole from black womanhood. But it's okay and we're supposed to be on Joe's side because Joe is supposed to be better at being black than the actual black women in the film.

With Loqueesha out of commission, the film's audience is treated to scenes of broadly drawn representations of "the people" who once tuned in. These sad sacks are scowling and looking suicidal, despondent that the genius who once gave their lives meaning has been replaced by a cruel pretender.

Like *The Test, Loqueesha* offers an insultingly unearned happy ending for a protagonist who behaves appallingly, learns nothing, and grows and matures in no way whatsoever, and is rewarded rather than punished.

Rachel returns after a forty-minute absence to speak the only truths in the movie: Joe is a racist and a misogynist who callously exploits regressive stereotypes and speaks in a racist white approximation of Ebonics.

Loqueesha is having none of that. It alone knows what a boon to humanity Joe/Loqueesha represents. So even in her anger Rachel has no choice but to concede that Loqueesha's advice was "brilliant" and that she loves this horrible man who has spent the film perpetrating an ugly hoax.

Then they fuck. Seriously. She's so moved by Joe's claim that "I may be a fake and a phony, but I am the most authentic one you will ever meet," she hops into bed with him to sexually reward him for illustrating that he's the best black woman AND a terrific white man at the same time.

Joe doesn't even have to stop doing Loqueesha! The public votes for him to stay on the air as Joe AND Loqueesha. That might seem like a pathetic cop-out, but *Loqueesha* thinks that Joe has done nothing wrong.

In the film's estimation, the worst Joe did was "put on a funny voice" in order to "help people" by employing a "theatrical device" to tell the public not what they want to hear but rather what they NEED to hear.

Loqueesha closes with a dedication to "Mom & Dad." I have no idea what Saville's parents could have done to earn such a dishonor, but whatever it is, it can't be that bad. The same is true of Detroit, where the film takes place, although it is so badly shot that it's not always apparent what planet this Detroit is on.

Saville could have set *Loqueesha* anywhere else and saved Detroit the shame of being associated with Saville and his cinematic endeavors. Yet, he chose to cruelly punish this already beleaguered city by making it the setting for this travesty.

Hasn't Detroit been through enough without it being linked to *Loqueesha* for eternity? Why must Saville degrade and embarrass this most luckless of American metropolises? From the proud home of Motown and the American auto industry to the humiliated home of the *Loqueesha* industry is one hell of a fall, but I have faith that Detroit, in its resilience, will be able to overcome *Loqueesha* as it has overcome so many challenges before.

THE WORST OF
EVERYTHING ELSE

DALE ALAN COOPER, IMPRESSIONIST FOR CHRIST, A TIME TO LAUGH (1974)

Dale Alan Cooper, a terrifyingly sincere young Bible student, impressionist, and evangelist who billed himself a "Dependable American Christian" as well as an "Impressionist for Christ," had two primary goals for his 1974 album *A Time to Laugh*. First and foremost, he wanted to strengthen the faith of the devout and bring lost souls to Christ.

A distant second, Cooper wanted to make people laugh with impressions of famous folks like John Wayne, Henry Fonda, Tiny Tim, and William F. Buckley.

In *A Time to Laugh*, Cooper is consequently a poignant combination of hack impressionist chasing cheap laughs and fire-and-brimstone preacher trying to save his flock from eternal damnation.

He's consequently operating at cross purposes. He wants to entertain the nice Christians in the audience, but not to the point where they forget about the agony they will endure unless they emulate Christ in word and deed.

A Time to Laugh is outsider art. It's transcendent accidental anti-comedy that predicts seemingly the entirety of Neil Hamburger's shtick, particularly *Laugh Out Lord*, which cynically combined comedy and Christianity, and *Left for Dead in Malaysia*, where Hamburger is performing for a crowd that doesn't speak English, and wouldn't laugh even if they did.

In *Left for Dead in Malaysia*, the indifference of the audience becomes a character in and of itself just as the most compelling presence on *A Time to Laugh* is not Cooper but rather a baby that starts crying early on side A, can be heard throughout side A, then makes a triumphant reappearance on side B.

Cooper has a sad, desperate, weirdly angry energy that silently but powerfully implores, Jeb Bush style, please laugh and please believe.

When the baby cannot be heard I started worrying about it. Was it okay? Was it having stomach problems? Why didn't its parents take it home? Why did the parents even take it to the show to begin with?

It's not an encouraging sign when a comedy record begins by assuring audiences that God *wants* us to laugh.

In a hypnotically clunky bit of oration, Charles Burgin, a minister from Louisville, Kentucky, kicks things off with an appropriately godly introduction in which he stiffly announces, "Sacred scriptures, the book of Ecclesiastes, in chapter three, the writer informs us, 'to everything there is a season and a time for every purpose under heaven, a time to weep and a time to laugh.' This is the reason for, and the purpose of, this record album: to provide YOU an opportunity to laugh."

The minister drones on, "Our speaker on this album is a young man gifted with a rare talent indeed—the talent of voice imitation, known today as impersonation. Dale Alan Cooper is a Christian and a member of the Southland Christian Church of Louisville, Kentucky, and a student at Louisville Bible College of Louisville, Kentucky.

"Dale Cooper feels that God gave him this talent, which he therefore must use for the glory of God and the winning of the souls of man. Dale owes all credit to the Lord, and shares what is in his heart through this medium of impersonation. Dale feels he can implant the message of Christ through the voices of the many widely known celebrities he imitates. Dale feels a Christian should have a joy in his heart and find a time to laugh. And now, ladies and

- 208 -

gentlemen, we present Dale Alan Cooper, an impressionist for Christ, in *A Time to Laugh*."

A Time to Laugh might not have been recorded in a church, but Cooper's heartbreaking act transforms whatever building it was taped in into a Cathedral of Sadness all the same.

It's an even worse sign that neither the audience, nor the impressionist, nor the stern, dour man of the Lord introducing him seem to genuinely believe that laughter *isn't* inherently wicked and heretical.

The halting, stilted, hypnotically clumsy rhythms of Cooper's performance consequently seem attributable to his inexperience, youth, and lack of talent, but also to a dogged fear that attempting to make people chuckle at a Paul Lynde impersonation is inherently sinful and will pave the road to hell.

Cooper does not introduce himself. Instead, he laughs the titular creepy laugh, then announces, "I'm Alfred Hitchcock," as the prelude to his first extended bit, which imagines the legendary Master of Suspense directing a star-studded war movie called *The Monster* with a cast made up of the most imitated men in Hollywood history, including John Wayne, Jimmy Stewart, and Walter Brennan.

Cooper, a college student in 1974, has the frame of reference of someone who grew up during the Great Depression.

Cooper's John Wayne talks so slowly and deliberately that he seems to be suffering some manner of mental impairment. Jimmy Stewart stutters adorably, and Cary Grant yells, "Judy, Judy, Judy!" Kirk Douglas is feral and sub-verbal; William F. Buckley is effete and erudite; and his Mark Twain consists mostly of yelling loudly for emphasis at the end of each sentence.

The impressionist for Christ's take on the most famous people in the world is often weirdly off-brand. In his muddled telling, Boris Karloff is Dr. Frankenstein instead of his monster and John Wayne is reborn as a slow-talking simpleton tossing out Henny Youngman one-liners like, "My folks moved a lot but somehow I always found them."

Cooper is weirdly invisible here. He's always either clumsily attempting to channel the voices and ways of the rich and famous or clumsily copying the cadences and affectations of preachers and evangelists.

Dale Alan Cooper is missing. Yet, at the same time *A Time for Laughter* is agonizingly personal and utterly revealing all the same. It's one thing to bomb at an open-mic night in a way that will be seen and instantly forgotten by a small group of people.

It's another to document your prodigious creative and personal shortcomings for posterity by recording an entire album of your faith-and-impression-based comedy stylings.

At the end of side A, Cooper crossbreeds his soul-consuming passion for bad religion and even worse comedy by putting the words of the Lord into the mouths of the famous folks he's unconvincingly portraying.

Despite his introduction, the audience does not, in fact, seem to know whether it is appropriate to laugh at the earnest young man and his material, even if he has explicitly given them permission to do so.

So, they listen in awkward silence while Cooper reads holy words in the familiar tones of John F. Kennedy or Richard Burton.

The humor ostensibly comes from the incongruous juxtaposition of secular celeb shenanigans and righteous words, but judging by the egregious lack of laughter, the audience apparently worries that there's something sacrilegious about laughing at God's words no matter how "humorously" they're delivered.

The scariest thing about side A of *A Time to Laugh* is that it's the fun half. Cooper is at least trying to make us laugh. On side B he does a painful routine imagining Paul Lynde as Adam, Flip Wilson's Geraldine as Eve, and William F. Buckley as the snake that tempted Eve that plays like a parody of hack comedy.

In his hippest bit, Cooper imagines David Brinkley interviewing Henry Fonda about the perils of drug use, something he might have some familiarity with, being the father of a pair of countercultural icons, only for the elderly movie star to comically misunderstand the newsman's slang.

After that tepid bit of milquetoast drug humor, Cooper stops attempting comedy and lays in with the God rap something heavy. First, he brings out a friend from Bible College who plays a pair of gloomy country gospel songs on an acoustic guitar that may be nothing special in another context, but here meld music and Christianity in a manner so organic that they render Cooper's bizarre tonal shifts even more jarring by comparison.

The God Cooper is serving is not a shiny, happy populist Jesus who loves you. He's an angry, Old Testament deity full of wrath and righteous indignation. It is therefore particularly strange for him to be the driving force behind what is ostensibly an evening of comedy and fun.

Cooper isn't one of those preachers who feels the need to be funny, or warm, or even remotely sympathetic. Instead, he's a glowering scold for Christ who rails against false prophets and false teachers and the sinful, lustful degenerates who have constructed "homosexual churches" in blasphemous defiance of God's will.

Unless, "As we find Paul warns Timothy in second Timothy four, three, 'For the time will come when they will not endure sound doctrine but after their own lust shall they heap to themselves teachers and having itching ears and they shall turn away, their ears from the truth and shall turn to fables,'" is your idea of a top-notch zinger, Cooper's sermon is defiantly not just devoid of a single identifiable joke; it lacks even a single moment of levity.

If there are good gags or solid bits to be found in the Bible, Cooper has not discovered them. His sermon is a stone-cold bummer, with much, if not most, of the material stolen from the New Testament. It's all doom and gloom time once Cooper puts his Tiny Tim and Bill Cosby impressions into cold storage, so that he can remind listeners that under an unrelenting sun, Jesus had nails pounded into the palms of his hands to ensure humanity's eternal salvation.

It's as if Cooper is punishing the audience for the ungodly nature of his comedy and comedy in general.

Cooper earnestly closes *A Time to Laugh* by dedicating the album to "the Lord Jesus Christ, the son of the living God. And I pray and I ask every Christian to pray with me that this record will strengthen other Christians and also influence people to accept Jesus Christ."

He failed. Oh, sweet Jesus did he ever fail.

Rumor has it that *A Time to Laugh* is so bad that a group of devout Christians listened to it once and became militant atheists. They figured that if Cooper was truly God's instrument on Earth, then He must be a half-mad supreme being with nothing but contempt for the flesh puppets he unleashed upon this poor planet.

A Time to Laugh barely exists. It sold almost nothing. Almost no information exists about it online.

Cooper's fusion of hack comedy and old-time religion is about as palatable and tasty as a lukewarm corn tortilla with half a bottle of Ativan and a Spider-Man Funko Pop folded inside. Separately those ingredients might all serve useful purposes and have their place in this world. Combined, they make no sense and violently refuse to congeal into something edible, let alone tasty. The same is true of Cooper's third-rate comedy and dour preaching.

Who wants to be lectured on how the world *and* the afterworld works by a Bible College student who's probably never gotten so much as a hand job?

Peter John-Byrnes, the friend who alerted me to this wonderful obscurity's existence, did some online sleuthing and discerned that Cooper is still alive and serving the Lord, albeit in a more traditional sense as a pastor serving up scripture without a side order of guffaws and Richard Nixon impersonations.

Cooper seems to have retired the shtick a long time ago, but I wonder if he's ever preaching and feels a Flip Wilson impression coming on and wonders wistfully, if only for a bittersweet moment, about the wacky, hacky, tacky road not traveled.

MCGRUFF THE CRIME DOG, MCGRUFF THE CRIME DOG'S SMART KIDS ALBUM (1986)

What I find fascinating about *Cartoon Rescue All-Stars to the Rescue* is the brazenly off-brand nature of the enterprise. Cartoon characters are unapologetic hedonists concerned only with their own pleasure.

They aren't about to channel Nancy Reagan and deliver rants about the evils of marijuana. That's more McGruff the Crime Dog's thing.

McGruff is the most kid friendly of Drug Warriors. Though perpetually clad in a trench coat, the unofficial uniform of 1970s flashers and porn movie theater devotees as well as gumshoes, McGruff serves as the affable canine face of law enforcement.

McGruff is cute but not *too* cute, to the point where children would be tempted to scratch behind his ears and ask him if he's a good boy while he's lecturing them about not getting kidnapped or experimenting with heroin.

McGruff was conceived as an enemy of crime who, on an existential level, "was tired" and embodied the world-weary detective tradition of Philip Marlowe and Columbo.

McGruff was not too world-weary, however, to make multiple forays into the world of music, most notably with the shockingly infectious 1986 anti-drug manifesto *McGruff's Smart Kids Album*.

It's eleven tracks and just under a half hour of sadistically catchy jams that are as sophisticated musically as they are egregiously terrible from a lyrical and vocal standpoint.

The only thing keeping this McGruff the Crime Dog album from being an absolute delight, a stone-cold banger, is that it's a McGruff the Crime Dog album that makes the bold if inexplicable choice to center on a man who nails McGruff's gruff growl during the spoken-word portions of songs, but cannot sing. At all.

The man voicing McGruff here has a poignantly terrible rasp of a croon that regularly wanders far off key, strains audibly throughout to hit even modestly challenging notes, and has no range whatsoever.

Listening to *McGruff's Smart Kids Album* on repeat, my heart broke for the poor man who was forced to sing an entire album when he barely has the voice for a thirty-second jingle.

The cassette's weird, fascinating tension consequently comes from the voice actor playing McGruff's inherently doomed attempts to showcase a talent he does not possess (singing) as well as the impossibly vast gulf between its breezy, assured musicality and caveman-primitive lyrics.

It's hard to tell who *McGruff's Smart Kids* is even for, aside from the titular smart kids, of course. Much of the album is pitched very overtly to elementary school–

age children who might be offered drugs at some point in their adolescence and need to cultivate the strength to reject peer pressure.

The wonderfully titled "Crack and Cocaine," however, opens with the decidedly adult assertion, "Using crack and cocaine to get high/that's what you say you love," which seems targeted less at impressionable, at-risk moppets than stressed-out stockbrokers who have just started freebasing after work.

In "Crack and Cocaine" McGruff delivers some tough love, with the emphasis on tough, to the kind of hopeless addict who tells people like the narrator of the song, "Using crack and cocaine to get high that's what I love."

Over slick electronic piano that is one of the project's many nods to Yacht Rock, McGruff confronts a crack and cocaine addict with dour judgment in the form of the lyrics, "Just a snort or a smoke, in your greed/That's all you care about/But your life is a joke/And you need someone to help you out."

"Crack and Cocaine" is bound to raise some very thorny, very complicated questions in the minds of small children. It is then up to parents to decide whether they want to explain that by "smoke" the funny animal crime stopper is talking about freebasing cocaine in rock form, or whether he's specifically referring to smoking crack through a pipe, or "sucking the glass dick," as it is colloquially known.

Yes, it's almost as if a song directed at a proud freebaser of rock cocaine or a crack addict does not belong on a cassette targeted at keeping kiddies in school and off the pipe.

Despite its title, *McGruff's Smart Kids Album* has never been available in album form, which is one of SEVERAL curious things about it. I'm also struck by the weird, sad minimalism of its cover art, which depicts someone in a McGruff costume standing in front of a fake brick wall in a tableau that suggests he's equally likely to interview a witness to a homicide or perform his tightest five-minute set at Señor Frog's Chuckle Hut as an opening act in 1985.

Before it can teach kids about the dangers of freebasing cocaine, *McGruff's Smart Kids Album* gets off to a deceptively competent start with "Winners Don't Use," a jaunty jingle with upbeat ragtime piano that wisely doesn't challenge the cursed soul playing McGruff's supremely limited voice.

That opening ditty marks the final time poor McGruff does not embarrass himself vocally by attempting songs and vocals far beyond his meager ability.

The diamond pure core of *McGruff's Smart Kids Album* is a four-song mini-concept album breathlessly overhyping the dangers of mood-altering substances in McGruff's trademark strangled-dog rasp.

Listening to "Marijuana," I alternated between enjoying the song's infectious groove and thinking up counterarguments to its asinine assertions.

"NEVER TRY/Marijuana don't try it at all/It's a lie! It's like beating your head on a wall," McGruff primly asserts. All I can say is that if the shit that McGruff is smoking makes him feel like he's beating his head on a wall, he needs to find a new dealer.

I hate to disagree with this fear-mongering Reagan-era icon of law and order, but marijuana has done an awful lot of good for an awful lot of people. The music of the Beatles, for example, would be boring as shit if they hadn't started toking up.

But McGruff isn't ready to have that conversation yet, so he pretends that marijuana will destroy your life and send you on the fast track to eternal damnation.

In one of many spoken-word interludes, McGruff repeats the "gateway drug" fallacy when he states, "A lot of people think marijuana ISN'T dangerous. But they're wrong! Because not only does it harm a person's body and mind, but it often leads users to try other, even MORE dangerous drugs!"

What kind of drugs? Why inhalants, for starters! On "Inhalants" McGruff croaks a dire warning about there being "danger in inhalants" over an infectious New Wave/Funk groove that's half New Order mid-period B-side and half "Billie Jean" bass alongside wildly out of place kiddie backup vocals.

Whoever signed their children up to sing "Don't do inhalants" and "Breathing them is really no thrill!" for government propaganda purposes needs to lose custody of their young ones as a result.

Musically, some very talented people put a lot of thought and effort into making *McGruff's Smart Kids Album* sound infinitely better than it has any right to. Lyrically, however, these same folks seem to always go with their first lazy instinct, confident that in a world where "pain," "brain," and "insane" all rhyme, there's no point putting an iota more effort into a faceless, thankless gig than is absolutely necessary.

The wildly overachieving first half of *McGruff's Smart Kids Album* ends with its best song. It's a sultry, sexy, shockingly sophisticated number with a Steely Dan by way of early Santana vibe called "Alcohol."

The intricate, Latin-inflected guitar solo that begins the song transports listeners to a hazy black velvet fantasy world where the women are beautiful and scantily clad, the drinks are strong, and the pungent smell of opium fills the air.

Then the crooning cartoon canine breaks the spell by yowling, "Hey, O-PEN up your EYES/You've GOT to see/Alcohol fills your world with lies/Listen to me!" When McGruff is backed by adults with lovely voices, it's jarring because the only voices we've heard up to this point belong to either children or a man pretending to be a cartoon dog.

The second side of *McGruff's Smart Kids Album* is not as inspired as the first, but it ends on an agreeably bonkers note with "I'm Glad I'm Me," a self-esteem anthem so over-the-top in its overly caffeinated optimism that it begins to feel like a Devo musical manifesto minus the irony or satire.

On a sonic level "I'm Glad I'm Me" recalls Devo as well. It's a weird song, with elastic synths, a jittery cocaine groove, and robotic backup vocals that seem to come out of nowhere.

McGruff's Smart Kids Album unintentionally illustrates why the Drug War was doomed to failure. It treats every drug, from the wine spritzer your mom enjoys after work to crack cocaine as pretty much the exact same: dangerous, destructive, and deadly, with the ability to get users hooked the first time around.

That's not how it works. Marijuana is a much different substance than crack, just as inhalants are different than alcohol. Yet *McGruff's Smart Kids Album* paints them all with the same oversized brush all the same.

Because *McGruff's Smart Kids Album* is Drug War propaganda it is a goddamn lie. It's not a benign or harmless lie either.

Lying to children about the dangers of using drugs can have tremendously harmful consequences. I grew up in the Just Say No '80s, when adults subscribed to the curious notion that the best way to keep children on a straight and narrow path was to lie to them about the potential dangers of sex, drugs, and rock and roll.

So, when I began experimenting with marijuana and realized that it was nowhere near as destructive as I had been led to believe, I lost faith in the anti-drug programming I grew up with.

When people lie to you about something important you stop believing them. You don't trust them. You don't respect them.

McGruff's Smart Kids Album lies blatantly and unashamedly to children about drugs and alcohol for just under twenty-eight minutes, but its surprisingly catchy music makes the never-ending falsehoods easier to bear, if not believe.

MR. DELICIOUS, CARTOON PITCHMAN FOR THE RAX CHAIN OF FAST-FOOD RESTAURANTS (1992)

For some inexplicable reason, fast-food joints periodically experience strange identity crises and decide that they need to market their wares to adults.

Burger-slingers get all fancy and become convinced that there is a fortune to be made from fast food for grown-ups. Sometimes these inevitably unsuccessful attempts to make shake shacks upscale take the form of menus full of salads or sit-down dining or premium hamburgers made from the meat of cows rather than horses.

Roast beef franchise Rax took the myopic insanity of trying to rebrand burgers and fries as classy food for adults to a whole new level with the introduction of controversial cartoon spokesman Mr. Delicious.

Mr. Delicious' message was twofold: my life is a waking nightmare and the food at Rax is tasty and affordable.

Consumers, alas, were so distracted by a cartoon fast-food pitchman obsessing on the nature of life's unfathomable cruelty that the second half of his message—the one about how you should eat at Rax—failed to register.

In his introductory TV commercial, Mr. Delicious introduces himself as a cartoon fast-food spokesman who hates cartoons, fast food, and himself.

Anticipating the audience's objections, Mr. Delicious concedes, "I know what you're thinking: He's a . . . cartoon. Cartoons are mostly for people who wet their pants."

Even though Mr. Delicious is a cartoon himself, he's not afraid to throw down the truth gauntlet and concede, up front, that cartoons are for babies, old people, and the incontinent.

Not Mr. D. He explains that he's a "special cartoon for adults." Usually "special cartoon for adults" means animated porn. With Mr. D, however, it means something different.

Each subsequent radio spot and television commercial gives us further insight into Mr. Delicious' depression and anxiety.

In a second television commercial, Mr. Delicious segues awkwardly from promoting Rax's value meal full of "adult-sized delectables for only ninety-nine cents each," to complaining that he's "a little over-extended," because, "perhaps the Rax executives aren't paying him enough to compromise his integrity."

What integrity? Is Mr. Delicious in Fugazi? Is he a Marxist? What has he done in his life as a cartoon mascot that would lead people to think he'd sold out?

Why would I want to visit a restaurant that underpays Mr. Delicious so egregiously that he complains about it in commercials? From there we experience a hard pivot back to the land of the hard sell when he explains, "On the other hand, you can't eat integrity. But you certainly can eat a hearty roast beef sandwich for ninety-nine cents."

Mr. Delicious' radio commercials were twice the length of his TV spots. That afforded the subversive geniuses behind the commercials an opportunity to give us a longer, more involved look inside the agonizing misery of Mr. Delicious' existence.

The first radio spot begins the same way the TV commercials do before veering quickly into psychodrama when Mr. Delicious concedes, "Mr. Delicious doesn't appreciate unnecessary commotion while he's eating. It brings out the dangerous, hostile side in Mr. D. At least that's what his analyst says."

Mr. Delicious does not specify exactly why unnecessary commotion brings out the dangerous, hostile side in him. I am going to assume that Mr. Delicious saw and did things in Vietnam that no one should ever see or do. Ever since then Mr. Delicious just hasn't been right in the head.

Mr. Delicious' rage then turns outward as he talks witheringly of an unnamed fast-food giant whose "bright yellow formica" upsets his stomach before he returns to the consumer-friendly theme of barely concealed rage when he enthuses, "Mr. Delicious always leaves Rax with a few bucks left. That's just grand because his analyst charges a lot to keep Mr. D's hostility all locked up."

But the most unintentionally revealing part of this unusually revealing fast-food commercial is when Mr. Delicious, in a deadpan voice hypnotic in its lack of energy and excitement, says of himself, "He can rest his feet on carpet, since Rax has confidence that Mr. D won't drop his twisty fries. He can lose himself in a cheap romance novel without his elbows sticking to the table."

Why is Mr. Delicious into cheap romance novels? What need do they fulfill in his sad life? Is he a frustrated romantic or a man in need of escape? The image of Mr. Delicious sitting by himself, reading a bodice ripper as he picks absentmindedly at his salad and baked potato is at once funny and sad.

It only gets darker, sadder, and weirder from there. In another radio spot, Mr. Delicious regales us with the details of his "bout with midlife crisis in 89." He goes on to explain, with the perfect note of self-loathing. "Fortunately (Mr. Delicious) was able to sell the Porsche back to the dealer. But much to his chagrin, he discovered that custom-designed hair weaves are nonrefundable. Same for the rotating glitter disco ball he installed in his basement and that vacation to Bora Bora he took with those two young friends that left Mr. Delicious feeling empty and unfulfilled, unlike the robust sandwiches, baked potatoes and refreshing drinks on the Rax menu for only 99 cents each."

The sly, suggestive way Mr. Delicious says "friends" implies that those younger friends were more like fuck-buddies he took to Bora Bora for the sexual adventure of a lifetime, one that found him lustily fulfilling all of his most depraved fantasies.

I'm also going to assume that Mr. Delicious' "friends" are a young man and a young woman, and that Mr. Delicious is a swinger, something Mrs. Delicious doesn't understand any more than she does his need to get wasted.

That's the theme of the final radio spot I could find online where, after the usual preamble about Rax's salad, pizza, and pasta bar, Mr. Delicious confesses, "Mr. Delicious stayed out a little too late last night and he isn't feeling very well. So, it's a good day for carbohydrates. Pizza and pasta will do the trick. Of course, having a wide selection of pizzas is helpful on a day when Mr. D is having trouble focusing. He's bound to grab a slice of something tasty. If you've ever enjoyed two for one night at the Rusty Anchor, you know how dehydrated Mr. D must be. Some free Coke refills will hit the spot. Besides, enjoying a long, leisurely dinner at Rax's will help him avoid the wrath of Mrs. Delicious, who isn't very fond of the Rusty Anchor."

Mrs. Delicious doesn't seem too fond of Mr. Delicious. He doesn't seem too keen on himself either.

Mr. Delicious was a fast-food spokesman unlike any other. With his briefcase, bowtie, plaid suit, "Dickety-dee" catchphrase, and aura of ineffable sadness, Mr. Delicious wasn't just different from every other fast-food pitchman; he was the antithesis of everything a spokes-cartoon is supposed to be.

Where the Ronald McDonalds of the world are cheerful and upbeat, Mr. Delicious is depressed, a sad sack who talks about his unhappy marriage, midlife crises, and failed hair transplants as much as he talks about Rax's roast beef sandwiches, pizza buffets, and free Coke refills.

Where other fast-food pimps are carefree, Mr. Delicious is a man of constant sorrow. He's a melancholy figure on the verge of giving in to hopelessness completely.

Mr. Delicious suggests a fast-food analogue to OK Soda, the notorious, failed attempt to market a soda to Gen-X slackers by co-opting their cynicism, irony, and hostility toward being sold consumer goods.

As a droll, absurdist parody of hard-sell hucksters like Ronald McDonald and Burger King, Mr. Delicious is inspired. As an actual advertising campaign, however, he was doomed from the beginning. It turns out there's a reason fast-food spokespeople are not suicidal, low-energy losers.

Mr. Delicious did not succeed. Rax declared bankruptcy not long after his introduction. The failing chain eventually brought back as their mascot a smiling reptile named Uncle Alligator who kept his private life private and stuck to promoting hamburgers and fries.

It's unfortunate that Mr. Delicious did not stick around longer because his unique persona opened itself up to ad campaigns no other fast-food restaurant would even consider, let alone implement.

If I were a copywriter for Mr. Delicious, I'd pitch the following decidedly adult, Mr. Delicious–friendly ideas for subsequent commercials:

* Mr. Delicious' young "friend" had an unplanned "accident" because she and Mr. Delicious didn't take the necessary precautions. Now Mr. Delicious needs the money he's saving by eating at Rax to pay for a "procedure" to take care of Mr. Delicious' young friend's little "problem."

* Mr. Delicious wants to end it all, but first he's going to binge on Rax's pasta and pizza buffet.

* Mr. Delicious bet on the football game and now some very not-nice men will break Mrs. Delicious' kneecaps if he can't come up with the two thousand dollars he owes.

* Mr. Delicious brought home some unwanted "souvenirs" from his trip to Bora Bora and needs to visit the clinic for some shots.

We'll probably never see another fast-food pitchman like Mr. Delicious. Commercially, that's probably wise, but creatively it's unfortunate, as his brief, curious existence single-handedly made the world of fast-food advertising weirder and more interesting.

9 CHICKWEED LANE
(1993-PRESENT)

When I was a child, I was obsessed with newspaper comic strips. I adored Calvin & Hobbes, Bloom County, The Far Side, and Peanuts and devoured them in daily form and in big collections. When I was a boy, I dreamed of having my own nationally syndicated comic strip.

I even wrote letters to my favorite creators asking for advice on how to break into the business. As I got older my obsessive comic strip fandom faded and was replaced by newer, less dorky enthusiasms. I still read comic strips from time to time, but I now largely see comic strips, like newspapers, as a beloved component of my past rather than part of my present or future.

Oh sure, there are still cartoonists that I dig, like Tom Tomorrow and Ward Sutton, but the comic strips I am most associated with, and write about the most, tend to be on the bad and tacky side: the uber-mediocrity of Garfield; the anti-marriage manifesto The Lockhorns, and the insanely patriotic, patriotically insane political cartoons of Ben Garrison.

I write about things that I love, but also about things that are terrible. So, it is perhaps not surprising that I was recently added to a Facebook group devoted to 9 Chickweed Lane, a comic strip with which I was only vaguely familiar.

At first, I resented it. I did not choose to be part of the group. It did not seem to speak to my interests, random, chaotic, and masochistic though they might be. But it wasn't long before I came to understand why fate had pushed me in the comic strip's direction.

The members of this group were mortified and horrified by the world of 9 Chickweed Lane and its erudite fop of a creator, Brooke McEldowney, a cartoonist/classical musician and graduate of the Juilliard School of Music who brings the full force of his academic credentials and intellectual pedigree to every unspeakably pretentious, self-satisfied, endlessly masturbatory panel he creates.

According to Wikipedia, "McEldowney's comic strip primarily focuses on the relationships between its multigenerational female characters, beginning with a single mother, Juliette, and her teenaged daughter, Edda. Although he did not originally intend to have the characters age, they have done so, though not at real-time."

To my philistine, uncultured eyes, however, every comic strip seems to be exclusively about how unbelievably horny the men in the strip are for their impossibly willowy, ethereal partners and how equally horny the women are for their erudite and urbane husbands.

A typical arc on 9 Chickweed Lane involves Edda, our impossibly gorgeous, lithe blonde heroine and primary sex object, finding an old school uniform that, of course, still fits her, which makes cellist husband Amos even hornier than usual, and leads to an explosion of mind-blowing sex. That's no small feat considering that Amos is, ordinarily, if the not the single horniest man in the universe, then certainly in the top ten.

Edda is the mother of twins, but giving birth to two human beings at the same time did not compromise Edda's slender beauty in the least. She did not gain even an ounce of cellulite on her perfect body and the twins intuitively understand that the only thing that matters in the universe is their parents' insatiable lust for each other. These poor unfortunate souls must take a back seat to mommy and daddy's raging libidos along with everything else.

The characters in *9 Chickweed Lane* are the sort that describe their husband or wife as their "lover" because they think that makes them sound scandalously sensual, and because they want other people to think about them having sex.

It feels like the only "gag" in *9 Chickweed Lane* is how unbelievably horny all the characters are for each other. Today's strip, for example, features a gorgeous and educated woman in a tight miniskirt drinking coffee in a diner with her clearly educated and cultured partner. She slides her hand over to his bathing suit area and, judging from the expression as he spills coffee all over his face in surprise, manually stimulates him to completion.

If you're wondering how a comic strip could get away with something like that it's probably because McEldowney is so self-consciously "artful" and "elliptical" that only the most sophisticated and observant of readers, those with Ivy League educations and extensive knowledge of classical music, will even discern that one of the strip's many total hotties is yanking her partner's crank under the table.

Many of the comic strip's characters are highbrow artists of some sort, dancers and classical musicians like *9 Chickweed Lane*'s creator, and undoubtedly bring the same passion, artistry, and grace to giving world-class hand jobs that they do to performing the work of Mozart.

9 Chickweed Lane's double-barreled combination of horny and pretentious is what makes it so morbidly fascinating as well as creepy. It's not hard to imagine McEldowney gazing with reverence and lust at a particularly randy strip and throwing himself a little one-handed pants party in appreciation of his horny yet highbrow genius.

I hope that *9 Chickweed Lane* reflects the real-life passion of a creator hopelessly in love and lust with a wife he adores beyond all things because the alternative is too heartbreaking to even consider.

I had hoped that McEldowney was an anomaly in an otherwise sexless comic strip world, but that is apparently not the case. *Luanne* has somehow devolved into a similarly oversexed strip, albeit with less faux sophistication. Heck, even *Arlo & Janis* regularly delves into semi-raunchy territory.

I can't unsee or unlearn what I have seen and learned about *9 Chickweed Lane.* Now neither can you. The comic strip world seems to be going through something of a sexual revolution and I don't like it one bit.

WYCLEF JEAN'S AMA
(2016)

When Wyclef Jean, or rather Wyclef Jean's PR team, agreed for him to do an AMA (Ask Me Anything) for Reddit in 2016, he clearly imagined that he was in for an hour of softball questions that'd help him sell records. Wyclef naively imagined that his Reddit interrogators would see him the way he sees himself—as a humanitarian, great artist and cultural icon, a modern-day Bob Marley.

Instead, the trolls of Reddit treated him like the con artist, deranged narcissist, and comically oblivious caricature of an egomaniacal celebrity he actually is.

The top question (from a user named skybrew) in the righteous bloodbath gives a sense of the enraged tone of the rest of the AMA, which threatens to give cold-blooded online pile-ons a good name:

"I have a question for you, how do you sleep at night knowing that the money people were donating to your charity Yele could have been spent improving the lives of 'your people' but instead you spent it on yourself and your celebrity friends? How do you justify $600,000 in donations went to Yele's headquarters, which have since been abandoned, $375,000 to cover 'landscaping' costs, $470,000 spent on food and beverages, you paid yourself $100,000 to perform at a 'Charity' event for your presidency bid, $100,000 to your mistress, $30,763 to fly Hollywood Lindsay Lohan from New Jersey to Chicago. You have stolen a total of $9 million dollars of the $16 million donated to Haiti. Do you feel like the biggest douche bag on earth or do you like stealing from the mouths of the poor and needy?"

Wyclef did not answer that question, understandably, but he did have the exquisitely terrible judgment to answer the loaded, "With all that money you stole from those poor Haitians, why couldn't you help Lauryn Hill out with her tax bill?" with a breathtakingly weak, "it's so important that u understand that if u fully do real research u will understand that whenever u decide that u are going to do more then sing and dance u have to be ready for the lies that comes with it i have never stolen from my people i brought Haitian pride to my people and despite what they tried to do i am growing stronger everyday and will continue to do my part as i can see you are doing your part as well."

Redditors were not impressed by Wyclef's E. E. Cummings-meets-Prince-meets-Corey Feldman after a night of binge drinking approach to grammar and capitalization.

Nor were they impressed by the pathetic self-mythologizing of Wyclef's non-answer as to why he can't help Hill out with some of the ill-gotten loot he purloined from a charity set up to feed and clothe the suffering souls of Wyclef's Haitian homeland.

It did not escape Redditors' attention that Wyclef's defense of his unconscionable acts of thievery from the poor was a combination of self-promotion mixed with self-pity. He's getting stronger every day? He brought Haitian pride to the Haitian people by robbing them?

Redditors sharpened their pitchforks and their wits and peppered the uncommunicative superstar with questions like the following:

- As a young songwriter myself, I have a question for you. What's a good fake charity I could start up to rob people of money who really need it?

- Hey Wyclef, I hope you have time to answer this with how busy you are answering the other ones but anyway, what's the first thing you're going to do when you get to hell?

- Why are you amoral?

- What was a better detriment to Haitian culture? You or the Earthquake?

- What was the worst decision you've ever made: doing this AMA, embezzling money from a charity for your own personal enrichment, or Crossfit?

It's not that Wyclef is completely averse to answering questions. He just prefers to answer softball questions briskly and blandly.

Wyclef isn't big on periods or capitalization so perhaps it's unsurprising that his non-snappy answers to fawning questions tend to be sentence fragments.

Jean did answer another relatively tough question in, "On August 5, 2010, you announced you were running in the 2010 Haitian presidential election, but you did not meet the residency requirement of having lived in Haiti for five years before the November 28 election. What would you have done if you were allowed to run and/or elected?" but his answer, "well i think its starts with Education and jobs over 50 percent of our population youth. . . . Haiti do not need hand outs it needs job creation," gives a good sense of how little Jean cares about this enterprise and the peons roasting him.

It's a good thing Wyclef wasn't elected president of Haiti. Can you imagine a president who can't spell basic words and ran a fraudulent charity? What an embarrassment that would be!

The only remotely newsworthy moment of the AMA occurred when Wyclef answered a question about Bernie Sanders by gushing, "i think he is a voice that the youth have been waiting to hear," but even that prompted a Redditor to note that Wyclef might be the first person to get down-voted for praising Sanders.

The rest of Wyclef's answers give a sense of the bland, promotional mass interview that might have been. What was it like being on the *Chappelle's Show*? "One of my best memories that guy is smart and funny." Who was your favorite person to work/collaborate with? Michael Jackson or Whitney Houston. What would you do if you weren't a pop star? Teach music theory. If someone had never heard your music before, what would you want them to begin with? "Gone Til November."

All perfectly polite and professional. All incredibly boring. Instead of having his ego carefully buffed, Wyclef ended up having it destroyed by a public that was feeling its own malicious power and rejoicing in its ability to make a narcissistic fraud feel as low as humanly possible.

Wyclef was too oblivious and arrogant to do anything to try to save a public relations fiasco of historic proportions.

The former Fugees mastermind fails to live up to a fawning intro that gushes, "The music that Wyclef Jean has written, performed, and produced—both as a solo superstar and as founder and guiding member of the Fugees—has been a consistently powerful, pop cultural force for over two decades. In 1996, the Fugees released their monumental album *The Score,* which inspired notoriously prickly rock critic Robert Christgau to write: "So beautiful and funny, its courage could make you weep.""

The hilariously over-the-top hyperbole of Wyclef's introduction makes the massacre that follows even funnier and more deliciously rich in schadenfreude. The snark of the Reddit Ridicule Brigade was so beautiful and funny, its courage could make you weep, particularly if you're unlucky enough to be Wyclef on this fateful day of unexpected reckoning, when his sins would not only be exposed but used to relentlessly hammer away at his bloated self-image.

THE FYRE FESTIVAL
(2017)

When the first and final Fyre Festival became a boondoggle of epic proportions, it engendered a potent double schadenfreude. Nothing makes online cynics happier than other folks' misery. The suffering of the Fyre Festival set made them positively giddy.

The public understandably had a hard time feeling sorry for rich assholes willing to spend fifteen thousand dollars for the privilege of watching Blink 182 perform while on a yacht partying with supermodels and guzzling champagne. Rubberneckers glorying in the festival's spectacular demise were more interested in mocking everyone involved than in empathizing with them.

When Fyre went down in flames, Twitter's snark brigade laughed maliciously in the festival's direction. The unseemly but infectious glee the internet took in the Fyre into the ground's failure was even more intense when directed at the people who ran the festival, the hucksters who sold a superficial public in thrall to the empty glamour of social media influencers an impossible fantasy of hedonistic excess it could not ultimately deliver.

The Fyre Festival also afforded the public yet another opportunity to laugh at Ja Rule.

The 50 Cent nemesis' central presence at a much-hyped 2017 festival should have been a red flag. After all, you can't have a hip, A-list, prestigious new festival with a walking punchline as your face and voice.

To anyone paying attention, Ja Rule's presence gave the game away. It betrayed the actual nature of the festival and its behind-the-scenes players: desperate and D-list, a shoddy simulacrum of money, power, and prestige.

There was a time when Ja Rule was one of the most famous rappers alive. Unfortunately for the Fyre Festival, that time was 2002. Billy McFarland, the cofounder of the Fyre Festival, was ten years old then. Consequently, when McFarland was a child, Ja Rule was as big as they came. We have an innate deference toward people who were famous when we were children. The world might have knocked them down a few pegs, but some part of us will always see them the way we did when we were kids, as heroes, idols, gods, figures of incredible glamour and prestige.

Even if they're Ja Rule.

McFarland and Ja Rule completed each other in some weird, toxic way. Hanging out with Ja Rule and starting a festival together that wouldn't just be a series of concerts but an immersive upscale lifestyle experience afforded the geeky wannabe tech mogul an opportunity to play rock star.

Ja Rule, in turn, who released exactly one album in between 2004's *R.U.L.E.* and the Fyre Festival in 2017, saw an opportunity to reinvent himself as an ambitious tech entrepreneur primed to make a second gaudy fortune selling the glitzy lifestyle he rapped about in his commercial prime to a new generation of suckers.

That Rule had recently gone to prison for not paying the government money that he owed them should have worried young entrepreneurs wanting to get into the Ja Rule business, the Billy McFarland business, or the Ja Rule/Billy McFarland business. If someone is willing to go to jail rather than pay taxes, then they're probably not going to lose sleep over not paying employees overtime, or paying them at all.

The Fyre Festival reminded the public how much they enjoyed laughing at Ja Rule. But it also provided targets for mockery of a more recent, more relevant vintage. The disaster doubled as a scathing indictment of the "influencer" mindset.

The idea of the "influencer" is that there are people so beautiful, glamorous, and worthy of envy that brands and companies throw money at them to share photographs on Instagram, Twitter, and Facebook showcasing their products, goods, and services.

It's like modeling only more superficial and unhealthy. It's a way of monetizing jealousy as well as lust and greed, of making cash money off the public looking at pictures of you on the permanent vacation that constitutes your lush life, and wanting to fuck you, be you, or both.

The Fyre Festival represented the influencer lifestyle in its purest form. Buy a VIP package for the festival and you wouldn't just be another nobody on the outside looking in.

For the right price, you could live that lifestyle. You could sneak into the frame and crash that glitzy, empty world. For thousands of dollars, you could live the life of an influencer for a weekend or two. You could pay to become one of the beautiful people.

The public's deep, not entirely unmerited hatred of influencers and the influenced helps explain why people were rooting for the Fyre Festival to fail and then gloried in its demise.

The idiotic dream of the Fyre Festival was that the hottest and most famous supermodels in the world (including Kylie Jenner, Bella Hadid, and Emily Ratajkowski) were going to be partying on what was once Pablo Escobar's private island, taking in performances from Major Lazer, Blink 182, Li'l Yachty, the G.O.O.D. Music family, and Migos while staying in luxury villas and eating gourmet food from the world's finest chefs. And you—yes, you!—could party with these aspirational figures for the modest price of tens of thousands of dollars.

In one of the many depressing aspects of the festival, this cynical ploy worked. The photo sessions with the world's most expensive models were a huge success. Paying supermodels vast sums to plug the festival was similarly a huge success, particularly since only one did the decent, legal thing and acknowledged that she was being paid to do an ad and didn't just find out about Fyre through organic means and take to Instagram to express her genuine excitement.

As a photo shoot, Instagram campaign, and outreach program to supermodels, Fyre Festival was a smash. That success brought in the money, attention, and heat that led to failure on an international, historic scale.

Deep into one of the documentaries, Andy King, a lovely, insanely committed gentleman who earlier said that he would have been willing to perform oral sex on a custom's guy in exchange for the release of bottled water after McFarland explicitly asks him to do so, argues that people only talk about how wonderful Woodstock was and never about the lack of water, drug overdoses, mud, terrible planning, and traffic problems.

That's not true. All the hassles and headaches are a major component of Woodstock mythology. We don't celebrate Woodstock because it was a smoothly run festival. No, we romanticize Woodstock—the *Get High on Yourself* of the late 1960s—as the essence of the 1960s counterculture precisely because it was a terribly organized festival that had to overcome incredible obstacles to deliver a transcendent spiritual experience for the muddy, drug-addled, clean water–hungry hippies in the crowd and onstage alike.

I think the fact that Insane Clown Posse, high school dropouts who perform in clown makeup and spray their fans with cheap soda, manage to successfully pull off an ambitious, high-profile festival of arts and culture every year in the Gathering of the Juggalos gives the rest of the festival industry a false sense of confidence. They think that it must be easy, when it is incredibly, almost prohibitively difficult.

I'll never forget a Gathering seminar where Violent J and Shaggy 2 Dope talked about how the port-a-potty industry refusing to work with them nearly kept that year's Gathering from happening before an unsung hero stepped in and did God's work by renting the clowns shitters.

This speaks to the precariousness of the whole industry: an absence of port-a-potties nearly kept the 2017 Gathering of the Juggalos from happening. The Fyre frauds lacked pretty much everything, not just places for people to relieve themselves.

Fyre Festival cofounders McFarland and Ja Rule made a series of crucial mistakes that ensured the kind of failure that people remember forever, that sets the gold standard/nadir for music industry fiascoes. Yet, the festival's founders still refused to cancel under the delusion that they still might be able to carry it off if luck was on their side and the universe played ball.

New festivals generally require a year to eighteen months of careful planning to handle the enormous amount of work and preparation involved in throwing a large-scale operation of that nature. The Einsteins over at Fyre decided they could do it all in six months. In an equally boneheaded move, they planned the festival during the busiest time of the year for the island they were befouling with their presence, a hugely important regatta that was the boating equivalent of Super Bowl Sunday. That ensured that resources would be both scarce and expensive.

The Fyre Festival planners could have made things easier for everyone involved by partnering with an outside firm with experience throwing music festivals. Alternately, they could have thrown the festival somewhere with a strong infrastructure capable of handling partiers needing airfare and accommodations and food and alcohol and water and something approximating order.

There's an element of magical thinking at play in the Fyre folks' belief that they could achieve as complete novices what veterans told them couldn't be done. People working eighteen-hour days convinced themselves that with enough hard work, luck, money, and star power they could make an insane dream a reality.

The Fyre Festival paid the shitty people over at FuckJerry, a meme factory turned digital marketing company, a lot of money to come up with striking iconography for the festival.

But when people think of the festival in the years ahead, they won't think of Kylie Jenner under a crystal blue sky but rather the apocalyptic tableau of FEMA tents in a stormy hellscape or, more likely, a sad little cheese sandwich and salad in a Styrofoam container. These images will live forever as an unforgettable visual representation of the gulf between the paradise festival-goers were promised and the unfortunate reality they encountered on the ground.

The picture of that sandwich should hang in an art museum. Like many other elements of the Fyre Festival, it succeeded spectacularly as an oddball piece of performance and pop art precisely because every other aspect of the debacle was such a spectacular failure.

The would-be festival-goers revolted and changed the narrative from one of glamour and luxury to one of dark comedy. Instead of the next Coachella, the Fyre Festival was received as a riotous joke at the expense of millennials, social influencers, tech bros, and Ja Rule.

These decadent millennials were going to live like the richest of the rich. Instead, they ended up getting a taste of what life is like for people in poor countries outside the United States.

And what of Ja Rule? Ja Rule emerges as an oddly slippery figure here. When it's time to toast to living like movie stars, partying like rock stars, and fucking like porn stars, he's front and center with that big superstar grin. But when it came time for accountability, he was nowhere to be found. He ultimately chose to point the finger at McFarland and present himself as another victim of his now-imprisoned cofounder's devilish ways.

Rule's defense seems to be that he came up with the idea for an exclusive festival on an exotic island with attractions like a million-dollar treasure hunt and, being an artist rather than a businessman, entrusted the day-to-day details to McFarland, and was mortified to discover that his partner was a con man rather than an upstanding businessman.

That is bullshit. Even if I can't imagine Rule staying up late crunching numbers with McFarland, he knew what was happening. Of course Ja knew. But it also seems possible, even plausible, that Ja didn't want to know what was happening behind the scenes for the sake of plausible deniability.

Watching the dueling documentaries on the Influencer Altamont that was the Fyre Festival, a strange, seemingly counterintuitive thought struck me. I couldn't help but notice that the Fyre Festival has incredible heat right now. It has incredible buzz. It has incredible name recognition. It's no exaggeration to say that people can't stop talking about the Fyre Festival, that it's enjoying a huge cultural moment after its initial huge cultural moment back in 2017.

True, all the Fyre Festival's buzz is negative. But infamy is the flip side of fame, and Billy McFarland is real fucking famous as well as infamous, as is his universally mocked brainchild, even if the context is that the whole world is laughing at them.

Something tells me we haven't seen the last of McFarland or Fyre. The legend of the Fyre Festival is simply too stupid and too famous for it to stay dead forever. At the very least, it merits a movie, *Serial*-style true crime podcast, or Netflix miniseries.

I would watch the fuck out of *Spring Breakers 2: The Fyre Festival Heist* or a reality show starring Ja Rule about his experiences post-prison and post–Fyre Festival. Best of all, we could turn a negative into a positive by ensuring that every dollar made from Fyre Festival–related projects went directly to the Bahamian workers fucked over by the festival instead of the charlatans and ne'er do wells behind it.

MARK DUPLASS' 2018 TWEET SUGGESTING LEFTISTS FOLLOW BEN SHAPIRO IF INTERESTED IN "CROSSING THE AISLE"

A few years back Mark Duplass, the prolific writer, director, actor, creator, and mumblecore pioneer, had an idea.

Duplass was concerned about the heated nature of online political discourse. He hated how polarizing the internet could be, how it divided us into warring tribes perpetually ready to do furious linguistic battle to prove the rightness and righteousness of our beliefs.

So, in an exquisitely misguided gesture, Duplass made an endorsement that proved controversial.

In a tweet he would later both delete and apologize for, Duplass wrote to Progressives looking to understand the other side, "Fellow liberals: If you are interested at all in 'crossing the aisle' you should consider following @ benshapiro. I don't agree with him on much, but he's a genuine person who once helped me for no other reason than to be nice. He doesn't bend the truth. His intentions are good."

To say that the response was bad would be a wild understatement. If there was a Hall of Fame for Well-Intentioned Gestures Gone Horribly Awry, Duplass' plea that Leftists give Ben Shapiro a try on account of him being a mensch with a heart of gold regardless of his politics would have made it in on the first ballot.

The internet instantly and brutally corrected Duplass on his conception of Ben Shapiro as a lovely man whose ideas deserved to be heard and considered by even the staunchest leftist.

With varying degrees of venom and mockery, people directed Duplass to Shapiro's long history of racist, sexist, homophobic, and transphobic statements.

Duplass' initial tweet displays a surreal lack of understanding about Shapiro. *The League* star seems to be mistaking Shapiro for David Brooks, who may be a superstar Conservative writer, but who also seems like a guy it would be fun to have brunch with even if you disagree with his politics.

Brooks cultivated an image as a Conservative it's okay for Liberals to like. Shapiro has cultivated a much different persona. Shapiro carved out a lucrative, high-profile niche for himself as a preeminent intellectual bully whose massive brain DESTROYS pretenders with FACTS and REASON.

Shapiro has gone out of his way to be seen as someone leftists DO NOT enjoy. So, it's crazy that Duplass would make what are extremely strong assertions regarding the goodness of Shapiro's soul despite seemingly knowing nothing about him.

Duplass made the mistake of assuming that his friendly relationship with Shapiro represents the Conservative provocateur's true essence, that it allows him to stand before God and the internet and piously proclaim that a figure rightfully hated for being a bigot is actually a nice guy.

People are complicated. They're flawed. They're erratic. That helps explain why superstars like Jodie Foster, Whoopi Goldberg, and Robert Downey Jr. can be friends and defenders of Mel Gibson, despite everything that he has said and done.

Mark Duplass is a rich, white, straight, powerful man who has enjoyed tremendous success in show business. Why wouldn't Shapiro be nice to a man like that?

Shapiro may have been nice to Duplass and helped him once solely for the sake of being a good dude, but that does not describe Shapiro's relationship with the LGBTQ community. Or African Americans. Or immigrants. Or the victims of police brutality.

To these people, Ben Shapiro is the enemy, an unfortunately huge cultural figure who has used his power and visibility to try to tear them down.

Shapiro could very well have found the original tweet as embarrassing as Duplass did, but when Duplass apologized for his misguided endorsement, Shapiro whined via social media, "So in 24 hours I apparently went from being a person with good intentions to a racist sexist bigot. Twitter toxifies any attempt to cross the aisle. There's no conservative Mark could have recommended who wouldn't receive the same blowback."

Shapiro was ALWAYS a racist sexist bigot. Twitter did not toxify Duplass' staggeringly misguided attempt to reach across the aisle; it merely pointed out to Duplass that the public Shapiro was not who Duplass imagined him to be.

Duplass withdrawing his misguided endorsement of Shapiro as someone liberals can learn from seems to have hurt the precious little snowflake's fragile feelings, but if I might paraphrase the words of a jackass no one should take seriously, facts don't care about your feelings.

Duplass wanted to make the perpetually enraged realm of online politics a little more civil. He wanted to prove that we're not so different after all. Instead, Duplass illustrated just how fraught with landmines our online political landscape can be.

KEVIN SPACEY'S "LET ME BE FRANK" YOUTUBE VIDEO (2019)

What do you do when society has canceled you? How do you move forward when you're so toxic that your colleagues are called upon to publicly condemn you lest they appear complicit in your transgressions? What's the next step after it's determined that your crimes are so extreme that you're cut out of a movie that has already been finished and replaced by an actor who is nominated for an Academy Award for his heroic work rescuing a troubled production from your unacceptable presence?

What do you do when decades of dark whispers about you being a handsy sexual predator explode into a firestorm of accusations, kicked off by a beloved *Rent* star, spurred by the avalanche of damning revelations of the #MeToo movement, accusing you of attempted sexual assault when he was fourteen years old?

If you're Kevin Spacey, you grab Granny's camcorder from the attic and decide to make a fun little YouTube video that should finish killing what's left of your career.

When Spacey's "Let Me Be Frank" video dropped, the question on everyone's mind was: "Why?" Why would someone savvy enough to have risen to positions of prominence in film, television, and theater be self-destructive enough to release something so damning and just plain weird?

The answer has to do with the way Spacey sees himself and his relationship to the public, and his inveterately doomed attempt to make the world fall in love with him as an entertainer, and not just respect him as an artist.

Even for an actor, Spacey is emotionally needy. Spacey has consistently illustrated a need not just for validation but adoration.

Early in his career, Spacey tried his hand at stand-up and while he ultimately chose the path of the Juilliard-trained thespian, he never lost the comedian's desperate hunger for the approval of the crowd.

To that end, Spacey tried to dazzle the public not just with his gifts as an actor but also with impressions of heroes like Jack Lemmon and Walter Matthau, colorful anecdotes that felt just a little too good to be true, and even song and dance.

Despite Spacey's conception of himself as a lovable leading man, the oily probable sex criminal was typecast as a bad guy early in his career for a very good reason. Spacey is an extremely unlikable performer. As an actor, Spacey just doesn't naturally convey arrogance and intelligence: he conveys the intimidating intelligence of someone who knows exactly how smart they are, and is a total asshole about it. That's what made Spacey's casting in *The Usual Suspects* inspired: Spacey's brilliant assholes use their intelligence as a weapon. They act as if the rules that govern the actions of mere mortals do not apply to them because they're smarter, sharper, better, more evolved, and more civilized than the rest of us.

Spacey was a natural for roles like bosses from hell (*Swimming with Sharks, Horrible Bosses*), an ambitious serial killer with a philosophy (*Seven*), and a brilliant criminal mastermind (*The Usual Suspects*).

Then in 1999 the worst possible thing happened to Spacey: he won the Best Actor Oscar for *American Beauty*. The film industry unwisely fed into Spacey's delusional sense of himself as a man the public was eager to root for and identify with rather than enthusiastically deride.

Despite what Spacey might want to believe, the public did not fall in love with him in *American Beauty*, so much as they rooted against Annette Bening's nightmare of a wife.

The movies that Spacey made after *American Beauty* illustrated that he tragically misunderstood the nature of his appeal in ways that would plant the seeds for "Let Me Be Frank."

Spacey decided that he, rather than someone like Robin Williams, would be perfect to play a lovable oddball mental hospital resident who thinks he's a space alien in *K-Pax*. Spacey similarly imagined that the public's love for him was so deep that he could get away with playing Bobby Darin in 2004's *Beyond the Sea* despite the actor being, at forty-five, nearly a decade older than Darin was when he died at thirty-seven.

Spacey was adrift before *House of Cards* brought him back by offering him a role smack-dab in his wheelhouse of charismatic bastards. Spacey has spent much of his career talking to audiences, often in the form of narration delivered directly to the camera, in his biggest, most beloved roles in *American Beauty*, *The Usual Suspects*, and *House of Cards*. Spacey's bond with his public is so strong that even his character's death in *American Beauty* did not keep him from serving as the film's narrator.

Spacey as Frank Underwood attempts a similar feat in "Let Me Be Frank," one of the weirdest amateur fan films ever made. It finds the actor reprising his *House of Cards* role of Frank Underwood for a three-minute-and-seven-second-long monologue delivered directly to the camera while wearing a Christmas apron. In the video, Spacey as Underwood comments bitterly on both the demise of his *House of Cards* character and the actor's own fall from grace.

Spacey/Underwood greets us as an intimate confidant who has stood by his side for a good half decade. He's a villain but also someone who has, in his own strange way always been true to us, the audience, his audience, people so mesmerized by Kevin Spacey as Frank Underwood that they'll happily lap him up in this bootleg, degraded form.

It's jarring seeing a dead character up and about and kibitzing with us, his dear friends, but as Frank mentions here pointedly, did we actually see his corpse? No, we did not, and considering that we are, at that very moment, watching a seemingly non-zombified Frank Underwood talk to us, we can't help but assume that—HOLY SHIT—Frank Underwood is still alive; Kevin Spacey should DEFINITELY still be playing him, and, furthermore, we should give actor Kevin Spacey the benefit of the doubt regarding charges of sexual assault and harassment because Spacey is a great actor who has been honest with us about who he really is through his iconic portrayals of evil sociopaths with sinister secret lives.

Spacey as Underwood is saying to the viewing public, clear as day, "If I were such a bad guy, which I am, and did the horrible things I am accused of, would I be talking to you now about what a bad guy I am and how I did horrible things? Of course not. The fact that I am a bad person guilty of horrible crimes PROVES that I am innocent of certain crimes and ultimately vindicates me!"

Spacey's peculiar brand works very hard to sell the Oscar winner as a razzle-dazzle entertainer with a powerful connection to his adoring fans, but also as an ACTOR, a thespian, someone skilled in the dramatic arts, a classically trained craftsman of the highest order.

Spacey's bizarre performance art begins with him washing and drying his hands while wearing a Santa Claus apron. Then the actor's lizard-like gaze fixes upon us.

Spacey begins by reaffirming his bond with the audience, a relationship he imagines is so strong that we'll take out a scale of judgment and place fresh charges of, among other things, trying to sexually assault a fourteen-year-old on one side and our enjoyment of Spacey's performance in *The Negotiator* on the other, and they'll come out more or less even.

This is not subtext. It's text. Spacey as Underwood starts off by whispering into our collective ear, "I know what you want. Oh sure, they might have tried to separate us, but what we have is too strong, too powerful."

There's something heartbreaking about the desperation of these words. Spacey believes that what has been hopelessly shattered into a million pieces, namely Spacey's reputation and relationship with Netflix/*House of Cards*/*House of Cards* fans, can be put back together through the magic of ACTING!

Spacey thinks he can do an end run around an industry that has judged him unemployable by appealing directly to his public through his chosen medium, ACTING!

Through Underwood, Spacey confides conspiratorially in us, "After all, we shared everything, you and I. I told you my deepest, darkest secrets. I showed you *exactly* what people are capable of."

Sounding every bit the smarmy politician, Spacey implores, "I shocked you with my honesty but mostly I challenged you and made you think. And you trusted me, even though you knew you shouldn't." Spacey continues before infamously lifting an empty mug to his lips to drink from thin air.

Growing more intense and undeservedly confident with each methodically delivered word, Spacey/Underwood insists, despite AMPLE evidence to the contrary, "So we're not done, no matter what anyone says and besides, I KNOW what you want."

This is not the first time in the video where it would seem weirdly appropriate for sleazy stripper music to come on and for Spacey to start seductively disrobing while purring, "You want to see Santa's yule log, don't you?!? Well, you've all been naughty AND nice, so I'm going to give you all a good look at Daddy Frank's candy cane!"

But, no, Spacey/Underwood merely strikes multiple inappropriately sexual notes before continuing, in an orgy of paranoia worthy of Richard Nixon, another President Spacey portrayed, "You want me back. Of course, *some* have believed everything and have waited with bated breath for me to confess it all. They're just *dying* to have me declare that everything said was true and that I *got* what I deserved. Wouldn't that be easy?"

At this point in the video Spacey/Underwood is carving something for emphasis, and, I suppose, to give him something to do with his hands while his brain and words spiral into madness.

Spacey/Underwood sternly insists, "But we both know it's not that simple, not in politics and not in life."

At this point, Kevin Spacey, a man accused of over a dozen sex crimes, who has been shunned from society, and Frank Underwood, a villainous fictional dead character Spacey played, turn the tables and point an accusatory finger our way.

Spacey isn't afraid to ask who the real criminal is: the guy who reportedly tried to drunkenly force himself on a fourteen-year-old sexually, or you, a person seemingly inclined to judge Spacey harshly without a proper criminal trial where a highly paid defense team could present the strongest possible legal defense? So, in a way, maybe YOU should be facing criminal charges instead of Spacey.

Speaking with the unimpeachable moral authority that comes with being accused of heinous sex crimes, Spacey/Underwood taunts, "You wouldn't believe the worst without evidence, would you? You wouldn't RUSH to judgment without facts, would you? DID you? No, not you! You're smarter than that."

Sounding increasingly southern, Spacey/Underwood drones on, "Anyway, all that presumption made for such an unsatisfying ending. And to think, it could have been such a memorable send-off! I mean, if you and I have learned nothing else these past few years, it's that in life and art nothing should be off the table. We weren't afraid. Not of what we said or what we did and we're still not afraid. Because I can promise you this. If I didn't pay the price for the things we both know I did do, I'm certainly not going to pay the price for the things I didn't do. Oh of course they're going to say I'm being disrespectful, not playing by the rules. Like I ever played by anyone's rules before! I never did and *you* loved it."

Spacey/Underwood is clearly talking about the actor with the dead career and the dead character he played and is somehow, inexplicably still playing, sort of, when he says that we love it when he doesn't play by the rules.

The key difference is that the rules Spacey didn't play by, according to the allegations against him, are those involving the age of consent and consent in general. I don't think anybody other than fans of pedophilia *loved* it when Spacey reportedly decided to violently flout the rules governing how old a person must be before you can have sex with them.

Sounding more than a little like Colonel Sanders, Spacey/Underwood blusters, "Anyhow, despite all the poppycock, the animosity, the headlines, the impeachment without a trial, despite everything, despite even my own death, I feel *surprisingly* good. And my confidence grows each day that soon enough you will know the full truth."

Spacey/Underwood then stops and, as if startled by the magnitude of what he's about to reveal, continues, "Wait a minute. Now that I think of it. You never saw me die, did you? Conclusions can be so deceiving! Miss me?"

Spacey/Underwood then leaves the kitchen and the video to a dramatic musical sting suggesting that we're ending on a cliffhanger and that we'll be seeing more of Spacey/Underwood in the not-too-distant future.

Everything that I just described happens in three minutes and seven seconds, including lots of dramatic pauses devoid of words, but full of the ACTING for which Spacey has become legendary.

The media can only really handle one idea at a time, and at the time of its release, "Spacey Releases Bizarre YouTube Video" fascinated the press and public in a way "Oscar-winner Spacey Charged With Felony Sexual Assault" did not. "Let Me Be Frank" may be career-definingly bizarre and terrible, but it distracted a public already inclined to think the worst of Spacey from even worse news.

As I write this, "Let Me Be Frank" has been viewed over six and a half million times. Those are six and a half million revealing glimpses into Spacey's psyche. In the space of just over three minutes Spacey did significant, even fatal, damage to a career that was already just barely hanging on.

Consider "Let Me Be Frank" the Zapruder film of disgraced movie star YouTube videos. Only in this case, instead of John F. Kennedy taking the bullet, it's the actor's flailing career being killed onscreen.

MIKE BLOOMBERG'S 2020 PRESIDENTIAL CANDIDACY

On February 4, 2020, something ended that never should have begun: Mike Bloomberg's ill-fated, often hilarious run for the Democratic 2020 presidential nomination. Billions were at the core of Bloomberg's persona and his ostensible appeal; clearly, someone who made BILLIONS of dollars in business would do an AMAZING job as president, right?

There's something strangely perfect about Bloomberg spending, by most estimates, half a BILLION dollars self-funding a campaign that went nowhere, accomplished nothing, and made the lilliputian businessman the laughingstock of the political world.

It's tempting to say Bloomberg got nothing for his roughly five-hundred-million-dollar investment, but that would not be accurate. For five hundred million dollars, Bloomberg got laughed at. For five hundred million dollars, Bloomberg got ridiculed. For five hundred million dollars, Bloomberg's sins, transgressions, and fatal flaws as a human being and politician spilled into public view, casting him in a light at once unflattering and relentlessly comic.

For half a billion dollars, Bloomberg paid to have the biggest "kick me" sign in American electoral politics placed just above his posterior.

Bloomberg's campaign intuited that the internet was the key to Trump's 2016 victory and that, with enough ad buys on social media, Bloomberg could purchase his way into being on equal footing with Trump, as well as Democratic front-runners Bernie Sanders and Joe Biden.

So, Bloomberg did what serious-minded souls out to change the world have always done: he recruited the services of meme factory FuckJerry, the plagiarism-happy hipster jackasses who helped make the Fyre Festival a thing.

Bloomberg's campaign pursued a similar strategy as the Fyre Festival. It threw money at popular Instagram accounts and "influencers" to create a huge wave of internet hype in a short amount of time.

Bloomberg was willing to look silly if it meant becoming the most powerful person in the world. A *New York Times* article on Bloomberg's Dresden bombing–like social media campaign described Evan Reeves, a "creative director for Jerry Media," being brought in to "build a self-aware ironic character around Mr. Bloomberg."

This self-aware, ironic character had nothing to do with the actual Bloomberg. If the real Bloomberg was self-aware or skilled in irony, he never would have run for the nomination in the first place. The idea of these shotgun marriages of convenience was to lead with self-awareness and shamelessness, to make a joke out of both Bloomberg's wild, indiscriminate spending and old white guy obliviousness, to depict Bloomberg as a guy who was so UN-hip and so out of it yet so open about it that he became ironically hip.

To cite a typical example, the account grapejuiceboys posted an image of a fake conversation between Bloomberg and their account where the former mayor inquires, "Hello Juice Boys. Can you post an original meme to make me look cool for the upcoming Democratic primary?" When they respond with "I don't think so tbh your vibe is kinda off," "Bloomberg" counters with, "I put Lamborghini doors on the Escalade" (lyrics from the 50 Cent/The Game song "How We Do") in a post demarcated as sponsored content from the Mike Bloomberg campaign.

"Your vibe is kinda off," is a euphemistic way of saying that Bloomberg's racist, discriminatory policies as the mayor of New York, most notoriously Stop and Frisk, helped destroy the lives of countless POC and black families, and that Bloomberg is a power-mad oligarch out to preserve an evil status quo.

By loudly broadcasting Bloomberg's desire to look cool and appeal to the kind of meme-savvy young people who helped get Trump elected, the campaign was angrily insisting that Bloomberg was not only in on the joke about him being an out-of-touch old codger; he was the source of the joke as well, at least from a monetary perspective. He was the source of the joke; the subject of the joke; the target of the joke; and, finally, the investor behind the joke.

If you do not think that jokes should have investors, well, you're not Mike Bloomberg or the meme maniacs behind FuckJerry. Also, you are correct. The whole point of memes is that they go viral in an organic way, that they reflect the funky, fickle, hard-to-anticipate will of the internet—the shitty, endlessly juvenile, cruel internet.

It's surprising and unfortunate that joining forces with FuckJerry did not lead to Bloomberg being taken seriously as a candidate for our highest office.

"Mike Will Get It Done" nervously insisted Bloomberg's slogan and commercials in a way that couldn't help but call to mind the catchphrase of a slightly more cornpone figure: Larry the Cable Guy of "Git-R-Done!" fame.

Bloomberg's ads did a terrible job of promoting him, his ideas, and his candidacy. But they did a wonderful job of selling a grateful nation on the necessity of the "Skip Ad" button.

Bloomberg's advertisements touted his leadership of New York. In a bid to out–New York Donald Trump, Bloomberg relentlessly played up his accomplishments as the problem-solving mayor of New York City. THE New York City.

You know, the famous one.

What Bloomberg did not seem to realize is that Americans and non-Americans have a violently bifurcated conception of New York and New Yorkers. On one hand, they hold New York in high esteem because it is an important city and an international metropolis, a vibrant hub of finance and culture that's home to Broadway and the publishing industry, and so much more. They similarly revere New Yorkers for being tough enough to make it in a city that has been endlessly mythologized as the center of the known universe and the only city that matters.

This idealized conception of New York coexists with a widespread conception of New Yorkers as a bunch of self-important assholes who think they're so fucking special because they live in New York. So, while Americans do, in fact, often hold New Yorkers in high esteem, they're also prone to thinking they're a bunch of pretentious, arrogant douchebags who can all go fuck themselves.

Bloomberg seemed to have banked on getting the first kind of response, that the ignorant rabble would be flattered that a rich man from New York City thought enough of our country to want to purchase its presidency. Instead, he received the second reaction. We, as a culture, told Bloomberg to take the entire Empire State and shove it up his ass.

Shortly before he dropped out, the merchandising arm of Bloomberg's campaign made a hat available for preorder with the words "Not a Socialist" on the front and "Bring in the Boss" on the back.

The problem with this hat is that it already exists, and is extremely popular, only usually it's red and has the words "Make America Great Again" on it and is worn by Republicans and supporters of Donald Trump.

The other problem is that this headwear feels violently out of sync with the tenor of our increasingly radical times. We are sharpening the guillotines and plotting revolution, but Bloomberg thought the problem was not that our country was being run and ruined by a narcissistic, deeply problematic New York billionaire with an appalling history when it comes to race and sex, but rather that the country was being run by the *wrong* narcissistic, deeply problematic New York billionaire with an appalling history when it comes to race and sex.

Bloomberg seemed to think that we did not vote for Trump *despite* his personality, persona, and background but rather because of them. Sadly, he could very well be right. The people might want an asshole, and a boss, but they nevertheless found Bloomberg's pitch unbelievably easy to resist.

How morally bankrupt was Bloomberg's blind ambition? As part of their meme blitz the Bloomberg campaign sought out the participation of widely reviled hack and notorious joke thief Fat Jew, a.k.a. Josh Ostrovsky.

However, and this is a very curious thing I am about to write, Fat Jew had too much integrity to sell out to a man convinced that he had a pathway to the nomination and presidency. The Fat Jew had no time for The Short Presidential Aspirant Jew.

For the first, and I would imagine the final, time, people found themselves respecting Fat Jew. Mike Bloomberg did the impossible: he made Fat Jew look good. He made him look better than good: he made him look like a paragon of integrity.

Bloomberg couldn't even secure the quasi-endorsement of Fat Jew in exchange for what I imagine is a fuck ton of money. How was he going to connect with people he did not personally pay off to further his political delusions?

So goodbye, Mike Bloomberg, and thanks for all the memes!

Oh, and in case you can't tell, I'm being sarcastic.

GAL GADOT AND FRIENDS' "IMAGINE" YOUTUBE VIDEO (2020)

Not too long ago, in those first anxiety-filled and terrifying months of the Covid Pandemic, Gal Gadot had a very sweet, very stupid idea.

She'd been moved by a viral video of a solitary trumpeter on a balcony in Italy playing a mournful solo version of John Lennon's "Imagine," a haunting rendition that wordlessly captured the fraught intensity of a terrible cultural moment, with its alternating currents of cautious hope and soul-wracking fear.

Gadot was so moved by this spontaneous moment of hope from an unknown musician using his art to comfort his neighbors that it inspired her to create a companion piece that was designed to honor its inspiration and build upon it, but that turned out to be its antithesis.

The *Justice League* star would recruit her super-rich, super-famous friends for an all-star circle-jerk sing-along as clumsily self-conscious, prefabricated, and dripping with condescension as its inspiration was spontaneous, organic, and pure.

If people were inspired by some random nobody on a balcony, then they would undoubtedly be moved to tears if they were to hear the WORDS to "Imagine" (you know, the good part!) sung not by one mega-celebrity like Gadot but by a FUCK ton of celebrities, A-listers like Amy Adams, Will Ferrell, and James Marsden.

They set out to create a funky, intimate "We Are the World" on their cell phones for the age of the coronavirus. Instead, they created something closer to "We Are the Worst."

Instead of inspiring appreciation among the unwashed rabble, the gaggle of celebrities singing the most overexposed song of all time led to rage and mockery.

The anger that Gadot & friends' rendition engendered helps illustrate how Trump was able to get elected president with seemingly the sum of show-business standing in staunch opposition to him, with the exception of contrarians like James Woods and Kristy Swanson.

Hillary Clinton ran with the universal support of Hollywood. Trump, because he had no other option, decided to turn a weakness into a strength by running AGAINST Hollywood. Trump couldn't get any real celebrities in his camp.

So, a man who represents the toxic cult of celebrity in its purest form decided to put the concept of celebrity on trial and find it GUILTY of being yet another cesspool of Marxist elitism looking down on patriotic Americans as inbred hillbillies swilling moonshine and marrying their first cousins.

I will be the first to admit that celebrities can be arrogant, tone-deaf, and condescending. But it's not like a group of megastars thought the ideal response to a cataclysmic crisis involved asking the common people to imagine a Socialist utopia with no materialism, or greed, or belongings, or God, just humanity united in cosmic interconnectedness through a painfully earnest screed by a wife beater, child neglector, and hypocrite whose monstrous ego ensured that the greatest rock band of all time never made it past a decade.

Oh wait, that's *exactly* what Gadot and her Super-Friends did! Like a freshman at the quad with an acoustic guitar, they thought they could reach us with the four millionth shitty cover of "Imagine," only this time with more unfortunate baggage than any one musical collaboration can bear, let alone one so staggeringly awful that to even call it music feels generous.

John Lennon has a powerfully bifurcated reputation. On one hand, there's the ultimate hippie flower child and countercultural icon with his long hair, granny glasses, and Quixotic yearning for a world of peace and love.

This is the reductive cartoon of Lennon commemorated on posters adorning dorm walls. Then there's the famously mean-spirited brute who hit his first wife, neglected his first child, and could be unconscionably cruel to the people who loved him most.

Gadot obviously sees Lennon exclusively through that first prism, as the beloved personification of the 1960s. Instead, a rightfully insulted public saw the song, and its writer, through the prism of Lennon's moral hypocrisy because it reflected that of the rich and powerful celebrities singing the song.

"Imagine" dreams of a world where we are all equal, but you needed to be rich and famous to get invited to Gadot's big celeb sing-along for coronavirus or whatever the fuck. Bear in mind, you don't have to be able to sing, but you DO need to be famous, and consequently better than the rabble you are singing at.

Elvis Costello said it best in "The Other Side of Summer" when he impishly inquired, "Was it a millionaire who said, 'Imagine no possessions?'"

On Gadot's "Imagine" it's not just one millionaire imagining no possessions: it's twenty-four millionaires joining forces to ask us to imagine a world without millionaires. It's folks with a combined net worth in the billions asking us to envision a world without massive economic iniquities.

"Imagine" is not quite "L'Internationale," but it's as close as a bunch of privileged movie stars hiding out in their mansions are going to get to a stirring Marxist anthem.

Then there's the actual performance of "Imagine" itself, which is so stilted and self-conscious that it makes three minutes feel like several lifetimes.

The awkwardness begins with Gadot on day six of the quarantine talking about how it has made her philosophical: "The virus has affected the entire world, everyone: it doesn't matter who you are, where you're from, we're all in this together."

She then segues into talking about the "Italian guy" on the patio playing "Imagine" and how there was something so "powerful and pure" about "this video" before saying, "And it goes like this," before beginning the interminable process of singing "Imagine" terribly alongside twenty-three other famous people.

Gadot's phrasing just before launching, regrettably, into song is telling. Gadot does not say that there is something "powerful and pure" about *that* video, the one with the lonely Italian trumpeter that inspired her; instead, she says that there's something powerful and pure about *this* video (the one she's making, one has to assume), one that "goes like this."

Then Gadot begins singing, after a fashion. If Gadot were trying to genuinely pay tribute to the video she's talking about, the phrase "goes like this" would either be followed by Gadot shocking the world by playing "Imagine" on the trumpet by herself, or her imitating the sounds of the lonely trumpeter with her mouth, a la Rahzel or *Police Academy* star Michael Winslow.

Nope, instead Gadot starts singing a cappella, one of many places where this video and its inspiration diverge dramatically.

GAL GADOT * KRISTEN WIIG
JAMIE DORNAN * LABRINTH
JAMES MARSDEN * SARAH
SILVERMAN * EDDIE BENJAMIN
JIMMY FALLON * NATALIE PORTMAN
ZOE KRAVITZ * SIA * LYNDA CARTER
AMY ADAMS * LESLIE ODOM JR.
PEDRO PASCAL * CHRIS O'DOWD
DAWN O'PORTER * WILL FERRELL
MARK RUFFALO * NORAH JONES
ASHLEY BENSON * KAIA GERBER
CARA DELEVINGNE * ANNIE MUMOLO
MAYA RUDOLPH

The miscalculations continue with the choice to have Kristen Wiig be the next celeb up to bat in this bizarre musical relay race. Wiig's persona is rooted in clammy, painfully self-conscious awkwardness. So, she is perhaps not the best choice for the leadoff spot in a project defined by awkwardness and self-consciousness.

"Imagine" is an exceedingly difficult song to pull off even if you are a professional musician backed by other professional musicians. When amateurs sing it a cappella half a line at a time, as they do here, it becomes impossible and unbearable.

Gadot is breathtaking in her beauty. She is also breathtaking in her misguided earnestness, in her delusional belief in the power of celebrity and good intentions to overcome tragedy and devastation.

Early in this slow-motion train wreck Sarah Silverman sings the three "meaningful" words she has been allotted in "living for today," at which point she begins to vamp, really throwing herself into the "whoa oh oh" part in a way that clumsily epitomizes the tonal weirdness at the project's core.

Silverman understandably seems to have no idea what tone to take. Do you play it earnest or tongue-in-cheek? Do you play up the sincerity to comic effect or do you leave behind the comedy because it has no place in this context?

Silverman splits the difference. She sings "living for today" earnestly and then puts a tongue-in-cheek spin on "whoa oh oh" that betrays a distinct discomfort with what she's being asked to do. Silverman is only onscreen for a few seconds, but her thought process is agonizingly apparent all the same. Her discomfort is palpable, but nowhere near as palpable as our own.

The celebs film themselves in tight close-ups and without makeup, presumably because shooting themselves in front of their swimming pools or sprawling mansions would undercut the song's anti-materialist message. We're supposed to be able to relate to these de-glammed stars as scared and uncertain human beings just like us, except that they're in a big group text with Gal Gadot and seem to think that singing half a line from "Imagine" will give the masses the strength to carry on.

Watching these celebrities slaughter "Imagine" illustrates a surprising truth about the song. Despite having some of the most famous lyrics in human history "Imagine" works better as an instrumental. That Italian trumpeter captured the fragile mood of the moment and the song's hopes more powerfully than Gadot's celebrity orgy of subpar singing and clumsy sermonizing.

I hate the phrase "cringe" because in real life it takes a LOT to make us cringe, but in the glib world of social media that phrase is tossed around to describe anything anyone finds awkward. But "cringe" is the perfect phrase to describe the video, in no small part because I physically cringed throughout it.

Gadot and friends did end up uniting the public after all, but not in the manner intended. Instead, they gave Hollywood-hating Conservatives and class-conscious Progressives something to despise equally. We all came together to make fun of this stupid video.

Watching and listening to celebrities destroy John Lennon's words, I suddenly found myself experiencing a weird surge of sympathy for Mark David Chapman.

JEREMY RENNER'S APP

There's something poignant as well as hilarious about celebrities who bizarrely overestimate their popularity and misunderstand the nature of their appeal. So, I couldn't help but feel bad for Jeremy Renner when the world greeted his efforts to make the leap from respected actor to multi-hyphenate entertainment superstar with a derisive snort.

As product launches go, Renner's attempt to rebrand himself as a Sammy Davis–like supernova who acts and sings and has his own app and Amazon store was roughly as successful as New Coke and Garth Brooks's alter ego Chris Gaines.

The Jeremy Renner app lived as a joke. It died as a joke as well. A public that never stopped deriving malicious delight at the idea of a Jeremy Renner app, as well as its actual existence, got one last laugh when a frustrated Renner posted the following message shutting down the app:

Goodbye . . .

The app has jumped the shark. Literally. Due to clever individuals that were able to manipulate ways to impersonate me and others within the app I have asked ESCAPEX, the company that runs this app to shut it down immediately and refund anyone who has purchased any stars over the last 90 days. What was supposed to be a place for fans to connect with each other has turned into everything I detest and can't and won't condone. My sincerest apologies for this to have not turned out the way it was intended. To all the super-fans who have supported me with your words or encouragement, amazing art, stories, and time shared on the app, a genuine THANK YOU and I hope to see you on Instagram, Twitter, youtube and facebook.

With all due respect, Mr. Renner, Sir, as much as I would love to keep track of your doings, and see trailers for your movies, and hear snippets of your new songs, and watch your music videos and see pictures of you frolicking with your friends and family, I simply can't follow you on Instagram, Twitter, YouTube, or Facebook because doing so will only remind me of the paradise I lost when your app shut down.

Renner wasn't going to let the app continue to flounder and embarrass itself. Yet, in a wonderfully representative development, Renner literally posted a message on his app to shut it down immediately, yet a good twenty-four hours later I was nevertheless able to download the Jeremy Renner app, create a profile, and make at least one post announcing my excitement at being part of such a worthwhile experiment. I decided to poke around and see for myself why the best idea in the world, launched by our most beloved and most cyber-savvy celebrity, led to one of the biggest failures in the history of apps.

One of the consequences of downloading the app is that every time I open my phone, I am forced to look at Jeremy Renner's stupid fucking face alongside the logos for Lyft and the Weather Channel, apps that do serve a purpose. And every time I look into Renner's eyes, I am reminded that Jeremy fucking Renner has a stupid app for some reason and it makes me hate his actorly mug anew.

Sometimes I'll open the app and be greeted by a black and white glamour shot of Renner's face, and my weird anger toward Renner, his face and his app reaches a fever pitch. Renner stares soulfully at you on the icon for his app, silently imploring, "It's me, actor Jeremy Renner. I have my own app now for some reason."

All the Jeremy Renner app really does is link to Instagram and Facebook and Twitter and give fans more pictures of Jeremy Renner than they could ever possibly want or need.

When a single Google search for your name can do as much as your entire business, maybe you should start thinking about how much value you're really offering the public.

Whoever was behind this embarrassment obviously hoped that the app could grow into a lifestyle brand, a male Goop. But where Gwyneth Paltrow inspires love and feverish hatred, Renner inspires shrugs. He's just some guy who is good at pretending to be different people. He's a man, not a brand, and he's certainly not a movement.

I doubt anybody defines themselves by their Jeremy Renner fandom, but if they do I think they've just established a useful baseline for the male version of being basic.

On Jeremy Renner's Instagram feed there are many, many photographs of Jeremy Renner, sometimes singing, sometimes acting, sometimes just fooling around. Sometimes he smolders. Sometimes he's goofy and casual.

Collectively, his Instagram screams, "Here are a bunch of photographs of me, I guess."

Then there's his Twitter account, which is mostly images culled from Instagram and Facebook, accompanied by clunky knots of hashtags.

One post on the app is a tall tower of onion rings. It looks tasty, I suppose? Another post is a sunset with the caption, "I hope everyone had a great weekend." In another, he's fishing and looking very autumnal in a vest.

It's boring! It's basic! It's blandly promotional! And it's all in one place for you to ignore because who needs to experience Jeremy Renner in any form other than as an actor in movies?

As his wonderfully failed attempt to go from being an actor to a business, man, not just a businessman, betrays, Jeremy Renner is just an actor. Now, Renner is a really good actor who can be great in the right role, but that's all he is. He isn't an icon. He isn't a way of life. He isn't James Dean or Humphrey Bogart or Robert Mitchum or Elvis Presley. He's not even James Franco. He's just another boring white guy who is good at performing words someone else wrote.

Since the Jeremy Renner app was still up when I wrote this, in glorious defiance of Jeremy Renner's wishes and his explicit command, I was able to hop onboard this digital Titanic after it hit that pesky iceberg. I meandered around, hoping to see some of the aggressive trolling Renner bemoaned in his post before attempting to shut down the app. Alas, the digital snark had been scrubbed from the doomed project, so it was less a profane disaster than a boring failure.

The worst part of the Jeremy Renner app, and there's a lot of competition, is that the song samples don't stop after you leave the app, so it feels like Renner's terrible music is following you, that it won't accept near-universal rejection and is intent on convincing you to take Renner seriously as a singer.

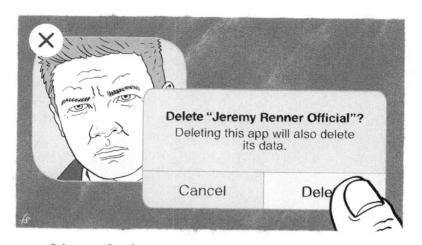

It's as if, after earning a fair amount of goodwill through a career full of fine work and excellent choices as an actor, Renner finally felt he had the leverage to tell a deeply unimpressed public, "Actually, I'm a musician too! Here's my new song." The world was all, "Whatever," and then he followed with, "Oh, I've got an Amazon store too! So, you can buy all the things you need to live the Jeremy Renner lifestyle!!" To which, we collectively responded, "Okay, this is getting weird." Then, with a wild gleam in his eye, Renner angrily shouted, "Not to mention my app! It's the one-stop shop for all things Jeremy Renner the world has been hungering for!" and we started wondering whether we should cancel someone just for being annoying and making bad music, not for doing anything wrong morally.

In one of the many splendid idiocies that makes the Jeremy Renner app such a singularly useless treat, if you click the web link on the Jeremy Renner app it takes you to the clunky, primitive-looking JeremyLeeRenner.com, "an unofficial website devoted to actor and musician Jeremy Renner."

An *unofficial* website! On Jeremy Renner's official app! That perfectly encapsulates the app's surreal miscalculation and terrible execution. Of course, the first story on Jeremy

Renner's *unofficial* website is that the Jeremy Renner app, the great hope of Jeremy Renner nation, was shutting down and taking with it the dreams and hopes of superfans like myself.

With the Jeremy Renner app, Jeremy Renner created a paradise, a digital Garden of Eden overflowing with the Fruit of Life, but cyber-snakes who thought the Jeremy Renner app was a joke had to ruin it for everybody.

This is why we can't have nice things. Jeremy Renner gave humanity a gift in the form of his app, and we made him look like a buffoon in return.

ERIC CLAPTON'S
"THIS HAS GOTTA STOP"
(2021)

The older I get, the less invested I am in my opinions. This is particularly true where hate is concerned. Life is just too goddamn short and precious to waste despising musicians, actors, and filmmakers, particularly artists everyone else seems to hate.

This laissez-faire attitude is partially attributable to age and partially attributable to a solid decade of evangelizing on behalf of Phish and Insane Clown Posse, two of the most hated and misunderstood acts in the history of pop music.

But rewatching *The Doors* recently reminded me that there are nevertheless musicians, actors, and filmmakers I genuinely hate with an intense, distinctly personal passion, chief among them Jim Morrison.

Hatred is not too strong of a word to describe my feelings toward Morrison. I hate damn near everything about him: the pretension, the ego, the insufferable self-indulgence, and the mindless hedonism.

My father told me you should save your hate for things and people that really deserve it, like Adolf Hitler. He was a seriously bad dude. He was so bad he was LITERALLY Hitler. Eric Clapton falls into this category as well.

I've mellowed with age, but villains like Eric Clapton nevertheless bring out the hater in me. I've always disliked Clapton and not just because I worked for a summer at a Goodwill in 1996 perpetually tuned into the Easy Listening station, where the musical sleeping pill that is "Change the World" was in heavy rotation.

My lifelong dislike of Clapton metastasized into hatred with the deeply unsurprising revelation that a man notorious for a 1976 racist rant against immigrants and people of color had hopped onboard the anti-mask, anti-vaccine bandwagon, after having a bad reaction to being vaccinated.

Clapton personally experienced side effects, so obviously the vaccine must be an evil instrument of Fascist oppression.

Clapton is so strongly against asking people to show basic consideration for the sake of curbing the spread of a deadly pandemic that he regrettably made a single about it that I can say without hyperbole is the single worst song in the history of the universe.

"This Has Gotta Stop" sleepwalks haphazardly out of the gate with a sleepy melody that feels like they rearranged some of the chords on "Change the World" and cynically passed it off as a new composition.

Clapton's middling manifesto opens with placeholder lyrics that the awful exemplar of boomer arrogance figured he might as well keep because there's no point trying at this stage of his career.

A delusional Clapton imagines this song will change minds and inspire social change despite beginning with the lines "This has gotta stop/Enough is enough/I can't take this BS any longer."

"I can't take this BS any longer!" That somehow wasn't just good enough to make it into what Clapton thinks is an important song, an anthem even: it made it into the chorus.

Clapton is so proud of the lyric "I can't take this BS any longer" that he repeats the line no less than five times.

That would seem to leave the song nowhere to go but up, but Clapton somehow keeps finding new bottoms.

Clapton just barely tries to sound tough when he taunts, "If you wanna claim my soul/You'll have to come and break down this door," with a dearth of energy that suggests that if you were to break down Clapton's door you'd find an old man sleeping in a fetal position in the corner, possibly sucking his thumb and drooling on himself.

At this point, really, Clapton's soul isn't worth claiming. Clapton invokes the kids, the precious children, when he whines, "Thinkin' of my kids/What's left for them/And then what's coming down the road/The light in the tunnel/Could be the southbound train/Lord, please help them with their load."

You know what might help them with their load? Getting vaccinated. That way they won't die after contracting Covid at one of Clapton's shows.

"This Has Gotta Stop" might just be the least urgent message song ever written. Clapton sounds exhausted, alright, but it's not the righteous exhaustion of someone who can't put up with injustice one moment longer.

His is instead the bone-deep exhaustion of someone with nothing left to say and no reason left to live, who is ready for the sweet release of the grave, and a nap that will last for all of eternity.

Seldom has a song that falls listlessly under the heading of "Easy Listening" been so difficult to listen to.

PRAISE FOR "THE JOY OF TRASH"

"Is anyone as adept at insightful dives into the bizarre avenues of pop culture as Nathan Rabin is with 'The Joy of Trash'!?!"

- Andrew Helm, writer of "A Talking Cat!?!"

"Nathan Rabin does not merely poke fun at bad media. He exactingly, methodically lies each of its sins bare with the thrilling precision of Hercule Poriot revealing the true identity of the murderer. Except instead of explaining how some gardener shot poison through a blowgun he's dismantling Loqueesha to its atomic components. It's an incredible spectacle."

- Justin McElroy

"This is not a condemnation, it's a celebration of how, despite the pop-culture garbage we're forced to wade through every day, we can still rise above it. And make fun of it. In a celebratory way. I think I mixed up my metaphors here."

- Patton Oswalt

"Nathan Rabin is one of my favorite pop-culture critics and historians. He takes on the good, the bad, and what some might refer to as the "ugly." To me, it's all beautiful. Especially the ugly. Like a crab scuttling along this nation's depths, he collects forgotten, shimmering, neglected objects and reveals them to a most grateful world. Another great book by a terrific writer.

- Mike Sacks, "Poking a Dead Frog," "Passing on the Right: The Batty Battison Story"

ALSO FROM DECLAN-HAVEN BOOKS AND NATHAN RABIN AND FELIPE SOBREIRO

The Weird Accordion to Al

The Weird Accordion to Al:
Ridiculously Self-Indulgent,
Ill-Advised Vanity Edition

The Weird A-Coloring to Al

The Weird A-Coloring to Al:
Colored-In Special Edition